The Politics of Population

The International Conference on
Population and Development

Cairo 1994

The Politics of Population

The International Conference on
Population and Development

Cairo 1994

Stanley Johnson

Earthscan Publications Ltd, London

First published in the UK in 1995 by
Earthscan Publications Limited

Copyright © Stanley Johnson, 1995

A catalogue record for this book is available from the British Library

ISBN 1 85383 297 9

Typeset by Photoprint, Torquay, Devon
Printed and bound by Clays Ltd, St Ives plc
Cover design by Dominic Banner
Picture research by Brooks Krikler

Published with the generous support of the
United Nations Population Fund (UNFPA)

For a full list of publications please contact:

Earthscan Publications Limited
120 Pentonville Road
London N1 9JN
Tel: 0171 278 0433
Fax: 0171 278 1142

Earthscan is an editorially independent subsidiary of Kogan Page Limited
and publishes in association with WWF-UK and the International Institute
for Environment and Development.

Contents

5

Contents

Preface

It is easy to be cynical. Nowadays, one mega-conference seems to succeed another. The Earth Summit, as the United Nations Conference on Environment and Development (UNCED) held in Rio de Janeiro, Brazil, in June 1992 was generally called, seemed at the time to be the conference to end all conferences. Like the Congress of Vienna, the Earth Summit aimed to set up a new world order. This time, however, the focus would not be on the balance of power, on diplomatic alliances and rivalries, but on the new verities, the new imperatives governing the way the world should conduct its affairs, particularly those having to do with the protection of the environment and the pursuit of higher living standards for the mass of the world's poor. The message was interdependence, not independence.

One hundred and seventy five nations were represented at Rio and over a hundred heads of state attended. There were 1500 officially accredited non-governmental organisations, as well as 7000 journalists. In Agenda 21 UNCED adopted a 600-page tome which seemed to cover every subject under the sun. The whole of life was there. As the weary participants made their way home after the two-week session, they could have been forgiven for supposing that the massive process of intergovernmental consultation and negotiation which had preceded the conference, which had continued in Rio itself and which ultimately had resulted in some hard-won international agreements, of which Agenda 21 was probably the most important and certainly the most voluminous, had surely obviated the need for another mammoth meeting at least for the foreseeable future.

Yet, as one great wave crashed on to the beach, new waves were curling their crests behind. Even as the UNCED negotiations proceeded, preparations were being made for further mega-conferences. The UN Conference on Human Rights would take place in Vienna in 1993 and a year later the International Conference on Population and Development, or ICPD, would be held in Cairo. (The decision to hold the ICPD had indeed been taken by the United Nations Economic and Social Council, ECOSOC, as long ago as July 1989. By the time of the Earth Summit, the first meeting of the ICPD Preparatory Committee had already taken place and others were planned.)

Beyond the ICPD loomed the "Social Summit" to be held in Copenhagen in March 1995 and beyond that lay the great women's conference planned for Beijing in August of the same year, with yet another meeting, known as Habitat 2, already being organised for Istanbul in 1996. As the poet William Wordsworth so aptly put it, "hills peep o'er hills and Alps on Alps arise".

Given this perspective, given the fact that, among all the reams of paper covered with ink at these UN gatherings, one will never find a single binding commitment, a single justiciable paragraph or even sentence, a degree of cynicism seems inevitable — and forgivable. If the output of these mega-conferences can be considered law at all, it is certainly the softest of soft law. Those who participate in these UN-sponsored gatherings certainly take them and themselves seriously — one only has to go into a meeting room when one of these mega-conferences is in session and watch the solemn-suited rows of delegates with their name cards and headphones to realise just how serious, how portentous, how self-deluding the proceedings can sometimes be. For the outsider, it can seem more than a trifle unreal. The airconditioned meeting rooms in New York or Geneva, Rio, Cairo, Copenhagen, Beijing or wherever are about as far from the village pump as you can get.

Why then a book about the Cairo population conference? What distinguishes the ICPD from the host of other gatherings? What was specially memorable about those nine days in September 1995? Now that the dust has settled along the banks of the Nile, can it plausibly be argued that the Cairo population "summit" represented — as some of the more enthusiastic participants have argued — a "quantum leap forward" in the way the "population issue" is to be handled from now on?

The argument advanced in this book is that the answer to this last question is an emphatic yes. Cairo was more than a way station on the road from Rio to Istanbul. The Cairo process and the Cairo Programme of Action taken together do indeed add up to something new and original and important and should be recognised as such even by the most cynical of cynics. Though the confrontations which took place before and during the meeting were not, happily, physically violent, the clash of ideas — as we shall attempt to illustrate — certainly was. Out of that clash and turmoil, a new synthesis, a new paradigm emerged. The heart of that new synthesis, that new paradigm, is the priority to be given to women as the agents of change.

The Cairo conference on population and development established a detailed agenda for gender equality, equity and the empowerment of women within the wider context of social development. If the Cairo programme is fully implemented at national and international level, there will indeed have been a new ordering of human affairs. With the full "empowerment of women", as proposed in the Cairo programme, the goals of sustainable development will be that much easier to achieve. And the goal of population stabilisation will no longer be a distant dream but a real, practical possibility.

Glossary

ADB	African Development Bank
CEDAW	Convention on the Elimination of all Forms of Discrimination Against Women
CELADE	Latin American Centre for Demographic Studies
CPR	contraceptive rate
ECA	Economic Commission for Africa
ECE	Economic Commission for Europe
ECLAC	Economic Commission for Latin America and the Caribbean
ECOSOC	United Nations Economic and Social Council
ESCAP	Economic and Social Commission for Asia and the Pacific
ESCWA	Economic and Social Commission for Western Asia
FP	family planning
ICPD	International Conference on Population and Development
IEC	information, education and communication
IGO	intergovernmental organisation
ILO	International Labour Office
IPPF	International Planned Parenthood Federation
IUSSP	International Union for the Scientific Study of Population
IWHC	International Women's Health Coalition
MCH	maternal and child health
NGO	non-governmental organisation
OAU	Organisation of African Unity
ODA	official development assistance
PAI	Population Action International

PrepCom	Preparatory Committee
TFR	total fertility rate
UAPS	Union for African Population Studies
UN	United Nations
UNCED	United Nations Conference on Environment and Development
UNESCO	United Nations Educational, Scientific and Cultural Organisation
UNFPA	United Nations Population Fund
USAID	United States Agency for International Development
WEDO	Women's Environment and Development Organisation
WEOG	Western Europe and Other Group
WHO	World Health Organisation
WPPA	World Population Plan of Action

Chapter 1
Setting the Scene

To appreciate Cairo's achievements as well as its shortcomings, one must understand the context. What is the "population problem"? How has it been perceived over time? How have these perceptions been translated into political realities? What are the historical antecedents of the Cairo conference and how did they influence the outcome of the ICPD?

The broad outline of the world's demographic evolution is by now familiar. School children and politicians recite the statistics almost by heart. It took mankind all of recorded time until the middle of the nineteenth century to achieve a population of one billion, less than a hundred years to add the second billion, and only thirty years to add the third. At the end of the 1960s, it was anticipated at the then current rates of increase that there would be four billion people by 1975 and nearly seven billion people by the year 2000. What had begun as a plane taking off over an immensely long runway had turned in a frighteningly brief period of time into a rocket accelerating rapidly towards the stratosphere.

The immediate cause of the massive demographic expansion which the world was experiencing at the end of the 1960s could be summarised in a single sentence. The fall in death rates in developing countries had not been matched by a fall in birth rates. The developing world had experienced one "demographic revolution" — the transition from high mortality to low mortality. But it had yet to undergo the second demographic revolution, the transition from high fertility to low fertility.

An increasing gap was opening up between the birth rates for countries in the developed regions of the world which ranged from 16 to 20 per 1000 and those of the developing regions which ranged from 36 to 49 per 1000.[1]

The first national population policies evolved as governments came to understand the consequences of rapid population growth and high fertility both for their national development efforts as well as for the welfare of families and individuals. Several countries, particularly in Asia, actively promoted policies aimed at facilitating fertility reduction and lowering population growth rates. Indeed, by the end of 1969, the governments of about thirty less-developed countries, comprising almost two-thirds of the combined populations of the less developed regions, had adopted national family planning programmes as integral parts of their development policies.

The fact that these first national population policies were, as it were, home-grown and not foisted on the developing world by the rich industrialised "neo-Malthusian" northern nations is sometimes forgotten. Speakers on the fringes of the Cairo conference made play with colourful phrases such as "condom diplomacy", arguing that contraceptives had now "displaced the sola topi" as the symbol of imperialist domination, but the reality of the 1950s and early 1960s was far otherwise.

In 1959, a Presidential Committee on the American foreign aid programme, chaired by General William Draper Jr, recommended that the US government should "assist ... countries ... on request in the formulation of ... plans designed to deal with the problem of rapid population growth". But President Dwight D Eisenhower had repudiated this recommendation, saying: "I cannot imagine anything more emphatically a subject that is not a proper political or governmental activity or function or responsibility."[2] If attitudes began to change in the United States, it was at least in part as a response to the expressed needs of developing countries who were embarking on population and family planning programmes.

What successes had there been, by the end of the 1960s, in turning the tide of human fertility? In what countries? Were those successes in any way replicable in other countries? In a small number of countries — including Japan, Taiwan, Singapore and China — significant reductions in fertility appeared to have been achieved. In other countries — India, Pakistan, Kenya and others — substantial and long-standing efforts were being made to provide family planning services either through government programmes or through the private sector, for example through national family planning associations, but the demographic impact of such programmes remained uncertain.

The growth in national concern over the implications of rapid population growth and the increasing number of official family planning programmes was reflected in the growth of international assistance in this field. Indeed, international assistance in the field of population, perhaps more than in most other fields, has played a vital role in reinforcing and underpinning national commitments.

The key players as they emerged on the international stage during the 1970s were national bilateral aid agencies, particularly the United States Agency for International Development (USAID) and other bilateral donors such as the United Kingdom, Denmark, Norway and Japan. The international agencies were also playing an increasingly important part, notably: the United Nations and its system of agencies, particularly the United Nations Population Fund (UNFPA); the World Bank (strictly a UN agency, but deserving a special mention); the International Planned Parenthood Federation (IPPF), whose local affiliates often played a pioneering role in pushing for action on family planning matters and in providing family planning services themselves either in the absence of, or as a supplement or alternative to, government services; and bodies such as the Population Council, the Ford Foundation, the Rockefeller Foundation, who truly were pathfinders in the field. Total international assistance for population activities amounted to only about $2 million in 1960 and $18 million in 1965, but it increased rapidly to $125 million in 1970 and to nearly $350 million by 1977. Between the years 1970–1974, the average annual rate of growth in international population assistance was around 20 per cent.[3]

Notwithstanding the increases in the resources available, both through national budgets and through international assistance, the whole question of how and why to curb rapid population growth remained deeply trammelled in controversy. Nor was the situation made any easier when, in July 1968, Pope Paul VI published the Encyclical *Humanae Vitae* which set out with great clarity precisely where the Vatican stood on the issue of birth control. For even though *Humanae Vitae* recognised that there might in certain circumstances be a case for contraception, the methods to be used were severely limited (essentially the "rhythm" method was the only one to receive any kind of official approval) while the notion of a state population policy intended to limit births remained anathema.

Less than a year after *Humanae Vitae*, on May 1, 1969, Robert S. McNamara, then the President of the World Bank, gave a speech at the University of Notre Dame, Indiana, on the subject of population. It was not the first time he had spoken on this topic. Indeed, McNamara's first address to the World Bank's Board of Governors on September 30, 1968, had caused considerable controversy, particularly among Latin American delegates, since he pledged the Bank's assistance for a new area of lending, namely population projects and programmes. What made the Notre Dame speech remarkable was that it was delivered before a Catholic audience. And it was a model of eloquence and passion.

Robert McNamara opened his remarks by saying:

> "I want to discuss with you this afternoon a problem that arose out of the recent past: that already plagues man in the present, and that will diminish, if not destroy, much of his future — should he fail to face up to it, and solve it. It is, by half a dozen criteria, the most delicate and difficult issue of our era, perhaps of any era in history. It is overlaid with emotion. It is controversial. It is subtle. Above all, it is immeasurably complex.
>
> "It is the tangled problem of excessive population growth. It is not merely a problem, it is a paradox. It is at one and the same time an issue that is intimately private — and yet inescapably public. It is an issue characterised by reticence and circumspection — and yet in desperate need of realism and candour. It is an issue intolerant of government pressure — and yet endangered by government procrastination.
>
> "It is an issue, finally, that is so hypersensitive — giving rise to such diverse opinion — that there is an understandable tendency simply to avoid argument, turn one's attention to less complicated matters and hope that the problem will somehow disappear.
>
> "But the problem will not disappear. What may disappear is the opportunity to find a solution that is rational and humane. If we wait too long, that option will be overtaken by events. We cannot afford that. For if anything is certain about the population explosion, it is that if it is not dealt with reasonably, it will in fact explode: explode in suffering, explode in violence, explode in inhumanity."

A few months after McNamara's Notre Dame speech, in October 1969, the Right Honourable Lester Pearson, a former Prime Minister of Canada, presented the report of the independent commission on international cooperation for economic development, which he chaired, to the Board of Governors of the World Bank. Like its successors the Brandt Commission, the Brundtland Commission and the South Commission, the Pearson report had a considerable impact at the time both on public opinion at large and among policy-makers concerned with aid, trade and development. Its recommendations for action were addressed to the developing countries, to the industrialised countries, and to international organisations.

As far as population was concerned, the Pearson report commented starkly:

> "No other phenomenon casts a darker shadow over the prospects for international development than the staggering growth of population.

It is evident that it is a major cause of the large discrepancy between
the rates of economic improvement in rich and poor countries."

One more quotation — again from 1969, obviously a vintage year for
quotations. Speaking in New York in his capacity as Secretary General of
the United Nations, U Thant said:

> "I do not wish to seem overdramatic, but I can only conclude from the
> evidence that is available to me as Secretary General, that the
> Members of the United Nations have perhaps ten years left in which to
> subordinate their ancient quarrels and launch a global partnership to
> curb the arms race, to improve the human environment, to *defuse the
> population explosion*, and to supply the required momentum to
> development efforts. If such a global partnership is not forged within
> the next decade, then I very much fear that the problems I have
> mentioned will have reached such staggering proportions that they
> will be beyond our capacity to control." (author's emphasis)

Looking back over a gap of 25 years, McNamara's moving and
courageous speech, Pearson's sombre vision, U Thant's almost apoca-
lyptic predictions encapsulate what seemed at the end of the 1960s to be
the bitter realities of the time. McNamara, Pearson and U Thant did not
speak just for themselves; they spoke for the ever-growing number of
men and women who believed that the population tide had sooner or
later to be turned back if there was to be any hope for the human race.
The issue, as McNamara so well put it, was whether the "rational and
humane solution" could be found.

The search for the "rational and humane solution" to the population
problem lies at the heart of population politics. For by the beginning of
the 1970s the fundamental debate centred not on whether or why
population growth should be checked, but rather on the means by which
this was to be achieved. The World Population Conference, Bucharest,
1974, provided the setting for the first great set-piece debate.

BUCHAREST, 1974

Though two World Population Conferences had been held before under
the auspices of the UN with the close collaboration of the IUSSP and
interested specialised agencies also — the first in Rome in 1954, the
second in Belgrade in 1965 — these earlier meetings were not
gatherings of official governmental representatives but rather technical
and scientific assemblies where experts could examine population
trends in different parts of the world and assess their implications. The
third World Population Conference, held in 1974, was the first official
governmental conference. The conclusions and the recommendations

coming out of that meeting had to be seen in an altogether different light from the resolutions emerging from Rome and Belgrade which in the final analysis committed no one except, perhaps, the individual participants themselves.

It was at Bucharest that the World Population Plan of Action (WPPA) was adopted and an attempt made, not wholly successfully, to define, amongst other policy and programme objectives, the goals and targets for reducing high rates of population growth and high levels of fertility. The speeches made by national delegates at the Bucharest meeting (as at subsequent meetings) are of consuming interest because they reveal the way different countries actually felt at the time on the key issues: population growth, family planning, abortion, and so on. China came in out of the cold at Bucharest to denounce both the "superpowers", arguing that "of all things in the world, people are the most precious".

The Bucharest conference witnessed the clash of competing ideologies and viewpoints. Put in its simplest terms, the contest was between those (like the United States) who saw population limitation as the precondition of, or vital concomitant to, economic growth and those of a different persuasion (for example the Marxist countries of Central and Eastern Europe) who believed that economic growth would of and by itself "solve" the problems of population. The position of the Vatican was an additional complication. Barely five years had passed since the publication of *Humanae Vitae*. Astute lobbying by the representatives of the Holy See both before and during the Bucharest conference ensured that most delegates were quite familiar with the Catholic church's position.

If Bucharest in the end managed to achieve a compromise, it was none the less a fairly fragile plant. There was no clear language about overall or global targets for population growth. Even the language which related to national target-setting was fuzzy. Where the draft Plan indicated that "countries which consider that their present or expected rates of population growth hamper their goals of promoting human welfare are invited, if they have not done so, to consider setting quantitative population growth targets", the Plan as it emerged from the buffeting of the conference merely invited countries to "consider adopting population policies, within the framework of socio-economic development".

Similarly, there was a proposal in the draft Plan to "make available, to all persons who so desire, if possible by the end of the Second United Nations Development Decade, but not later than 1985, the necessary information and education about family planning and the means to practise family planning effectively and in accordance with their cultural values". The alternative text which the conference adopted merely talked of the need to "encourage appropriate education concerning responsible parenthood and make available to persons who so desire advice on the means of achieving it".

In spite of the real disagreements on substance which existed, the Plan adopted at Bucharest was important in that it set the framework for national action and for international assistance in the field of population.

The decade which followed the Bucharest conference saw rapidly falling birth rates in some parts of the world (what the UN has called a "spectacular" decline). In 1950–1955, the birth rate for the world as a whole was 38.0 per 1000 persons. The corresponding figures for the more developed and less developed regions were 22.7 and 45.4. By 1975–1980, the birth rate for the world had fallen to 28.9 and, for the more developed and less developed regions, to 15.8 and 33.5 per 1000, respectively.[4]

In all world regions except sub-Saharan Africa, there had been substantial declines in fertility. The picture was mixed in the case of Asia, the most populous and, demographically, the most heterogeneous continent. Fertility remained high in most countries of Western South Asia while declines in fertility had been recorded in many countries elsewhere in Asia. Not only had fertility declines been observed in city states, such as Singapore, and islands, such as Sri Lanka, but they had also been observed in parts of some of the largest countries of the region: India, Indonesia and the Philippines. China, which comprised approximately one third of the total population of all developing countries, had experienced a particularly rapid fertility decline. Its birth rate was much below the average for the developing countries of Asia. However, little or no change in fertility appeared to have taken place in Bangladesh, Pakistan or the Islamic Republic of Iran.

There was also diversity in Latin America, but the decline in fertility was not limited, as it was a few years previously, to the countries of temperate South America and the Caribbean. There was evidence of decline in the largest countries in the region, including Brazil, Mexico, Colombia and Venezuela.

In all but a few of the developed countries, fertility was lower in 1980 than a decade earlier. In some countries, for example the (former) Federal Republic of Germany, crude birth rates had fallen almost to 10 per thousand. However, fertility in Eastern Europe remained higher than for the developed countries as a whole.

Evidence from the World Fertility Survey, a series of national inquiries begun in 1972 using a comparable methodology in a large number of countries, indicated that, in most developing countries of Latin America, Asia and Oceania, preferences were for moderate-sized rather than large families. The survey indicated that lack of access to modern contraception was a major problem. The evidence seemed to be that where effective governmental policies favoured their use, contraceptive methods could spread quite rapidly and accelerate the decline in fertility.

There remained, however, substantial differences in the approach to population questions which countries in different regions of the world adopted. The nations of East Asia remained in the vanguard but many Latin American and Caribbean countries developed over the decade an increasing consciousness of the social and economic consequences of their respective demographic situations, and — to a varying extent — showed a concern for associated problems such as adolescent pregnancy, though the question of abortion remained on the whole taboo. Many Latin American governments seemed to prefer not to look and not to know. Meanwhile in the Middle East and most of Africa the fairest assessment was that there was still a long way to go before the urgency of population issues began to impinge on the consciousness of policy-makers in any profound sense.

MEXICO CITY, 1984

The culmination of the post-Bucharest decade came with the International Conference on Population, held in Mexico City in August, 1984. Of particular interest was the position adopted by the United States whose representative threw a largish bombshell into the proceedings on the first day by arguing for "market-based solutions" to population and by threatening to withdraw US funding for international population programmes run by the UN and the IPPF (International Planned Parenthood Federation) unless it could be demonstrated that these bodies were not, directly or indirectly, supporting coercive abortion in China.

Nonetheless, in spite of the fireworks, the Mexico City conference marked some solid progress. On the opening day, Rafael Salas, the Conference's Secretary General and the Executive Director of UNFPA, said:

> "Our goal is the stabilisation of global population within the shortest
> period possible before the end of the next century."

This was possibly the most explicit commitment to a specific target so far made by a high official of the UN. Though the Mexico conference did not itself adopt the goal of world population stabilisation, there was none the less an underlying current of interest in such an idea and in the better provision of practical means to attain it. The final Declaration of the Mexico Conference observed that "millions of people still lack access to safe and effective family planning methods" and called for major efforts to be made "to ensure that all couples and individuals can exercise the basic human right to decide freely, responsibly and without coercion, the number and spacing of their children and to have the information, education and means to do so." The Mexico texts did not, of course, seek to argue that demographic objectives were the only purpose of family planning programmes. But the experience of the previous decades seemed to indicate that the provision of family planning services was a necessary, though not a sufficient, condition of successful attempts to limit human fertility.

It is impossible to maintain that the Mexico City population conference of August 1984, any more than the Bucharest conference of August 1974, produced a real consensus on the population question. The position adopted by the United States under the Reagan administration effectively precluded such a consensus, not to speak of the reservations made by the Holy See and to a greater or lesser extent shared by some of the Catholic countries of Latin America. (In Mexico City, as in Bucharest, the Holy See formally dissociated itself from the final resolution of the conference). However, a number of conferences, events or reports helped to bring the view points closer together.

EVOLVING PERCEPTIONS

Some of the events, such as the Colombo Conference of Parliamentarians (1979) or the Rome meeting on Population and the Urban Future (1980), were directly concerned with the population issue. Weighty reports, such as the Brandt Report or Global 2000 or the World Conservation Strategy, all of which came out in the early 1980s, treated population as part of a wider theme. It was the World Commission on Environment and Development (1987) chaired by Gro Harlem Brundtland, the Prime Minister of Norway, which, most famously, took a comprehensive view of the population-environment-development nexus. The Brundtland report "Our Common Future", is widely credited as having coined the concept, or at least the term, "sustainable development". The treatment of population issues given in the Brundtland report was a model of intelligent analysis and sensitive drafting. It set the stage for the last major highlight of the decade of the 1980s, at least as far as the great debate on population was concerned, namely the International Forum on Population in the Twenty-First Century, which was held in Amsterdam in November 1989.

The Amsterdam Declaration on Population and Sustainable Development made clear recommendations about national population goals ("a reduction in the average number of children born per woman commensurate with achieving, as a minimum, the medium variant population projections of the United Nations"). It indicated clear programme priorities ("an increase in contraceptive prevalence in developing countries so as to reach at least 56 per cent of women of reproductive age by the year 2000"). It gave a realistic assessment of programme costs (a minimum annual cost of $US 9 billion, to be compared with the 1987 total of national and international expenditures for family planning and other major population activities in developing countries of around $4.5 billion).

However, the Amsterdam meeting, crucial though it was as far as the intellectual debate was concerned, did not carry the *political* weight which attaches to some other international meetings. Though the United Nations General Assembly would later "take note with appreciation" of the Amsterdam Declaration, many looked to the Earth Summit, the United Nations Conference on Environment and Development (UNCED) which was to be held in Rio de Janeiro, Brazil, in June 1992 for a final political endorsement at the highest level of the Amsterdam vision.

In the event, UNCED's recognition of the centrality of population policies and programmes to the pursuit of sustainable development was less than vociferous. Though Agenda 21's Chapter 5 (on Demographic Dynamics and Sustainability) contained some workmanlike ideas amid the inevitable dense thickets of intergovernmental prose, UNCED could not in the end be said to have taken the consensus on population as far as many hoped. Rio's delegates were, for whatever reason, unable or unwilling to be even as specific as Amsterdam's. Perhaps it was something to do with the climate. Some even argued that Rio's treatment of the population issue was a step backward when compared to earlier internationally agreed texts.

At the end of the 1980s the world population situation was summarised by the UN in the following terms. Under the UN's so-called *medium* variant, total world population would grow from 5.3 billion in 1990 to 8.5 billion in the year 2025. The population of the more developed regions would increase by 12 per cent during that period and that of the less developed regions by 75 per cent. Europe's share of the world's population, which declined from 16 to 9 per cent between 1950 and 1990, would decline further, to 6 per cent by 2025. Africa's share, which increased from 9 to 12 per cent between 1950 and 1990, would rise to 19 per cent in 2025.

The *medium variant* assumes that the total fertility rate for the developing countries as a whole declines from 3.71 for the period 1990–1995, to 2.71 for the period 2010–2015 and 2.32 for 2020–2025.

Under the *low* variant, the world population would reach only 7.6 billion by the year 2025, and 7.8 billion by the year 2050. However, the low variant assumes more rapid falls in fertility. To achieve it, the total fertility rate for the developing regions as a whole would have to decline from 3.38 for the period 1990–1995, to 2.19 for the period 2010–2015 and 1.83 for the period 2020–2025. The long-range projection of the low variant, that is beyond the year 2025, would ultimately bring about an *actual decline* in total world population: to 6 billion in the year 2100 and 4.3 billion by the year 2150. So around one hundred and fifty years from now, world population could — hopefully in an orderly and rational manner and without the intervention of one or more of the Four Horsemen of the Apocalypse — have been clawed back to a level not seen since the beginning of the 1980s.

As the Cairo conference approached, the stakes, whether we looked at the near future, to the middle distance or to the far horizon, seemed thus almost unimaginably high. The difference between the high and the low projections was 327 million people by the year 2000, 1.8 billion by the year 2025, 4.6 billion by 2050 and 13 billion by the end of the next century. In other words people were talking about the difference between, on the one hand, a world which was demographically speaking out of control and, on the other hand, a world where the unprecedented proliferation of the human race (probably the single most distinctive feature of the history of the twentieth century) has at last been contained and even reversed.

Could the fertility levels implied in the "low" projections actually be attained in practice?

By the beginning of the 1990s, important reductions in fertility had been achieved in many parts of the world. The region of East Asia, which included China, had already attained the replacement level fertility of 2.1 children per couple. In Southeastern Asia, Indonesia had achieved a fertility rate of just above 3 taking the country as a whole, but some major provinces had already attained or were on the verge of attaining replacement levels. In Latin America, fertility had declined by at least one child per woman since the 1970s and stood at just above 3 at the beginning of 1990.[5]

In Europe, fertility at 1.7 children per woman was below replacement level (with the highest fertility in Eastern Europe at 2.0 and the lowest in Southern Europe at 1.5, the world record low being held by that staunch Catholic country, Italy, with a rate of 1.3 children per woman, followed closely by another Catholic country, Spain, with a rate of 1.4). Like Europe, Northern America had already attained replacement level fertility at the beginning of the 1990s, as had Australia and New Zealand.

According to the World Bank, the *"central observable event in the reproductive revolution is a substantial irreversible decline in human fertility"*.[6] That reproductive revolution was, however, by no means complete. Though substantial progress had been achieved in many areas of the world, there were other regions where reproductive revolution was either unfinished or had not properly started. The fertility rate per woman over the continent of Africa as a whole still stood at around 6 at the beginning of the 1990s, the highest rate being found in Eastern Africa with 6.8 and the lowest in Southern Africa at 4.2. In Western Asia (or the Middle East) the fertility rate stood at 4.7 and in Southern Asia, an area which included Afghanistan, India, Iran and Pakistan, the rate stood at 4.3. A survey by the Population Information Programme of Johns Hopkins University published in December 1992 indicated that between 20 per cent and 30 per cent of married women had an "unmet need" for family planning.[7]

The Johns Hopkins survey, World Bank studies and numerous other reports indicated that, if family planning programmes met all of the existing potential demand, they would have a dramatic influence on contraceptive prevalence in the developing countries and hence on fertility levels. Surveys indicated that with an increase in contraceptive prevalence from the current level of 51 per cent to over 60 per cent, fertility would fall from an average of about 4 children per woman to about three, or halfway to replacement level. In most countries outside sub-Saharan Africa, a further rise in contraceptive prevalence — to levels of 70–80 per cent — could bring fertility close to replacement.

To many, the main challenge facing the world as the Cairo conference approached was to consolidate existing gains while achieving new breakthroughs in fertility reduction in those areas where progress had been so far limited. New insights might be required; new or different approaches might need to be pursued if these more demographically recalcitrant regions of the world were to be able to follow successfully the trail which others had blazed. From a global perspective, the second "demographic revolution" — namely the transition from high fertility to low fertility — had still some way to go. Both national and international resources would be needed if further reductions in fertility were to be achieved.

Compared with other expenditures, the sums that appeared to be needed were not enormous. It was calculated that if the world was to reach an average family size of two children early in the twenty-first century, 70 to 80 per cent of all couples would need to use contraception by the year 2000. This would require a doubling of family planning users from about 350 million in 1990 to roughly 700 million by the end of the decade. Assuming that the cost of providing high quality family planning information and services is about $16 per couple per annum, annual expenditures on family planning would need to more than double from their current levels — to around $11 billion in constant 1990 dollars. Such a sum (which was less than one per cent of current Third World debt) could put the world firmly on the track towards population stability.

The consolidators, the incrementalists — all those who believed in the kind of perspective that is presented above — were not necessarily so foolish as to imagine that the opposition had disappeared. The Marxist battalions, opposing population limitation on the grounds that revolution will solve the problems of production, might be much diminished as a result of the world-wide collapse of Communism, but the Roman Catholic Church had certainly not given up the attempt to assert the absolute rightness of its own view of the moral and ethical issues relating to population and family planning questions, particularly those having to do with contraception, abortion and certain other aspects of human sexuality. On the contrary, *Humanae Vitae* had been followed — in the months before Cairo — by *Splendor Veritatis*, a document which held out little hope that any major doctrinal revision was in the offing as far as these matters were concerned. And though, in practice, many millions of Catholics around the world apparently ignored the dictates of Rome, the situation was not a happy one. The fact that the current Pope in particular had so much vision and charisma, was in so many ways such an heroic figure, made it all the more poignant that he was still on the other side of the argument, as it were, while adding to the personal anguish of those who were unable to conform to the Church's prescriptions.

THEMES AND AGENDAS FOR CAIRO

On the whole though, as the preparations for the Cairo conference gathered pace, there seemed to be some solid grounds for believing that the last pieces of the jig-saw would fall into place. There might still be intellectual and political disagreements at Cairo, as there were in Bucharest in 1974, and Mexico City in 1984, but those disagreements if they occurred should be less acute and less disruptive than they were in earlier years. There would certainly be some fireworks over the Nile, but few predicted major explosions or a shattering of the slow but sure progress towards consensus that the last years had witnessed. Barring unforeseen accidents or diversions, at the end of the day one message seemed likely to come through loud and clear: *by acting vigorously and effectively to turn back the tide of population growth and to reduce*

*human fertility, mankind would in a very real sense be taking back or
reasserting its duty and its ability to control its own destiny.*

After Brundtland, after Rio, after a score of international meetings and
resolutions which stressed the need to "integrate" population and
development, it was — of course — increasingly apparent that any
putative consensus on population issues could not be limited to the
purely demographic perspective. If a new international consensus on
population was to emerge at Cairo, it had to be based on the profound
conviction that coherent population programmes were a vital third side
of the "population-environment-development triangle" rather than a
bargain-basement substitute for development.

Were such beliefs sufficiently widespread and sufficiently solid to
generate the consensus which would be needed if the Cairo conference
was to achieve the success it deserved? Where, after the previous 30
years, did the great population debate stand? What were the intellectual
and other undercurrents which had determined the course of this
particular river?

At any moment, one or more of several themes might appear to
dominate the population discussion. Sometimes Malthusianism, having
flown out by the window, seemed to be creeping back through the door
and books with titles like *The Population Bomb, Standing Room Only* or
Our Crowded Earth reappear in the shop windows. At other times, the
economic arguments predominated. It was not population growth *per se*
which matters, or so we were told; it was the rate at which populations
were growing in any particular country and the ability of the national
economy to absorb the annual increase. This latter viewpoint certainly
predominated in the 1960s and early 1970s when weighty volumes like
the United States National Academy of Science's massive study, "Rapid
Population Growth: Consequences and Policy Implications",[8] were to be
found on the desks of officials in the World Bank, United Nations
Development Programme (UNDP), USAID and the Ford Foundation.

Or again, action in the field of population and family planning might
be promoted or supported primarily for health or human rights
motivations, with wider demographic considerations taking second
place. The right of couples to choose freely and responsibly the number
and spacing of their children had been enshrined as early as 1968 in the
corpus of international law and was certainly one of the factors which
led to increasing support at national and international level for maternal
and child health programmes which included family planning or for
stand-alone family planning programmes.

Over the years other themes began to emerge. The impact of
population on the environment, and the contribution of population
pressures to ecological degradation, began to be examined more closely

and this in turn necessitated some rethinking. If there were after all "limits to growth" in the long term, and real environmental problems in the shorter term (like desertification) associated with population pressures, perhaps the classic economic theories needed to be looked at again. Perhaps it was not just the rate of population growth; perhaps population *per se* was indeed a problem, particularly when seen in terms of its impact on non-renewable ecological resources. In which case, of course, the matter could no longer be presented as an issue purely for the developing world since it was clear that the rich industrialised world — in particular, the United States, Western Europe and Japan — consumed far more resources on a per capita basis than did most of the inhabitants of Asia, Africa and Latin America. Thus even though the industrial world might have much lower rates of population growth, and in some cases might have already attained replacement levels of fertility or lower, the impact of the average American person (or even the average American dog for that matter) on limited world resources might far outweigh that of, say, 100 villagers in Bihar or Rajasthan. The textbooks of the future may quite possibly treat the equation $I = PAT$, (where I stands for environmental impact, P for Population, A for affluence or per capita consumption, and T is a measure of the environmental damage done by technology in supplying each unit of consumption) with as much respect as they accorded Einstein's historic formula $E = MC^2$!

This latter theme emerged quite strongly at the Earth Summit in June 1992. Principle 8 of the Rio Declaration on Environment and Development stated that:

"To achieve sustainable development and a higher quality of life for all people, States should reduce and eliminate unsustainable patterns of production and consumption and promote appropriate demographic policies."

Chapter 4 of Agenda 21, the international action plan for achieving "sustainable development", was devoted to "changing consumption patterns" and was followed by a chapter on "Demographic Dynamics and Sustainability" which began with the clear statement that "The growth of world population and production combined with unsustainable production patterns places increasingly severe stress on the life-supporting capacities of our planet."

In practice it is always easier to call for changes in consumption patterns than to achieve them. The Earth Summit gave no clear guidance on this front. Some saw a linkage between reducing population growth in the developing world and reducing consumption in the industrialised world, reckoning that the one might be a quid pro quo for the other. Others saw a danger in seeking to strike this kind of a global bargain. Reducing population growth, reducing consumption were objectives to be pursued in their own right without being part of some international package deal.

The process of urbanisation forced another rethink of the classic approaches to population. Urban problems were not purely economic problems, capable of being "solved" through the application of economic measures. In the developing world, many urban problems were linked to the phenomenon of urbanisation, itself a function both of population growth and internal migration (the latter often a result of rural population pressures).

Ultimately, questions of population growth could be linked to the maintenance of world peace itself. The validity of such a linkage had over the years been increasingly explored. It was, for example, specifically mentioned by UN Secretary General Perez de Cuellar in his own speech to the International Conference on Population in 1984, when he said:

> "I consider these [population] activities are directly linked to the first objective of the United Nations, the preservation of peace, since future political stability, like economic development, will depend heavily on the way population policies are handled."

Events of recent years had tended to confirm the wisdom of that observation since population pressures had been at least a contributing factor in local or regional conflicts. The growth in the number of "environmental refugees", particularly in Africa, bore witness to the potentially explosive disruption that might be caused when the population-resources balance tilted out of kilter.

Population and human rights; population and development; population, resources and the environment; population and urbanisation; population and peace — all these were themes which had played their part in the process of building the consensus for action which increasingly took shape in the 1970s and 1980s.

If one single theme, however, can be said to have shaped the outcome of the Cairo conference, it was the theme "population and women". The new emphasis on women's rights and female emancipation has led not so much to an evolution, as a revolution, in thinking about population.

Historically (as noted above) the issue of human rights — and the impact of high fertility on the well-being of individuals and families — has long been to the fore in the population argument. The decade of the eighties gave a much sharper focus to this issue. A woman's right to bear a child, one of the most fundamental human rights of all, increasingly became linked to a woman's right *not* to bear a child. She was, in other

28

words, to be in control of her own body. Population policy, in so far as it encompassed information about and programmes for contraception and family planning, was clearly of the greatest relevance here, even though abortion — an area where different human rights appeared to come into direct conflict with each other like ignorant armies clashing by night — remained a matter of controversy. This was all the more tragic in the light of the evidence that illegal abortions in some parts of the world, particularly in Latin America, represented an enormous human and social problem, a problem that could be substantially reduced if the governments were ready to come forward with enlightened and compassionate legislation in this area.

And if family planning was an integral part of female emancipation, a solid blow struck against the beliefs which prevailed in some regions of the world, for example, in parts of the Middle East, as far as attitudes to women were concerned, so female emancipation (as expressed, for example, in the goals and objectives of the United Nations Women's Decade) was a necessary concomitant of successful family planning programmes. The link between fertility and social patterns extended in both directions. Nothing could be more fundamental.

But as subsequent chapters hopefully will make clear, the preparations for the Cairo conference — and the conference itself — gave a totally new level of importance to the question of the "empowerment of women", to such an extent that in substantive terms it became a dominant theme in the Cairo programme of action. The essence of the Cairo consensus was that it moved away from a modified Malthusian approach towards a holistic approach which takes in poverty, women's status and the structure of society as well as fertility *per se.*

If there was a "paradigm shift" at Cairo, women were at the very heart of it.

The other surprise both before and during the Cairo conference was the tenacity with which the Vatican "fought its corner" and the way in which two of the world's great religions — Islam and Catholicism — made common cause to oppose tendencies and texts which they disliked or distrusted. If women's issues dominate the Cairo text as adopted, the heated debates over abortion, reproductive rights and adolescent sex — and the social attitudes and spiritual and material values relating thereto — dominated the proceedings of the conference itself.

The combination of all these factors, as well as the personalities of some of those most closely involved — Gro Harlem Brundtland, Benazir Bhutto and Dr Nafis Sadik, the Conference's Secretary-General in particular — ensured a powerful, heady cocktail which grabbed the attention of the world's media against all precedent and expectation.

Chapter 2
Preparing for the ICPD

BACKGROUND

As we have seen, the International Conference on Population took place in Mexico City in August, 1984, almost exactly a decade after the World Population Conference held in Bucharest in August 1974. On 26 July 1989 the United Nations Economic and Social Council (ECOSOC) adopted resolution 1989/91 which called for the convening in 1994 of an "international meeting on population". Two years later, on 26 July 1991, ECOSOC adopted resolution 1991/93, in which it decided to call the meeting the International Conference on Population and Development, and further defined the objectives and the themes of the conference. Resolution 1992/37, adopted by the Council on 30 July 1992, accepted with gratitude the offer of the Government of Egypt to host the conference in Cairo from 5–13 September 1994.

The objectives of the conference were set out in Council resolution 1991/93 as follows:

(a) To contribute to the review and appraisal of the progress made in reaching the objectives, goals and recommendations of the World Population Plan of Action and to identify the obstacles encountered.
(b) To identify instruments and mechanisms in order to ensure the operational implementation of the recommendations.
(c) To maintain and strengthen the level of awareness of population issues on the international agenda and their linkage to development.
(d) To consider the desired focus of intensified action at the global, regional and national levels, as well as all necessary ways and

means of treating population issues in their proper development perspective during the forthcoming decade and beyond.

(e) To adopt a set of recommendations for the next decade in order to respond to the above-mentioned population and development issues of high priority.

(f) To enhance the mobilisation of resources needed, especially in developing countries, for the implementation of the results of the conference; resources should be mobilised at the international and national levels by each country according to its capacity.

In the same resolution, the Council emphasised that the overall theme of the conference would be population, sustained economic growth and sustainable development. Within that theme it identified six groups of issues (not listed in any order of priority) as those requiring the greatest attention during the forthcoming decade:

(a) Population growth, changes in demographic structure, including ageing of the population, and the regional diversity of such changes, with particular emphasis on the interaction between demographic variables and socio-economic development;

(b) Population policies and programmes, with emphasis on the mobilisation of resources for developing countries, at the international and national levels by each country according to its capacity;

(c) The interrelationships between population, development, environment and related matters;

(d) Changes in the distribution of population, including socio-economic determinants of internal migration and the consequences for urban and rural development, as well as determinants and consequences of all types of international migration;

(e) Linkages between enhancing the roles and socio-economic status of women and population dynamics, including adolescent motherhood, maternal and child health, education and employment, with particular reference to the access of women to resources and the provision of services;

(f) Family planning programmes, health and family well-being.

THE SIX EXPERT GROUP MEETINGS

ECOSOC, in resolution 1991/93, authorised the Secretary General of the conference to convene six Expert Group Meetings corresponding to the six groups of issues defined above. The Expert Group Meetings were organised by the Population Division of the Department of Economic and Social Development of the United Nations Secretariat, in consultation with the United Nations Population Fund (UNFPA). Each Expert Group included 15 experts, invited in their personal capacities, along with representatives of relevant units, bodies and organizations of the United Nations system and selected intergovernmental and nongovernmental organizations. Efforts were made to have a full range of relevant scientific disciplines and geographical regions represented. Each Expert Group Meeting lasted five days. The standard documentation for each meeting included a substantive background paper prepared by the Population Division in consultation with UNFPA, technical papers prepared by each of the experts and technical contributions provided by the participating UN regional commissions, specialised agencies and other organisations and bodies of the UN system, as well as intergovernmental and non-governmental organisations. At the conclusion of each meeting, a set of recommendations was adopted to be submitted to the Preparatory Committee of the conference at its second session, in May 1993. The number of recommendations in each set varied between 18 and 37, adding up to a total of 162 recommendations.

The first Expert Group Meeting, on population, environment and development, was held at UN headquarters from 20–24 January 1992. The second, on population policies and programmes, was hosted by the government of Egypt in Cairo, from 12–16 April 1992. The third, on population and women, was hosted by the government of Botswana in Gaborone, from 22–26 June 1992 and financed by a contribution from the government of the Netherlands. The fourth, on family planning, health and family well-being, was hosted by the government of India in Bangalore, from 26–29 October 1992. The fifth, on population growth and demographic structure, was hosted by the government of France in Paris, from 16–20 November 1992. The sixth, on population distribution and migration, was hosted by the government of Bolivia in Santa Cruz, from 18–23 January 1993.

At the second session of the Preparatory Committee (PrepCom) for the International Conference on Population and Development, held in New York in May 1993, delegates were provided with a synthesis of the Expert Group Meetings as well as the full reports of the meetings.

In addition to the six Expert Group Meetings, several roundtables were organized following PrepCom II. The roundtable on Women's Perspectives on Family Planning, Reproductive Rights and Reproductive Health was held in Ottawa, Canada, on 26–27 August 1993; and the roundtable on Population Policies and Programmes: the Impact of HIV/AIDS was held in Berlin, Germany, from 28 September to 1 October, 1993. Other roundtables took place during the first months of 1994.

REGIONAL CONFERENCES

Another key element in the preparations for the International Confer-ence on Population and Development to be held in Cairo in September 1994 was the series of regional conferences held during 1992 and 1993 in accordance with ECOSOC resolution 1991/93.

The Bali Declaration

The first of these regional conferences, the Fourth Asian and Pacific Population Conference, jointly sponsored by the Economic and Social Commission for Asia and the Pacific (ESCAP) and UNFPA, was held in Denpasar, Indonesia, from 19–27 August 1992. The conclusions of that conference, enshrined in the Bali Declaration on Population and Sustainable Development, served once again to underline the Asia and Pacific region's "pole position" as far as population policy and family planning programmes were concerned.

The Bali Declaration recognised that fertility, as measured by the total fertility rate (TFR), currently averaged 3.1 per woman in the Asia and Pacific region. However, there were substantial differences between and within the sub-regions of Asia and the Pacific. Fertility, at 2.1 per woman, was currently lowest in East Asia. It was highest, at 4.3 per woman, in South Asia. Similar marked disparities were exhibited in sub-regional levels of mortality. Thus, for example, infant mortality at 90 per 1000 births, in South Asia, was more than three times the level of the corresponding rate in East Asia where it was 26.

In the Bali Declaration,[1] the countries of the ESCAP region set themselves the ambitious target of attaining replacement level fertility by the year 2010.

> "In order to help reduce high rates of population growth, countries and areas should adopt suitable strategies to attain replacement level fertility, equivalent to around 2.2 children per woman, by the year 2010 or sooner."

The ESCAP countries also fixed the objective of reducing the level of infant mortality to 40 per 1000 births or lower during the same period and, in those countries and areas where maternal mortality was high, of reducing it at least by half by the year 2010.

The Dakar/Ngor Declaration

The Third African Population Conference, jointly organised by the Economic Commission for Africa (ECA), the Organisation of African Unity (OAU) and UNFPA, in collaboration with the African Development

33

Bank (ADB) and the Union for African Population Studies (UAPS), was held in Dakar from 7–12 December 1992.

The conference adopted the Dakar/Ngor Declaration on Population, Family and Sustainable Development,[2] which included a commitment by the participating governments to:

> "Integrate population policies and programmes in development strategies, focusing on strengthening social sectors with a view to influencing human development and work towards the solution of population problems by setting *quantified national objectives for the reduction of population growth with a view to bringing down the regional natural growth rate from 3 per cent to 2.5 per cent by the year 2000 and 2 per cent by 2010*."[3] [author's emphasis]

The Dakar/Ngor Declaration, in a section on "Fertility and the Family" declared that African governments should:

> "(a) Create a conducive socio-economic climate and sustained political will for the pursuit of such effective fertility policies as make for (i) setting fertility and family planning (FP) targets for all people of reproductive age and take measures to reduce infertility where needed; (ii) implementing legal measures to improve the status of women and their reproductive health; (iii) establishing strong maternal and child health (MCH) programmes; (iv) ensuring strong management and close collaboration between private and public sectors and communities in the implementation of their MCH and national FP programmes; (v) decentralising health care delivery systems for urban and rural areas; (vi) strengthening information, education and communication (IEC) in MCH and FP programmes; (vii) strengthening family institutions; (viii) addressing unmet family planning needs of adolescents and others; and (ix) promoting the education of men and women on joint responsible parenthood."

The Declaration went further than generalities where family planning was concerned (useful though the generalities listed above were in view of the African continent's very special demographic situation.) The Declaration committed African governments to:

> "Ensure the availability and promote the use of all tested available contraceptive and fertility regulation methods, including traditional and natural family planning methods ensuring choice of methods with a view to doubling the regional contraceptive prevalence rate (CPR) from about 10 to about 20 per cent by the year 2000 and 40 per cent by the year 2010."[4]

The Arab Population Conference

The Economic and Social Commission for Western Asia (ESCWA), the League of Arab States and UNFPA jointly sponsored the Arab Population

Conference in Amman, Jordan, from 4–8 April 1993. Though less forthright than their Asian and Pacific counterparts, the Arab delegates adopted as one of their objectives:

"Achieving appropriate population growth rates through provision of the services needed to attain national policy goals. In the case of countries wishing to reduce their population growth rates, this requires provision of the services needed to develop and enhance family planning and family protection services, including maternal and child health care, and the formulation of economic, social, health and education policies to help create the requisite climate in which couples will accept and react to these objectives."[5]

The Latin American and Caribbean Consensus

The last of the developing world's regional conferences, the Latin America and Caribbean Population and Development Conference, jointly sponsored by the Economic Commission for Latin America and the Caribbean (ECLAC) and UNFPA, was held in Mexico City from 29 April to 4 May 1993.[6] The conference adopted the Latin American and Caribbean Consensus, which, like the declarations from the other regional gatherings, viewed its subject matter not through narrowly focused spectacles but in the larger framework of social and economic priorities. In the Latin American and Caribbean case, the key was the search for "equity". This, by itself, was not surprising since social inequalities within the Latin American nations were certainly as high, if not higher, than those obtaining in other regions of the world. An analysis prepared by ECLAC and the Latin American Demographic Centre (CELADE)[7] and presented to the conference argued that achieving greater equity within Latin American societies was an important and possibly essential element in the control of fertility. The rich, as the old saying had it, got richer while the poor got children.

The search for equity between nations was no less important than the search for equity within nations. The region's external indebtedness accounted for a more than disproportionate share (almost a quarter) of overall Third World debt. The Consensus stated:

"External debt and its servicing place a heavy burden on Latin American and Caribbean countries that prevents resources being allocated for development; specifically, it prevents those countries from giving priority to social programmes aimed at raising the population's standard of living. Consequently, regional consensus-building mechanisms must be created to release resources now used to repay and service debt for the implementation of social development programmes, including those related to population and development."

Debt-servicing could force structural adjustment programmes with their difficult consequences for social expenditures (including family planning programmes) no less surely than the International Monetary Fund.

The Latin American and Caribbean Consensus on Population and Development recognised that:

> "One of the most outstanding demographic changes in Latin America and the Caribbean in the past 25 years is the pronounced decline in fertility, from 6 to 3.5 children per woman."[8]

However, there were wide disparities between the countries in the region, evidenced not only by differences in basic demographic indicators, such as fertility and life expectancy, but also in discrimination directed against women. Special efforts had to be made to "prevent any lack of equity with respect to women's education and employment status" and to reduce the high morbidity and mortality rates associated with child birth.

Given that this was an official governmental conference, and given the fact that the conference was being held in a Latin American country with a majority of the delegates being Latin American (and probably Catholic), it was not surprising that the meeting failed to address the abortion issue as directly as had some of the Expert Groups referred to earlier. However, Jyoti Singh, a senior UNFPA official who served as Executive Coordinator for the International Conference on Population and Development (ICPD), did allude forcefully to the topic of abortion in his opening speech in Mexico City, as did some of the Caribbean delegates.

The UNFPA circulated a paper which stated that throughout the region "abortion is pervasive and carried out in vast numbers". In the early 1980s, it was estimated that 3.4 million women had resorted to induced abortion, with a rate of 45 abortions for each 1000 women of childbearing age. (UNFPA estimated that each year throughout the world nearly 55 million unwanted pregnancies were terminated through abortion.[9])

The upshot of it all was that a grammatically opaque but none the less helpful reference was included in the final Consensus document:

> "Considering that abortion is a major public health issue in the countries of the region and that, while various views are held in this regard, none of them accepts abortion as a method of regulating fertility, it is recommended that governments devote greater attention to the study and follow-up of this issue, with a view to evaluating how prevalent abortion really is and its impact on the health of women and their families; governments should also promote universal access to proper guidance on how to prevent unwanted pregnancies."

On the family planning front, the Consensus stressed the need for quality and for a variety of choice of contraceptive methods, and sounded a note of caution about the use of female sterilisation, reported to be the most widely used method of birth control in the world (it was estimated that nearly one-third of the women who controlled their fertility had undergone this treatment.)[10] The Consensus asked for more attention to be given to the rhythm method of family planning "taking into account that some population groups show a preference for methods based on periodic abstinence". It also recommended that governments, though it might be "desirable to set targets as to either the number of users or fertility rates" refrain from "establishing quotas for the number of persons that may use the services provided". Targets — *si*; quotas — *non!*

The European Conference

Participants in the European Population Conference, which was jointly convened by the Economic Commission for Europe (ECE), the Council of Europe and UNFPA and held in Geneva, from 23–26 March 1993, included the major donors from Europe and North America. It was therefore a matter of particular interest that the conference made a strong plea for strengthened international cooperation in the population field. Recommendation 51 stated:

> "Cooperation with developing countries should be built upon a strengthened partnership based on the recognition of sovereign equality, mutual interest and shared responsibility with mutual commitments. While developing countries have a primary responsibility for their own economic and social development, including the formulation and implementation of appropriate national policies relating to population and development, *developed countries have a special responsibility to help create a favourable international economic environment and to increase the quantity and quality of their assistance, particularly in the field of population.*" [author's emphasis]

In its Recommendation 53, the European conference referred to the "large, and growing, unmet demand in developing countries for family planning services" and to UNFPA's estimates that 300 million women lacked access to such services.

> "Efforts should thus be intensified to ensure the availability of family planning services to all who wish to make use of them. Such efforts can be expected to help in achieving population growth rates which contribute to a sustainable use of natural resources."

As one of the basic principles of cooperation, the European conference attached "particular importance to gender perspectives, to the full involvement of both women and men in reproductive health programmes" and to improving the status of women who should be "free to make responsible decisions affecting their lives and those of their families, including decisions on reproduction".

The Recommendations of the European conference called on governments of the region

> "to be aware that poverty, population growth and environmental degradation are closely interrelated. While population growth and poverty result in certain kinds of environmental stress, the major causes of the continued deterioration of the global environment are the unsustainable patterns of production and consumption, particularly in industrialised countries."

The conference recommended that "common targets should be the promotion of patterns of consumption and production that reduce environmental stress, and the encouragement of social and economic development that meets basic needs and allows for better living conditions and appropriate fertility rates".

The call to change consumption patterns in the rich, industrialised world had, as we noted in the previous chapter, been a feature of the UN Conference on Environment and Development (UNCED) held in Rio in June 1992. UNCED's recommendations as to just how such consumption patterns were to be changed had been on the thin side, inviting much further study but little specific action.[11] The recommendations of the European conference in this respect were, if anything, pitched at an even higher level of generality. There was little, if any, talk in Geneva in March 1993 of a "global bargain" under which the West would change its lifestyles, and the South would change (or further change) its patterns of fertility. That kind of a deal was not on the table in Geneva, nor — by all indications — would it be on the table in Cairo in September 1994. There were undoubtedly many good reasons for the West to change its lifestyle, just as there were many good reasons for the South to reduce rapid rates of population growth but the two issues would not, and probably could not, be linked as part of an international negotiating process.

ICPD PREPCOM II, MAY 1993

As already noted, the participants in the Expert Groups attended in a personal capacity, while the series of regional population conferences took place at the official governmental level. Already in 1992 and 1993, national positions on key issues were being worked out and the framework for subsequent negotiations established. However, it was not until the second meeting of the PrepCom of the ICPD, held in New York in May 1993, that the main elements of a new action plan for world population began to emerge.

Goals for 2015

In her speech to the PrepCom on 14 May, 1993, Dr Nafis Sadik, the ICPD's Secretary General, invited delegates to consider a set of goals for inclusion in the new World Population Plan of Action.

> "I propose that all countries commit themselves to reach or assist others to reach the average of the developing countries in such areas as maternal mortality, infant mortality, life expectancy, education especially for women and girls, gender equality and availability of and access to a full range of modern, safe and effective family planning services to enable the exercise of choice.
>
> "Such an approach should be seen as a challenge for the whole international community rather than an imposition on any part of it. Setting goals for the international community is not an attempt to impose a rigid formula, or to over-simplify a complex problem, but rather a way to address the basic components of an acceptable quality of life for all members of our global family. The proposed 20 year time-frame offers the necessary flexibility of response by individual countries and the wider community."

Dr Sadik went on to say: "A call for quantifiable, reachable goals is unusual for a conference such as ours, but not unprecedented. Optimism as well as commitment will be needed for success."

Total size of the human family

Dr Sadik addressed herself first to the "total size of the human family". Looking forward to 2025, three scenarios were proposed by the UN's Secretariat's Population Division, based on different assumptions about fertility. The projections ranged from a high of 7.92 billion in 2015 to a low of 7.27 billion. The difference in world population between high and low projections was 660 million. The difference between the medium and low scenarios was 338 million. Of these, 266 million would be in today's developing countries and only 71 million in the developed regions.

Though Dr Sadik had suggested after the UNCED conference that attaining the medium projection should be the overall policy goal objective, in her speech to the PrepCom in May 1993, she was able to advise delegates of an important evolution in her (and UNFPA's) thinking and of the reasons for it.

"The needs and the impact of a population of 7.27 billion in 2015, the *low* projection, are very different from the high projection of 7.92 billion, or even 7.61 billion, the *medium* projection. *I believe that we must strive for the low projection. I believe that it can be achieved with sufficient commitment at the local, national and international level. There is ample evidence that the currently unmet needs of couples and individuals make up the difference between the medium and the low population scenario.* As many as 300 million people have no access to contraception, and there are many more who know that information and services are available but in fact have no access to them." [author's emphasis]

In formal terms, the Secretary General of the ICPD circulated a paper to delegates under the heading GOALS FOR 2015 which contained the following paragraph:

"The Secretary General of the conference believes that the low population projection can be reached by 2015, if family planning information and services are provided to all couples and individuals who need them and if policies are formulated and implemented to empower women to participate fully in socio-economic development. *She therefore urges the conference to set the goal of attaining the low variant population projection of 7.27 billion for 2015.*" [author's emphasis]

The last sentence, especially, was a clear and unambiguous statement. Dr Sadik did not mince her words; she did not duck and weave. She did not urge the conference to "consider the possibility of setting the goal . . . " or even to "envisage considering the possibility of setting the goal, etc." As Secretary General of the conference, and as Executive Director of UNFPA, she had a right and a duty to show leadership. In proposing to PrepCom II to adopt the "low variant" with all that that implied in terms of further falls in fertility, particularly in sub-Saharan Africa, South and West Asia, North Africa, and some parts of Latin America, Dr Nafis Sadik set the stage for a final immense effort in the international endeavour, now decades old, to "turn the tide" of human fertility.

Infant mortality   Dr Sadik also proposed other specific targets. She suggested that *infant mortality* in the developing countries, which had dropped from 92 per 1000 births in 1970–75 to 62 over the period 1990–95 should be reduced to the developed country levels (12 deaths per 1000 in 1990–95).

"Is it realistic to believe that infant mortality could be so dramatically reduced in 20 years? The answer must be yes. We know why these infants are dying. The remedies are affordable if the resources are available."

Maternal mortality She proposed that *maternal mortality* be reduced in the developing countries to 30 per 100,000 live births (the level of the developed countries) from the present 450 per 100,000 live births.

> "It is estimated that half a million women die each year as a consequence of pregnancy. Almost all these deaths are preventable. As many as half result from unsafe and illegal abortions."

The issue of *abortion*, she felt, had to be addressed as a health issue, not as a means of family planning. "The international community is expecting us to turn our attention to this subject. We must not shy away from it."

She proposed that the gap in *life-expectancy* between developed and developing regions should be closed (aiming at 75 years for developing countries by 2015, as against the projected 77.5 years for the developed countries).

She also recommended that the conference should also adopt the goal of *"universal access to and completion of primary education" by 2015*. She proposed, to achieve this, that access to quality education must be assured for girls and women, and obstacles removed that hampered their active participation.

Family planning Finally, Dr Sadik turned to the question of targets for access to family planning information and services. *"In no other area"*, she said, *"has such dramatic progress been achieved. In 1970–75, contraceptive prevalence in developed regions was between 65–70 per cent compared with 20-25 per cent in developing regions. In 1990 virtually no change had been recorded in developed regions while developing regions had doubled to 51 per cent."* However, there was still a very large measure of unmet demand in developing countries.

> "Clear evidence is found in the 50 million abortions that take place each year. All of these women would surely have preferred to have prevented rather than interrupted their pregnancies. This especially applies to adolescents, for whom pregnancy carries special risks."

The paper on GOALS FOR 2015 circulated to delegates proposed a target of *71 per cent for contraceptive prevalence by the year 2015*.

What in practice did this imply for fertility? Dr Sadik pointed out that there had been a steady decline in total fertility from 4.46 (in 1970–75) to around 3.26. "If steps are taken to meet unmet demand among couples and individuals for family planning information and services, this rate could well decline to 2.62 by the year 2015."[12]

41

GENERAL DISCUSSION AT PREPCOM II

Throughout the four days of debate at PrepCom II, governments, UN agencies and non-governmental organisations (NGOs) made a number of concrete recommendations on the structure, format and content of what became known succinctly as "the Cairo Document". The highlights of the debate were captured by journalists from the *Earth Negotiations Bulletin*, an invaluable reporting service covering international negotiations in the field of development and environment, published by the International Institute for Sustainable Development in Winnipeg, Canada.

> "Colombia, on behalf of the Group of 77, recommended a chapter on finance for international cooperation for population activities and suggested that more emphasis be placed on issues such as education, empowerment of women, the role of men in family planning, and migration. Denmark, on behalf of the EC, identified four key areas for organising the proposed section on guiding principles: Human Rights and Population; Human Development and Population; Sustainable Development and Population; and Partnership and Population.
>
> "Egypt proposed that the principles section be merged into the section on choices and responsibilities and that the preamble be expanded to include the right to development, national sovereignty, mutual responsibility and global partnership. Sweden, on behalf of the Nordic countries, stated that the draft outline must be better articulated with regard to the interrelationships and dynamics between population, sustained economic growth and sustainable development. Sweden also urged that the document should address follow-up measures, and suggested that Part II of the draft outline should give special emphasis to a limited number of issues or clusters such as: integrating population concerns into development; the role and status of women; and reproductive rights, reproductive health and family planning.
>
> "Australia urged that over-consumption and inequitable distribution of wealth be addressed and that additional resources are needed to improve both the quality and the availability of reproductive health services. Zimbabwe said that the document needs to consider financial provisions. Canada suggested that the Commission on Sustainable Development should participate in the monitoring of the results of the ICPD and that the conference should focus more on the causes, rather than the effects, of international migration. Poland and the Russian Federation called for distinctions to be maintained between regional and global recommendations, especially in light of the special socio-economic problems of countries in transition."[13]

Of particular interest given the position taken by the United States at the Mexico City conference was the US delegate's intervention. Speaking on behalf of the United States, Timothy Wirth, a former US senator, stressed the changes in US policy since President Clinton took office. He mentioned that the US was developing a comprehensive new approach to international population issues, including: freedom of choice regarding family size; access to quality reproductive health care; the empowerment of women; preservation of the natural environment; and sustainable development. He mentioned three major concerns to be addressed by the conference: women's health and status; population and the environment; and migration. Finally, he said that the US *"supported reproductive choice, including access to safe abortion."* This last comment, according to the *Bulletin*, "generated a round of applause".

Another interesting — and possibly courageous intervention — was made by India, which stated that the Cairo conference should not become an umbrella conference that crowded the agenda with important issues that were not directly related to population and development, such as the environment and women. India also made a number of specific recommendations for the restructuring of the conceptual framework to focus more on population.

The position of the Holy See was of particular concern. As we have seen, the Holy See at the Bucharest and Mexico Conferences had, at the end of the day, refused to join the consensus even though in certain cases the text of key documents had been sensibly modified or weakened in order to accommodate its objections. In Rio, at UNCED, the Vatican had again sought, and on the whole succeeded, in diluting the recommendations on population. Would Cairo be a repetition of Bucharest, Mexico and Rio?

Though no doubt there was still scope for the Vatican to fight some rearguard actions over terminology ("couples", as opposed to "individuals and couples" or — worst of all from the Vatican's point of view — simply "individuals"), the key issue for the Holy See looking towards Cairo 1994 was perhaps not so much contraception, as abortion.

ABORTION

Most of the Expert Groups had clearly recommended that women should have legal access to abortion counselling and services. The need for safe legal abortion had been stressed in the context of the various regional population conferences, including in that most Catholic of regions, Latin America. The Secretary General of the conference, who spoke with the authority of gender as well as position, had — as noted above — urged delegates not to shrink from the issue. Her deputy, Jyoti Singh, had used similar terms at the opening of the Latin America and

Caribbean regional population conference in Mexico in May 1993. Any new World Population Plan of Action worth its salt would surely have to address this issue head on.

During the debate on the Conceptual Framework, Archbishop Renato R Martino, speaking for the Holy See, stated that voluntary abortion under the guise of other perceived rights "violates the most fundamental right of any human being to life". He said that the Catholic Church did not propose procreation at any cost, but rather it opposed "demographic policies and family planning that are contrary to the liberty, dignity and conscience of the human being".

According to the *Bulletin*,[14] at the conclusion of the Holy See's intervention, Dr Sai, PrepCom's Chairman "welcomed the introduction of moral and ethical issues into the discussion. He then asked why the Vatican could support the blessings of modern medicine but could not make modern contraceptives available, saying that morals and ethics are a two-way street." Though not even the *Bulletin* recorded the fact, anecdotal evidence suggests that Dr Sai's well-aimed thrust met with applause from several, perhaps many, of the delegations present. Certainly in the debate which followed, several delegations, including Sweden and the United States, urged that attention should be given to this issue, above all in the health context. Argentina, predictably, expressed its opposition to any mention of abortion in the context of family planning.

A key paragraph on the subject of abortion was included in the "Chairman's Summary on the Conceptual Framework". Though it could not be considered as an agreed record of the meeting (pressures of time ruled that option out), the Chairman's summary, presented by Dr Sai on the last day of PrepCom II, could safely be deemed to reflect the general tendency of the meeting. The text of paragraph 37 of the Chairman's Summary[15] read as follows:

> "It was pointed out that among the issues that the conference needed to address were unacceptably high levels of maternal mortality and morbidity in many developing countries. Unsafe and illegal abortion, which in many countries was an important cause of maternal morbidity and mortality, constituted one of the most neglected problems affecting women's lives. It was seen by most delegations as a major public health issue which the conference needed to recognize and address as such. While many delegations suggested that all women should have access to safe abortion, others suggested that the best way to eliminate abortions was provision of effective, modern contraception information and services; a few delegations reiterated that abortion should not be promoted as a method of family planning."

QUANTITATIVE GOALS

Encouragingly, the Chairman's summary indicated that:[16]

"there was general support for the proposal of the Secretary General of the Conference to include a set of quantitative goals in the Cairo document. Such goals must take into account regional and national variations. Some delegations suggested that the proposed time-frame of 20 years could be segmented into 5- and 10-year frames. Progress towards achieving the goals should be monitored.

"The point was made by many delegations that the goals must be consistent with each other and with those set at other international forums. There must be no coercion of any kind in the programmes formulated to achieve those goals. Some delegations suggested the possibility of including other social and economic goals."

RESOURCES FOR THE NEW WORLD POPULATION PLAN FOR ACTION

On the question of resources for population activities, another issue which was unlikely to be finally resolved until the last minute of the Cairo meeting (if then), the Chairman's summary stated[17] that "the Amsterdam Declaration on a Better Life for Future Generations ... should be refined in this respect, so as to provide the Cairo conference with more precise estimates of the resources required over the next decade."

Reference was also made in the Chairman's summary to the proceedings of the European Population Conference. A paper presented to that conference by Halvor Gille, former Deputy Executive Director of UNFPA, had pointed out that the $9 billion estimate was in 1989 dollars; after adjustment for inflation it would be around $13 billion in the year 2000 if a similar change in purchasing power should apply as experienced in the 1980s.[18] Gille argued, moreover, that if the goals set by the Amsterdam Forum as regards the reduction of infant and maternal mortality were to be achieved, core population activities would not be sufficient; improved maternal and child health care such as antenatal and postnatal care, health education, promotion of breastfeeding and the immunisation of infants would also be needed, requiring an additional amount of between $4 and $7.6 billion annually.

A few weeks after the second session of the ICPD Preparatory Committee ended, Population Action International (PAI) published estimates of the resource requirements involved in stabilising world population below the 10 billion level.[19] PAI calculated that if the world was to reach an average family size of two children early in the twenty-first century, 70 to 80 per cent of all couples would need to use contraception by the year 2000, requiring a doubling of family planning users from about 350 million in 1990 to roughly 700 million by the end of the decade. Assuming that the cost of providing high-quality family planning information and services was about $16 per couple, annual expenditures on family planning would need to more than double to about $11 billion in constant 1990 dollars, or, adjusted for inflation, to an estimated $15 billion.

The goals put forward by PAI were obviously more ambitious, at least in terms of target dates, than those proposed by ICPD's Secretary General — and those proposals were in themselves, as noted above, bold enough. The new calculations were nevertheless of interest in providing, or attempting to provide, an answer to the question: how much would "going for broke", that is attaining replacement level fertility by the end of the century, cost?

PAI also addressed itself very directly to the question of donor contributions. It pointed out that at the Amsterdam forum the international community agreed that four per cent of overall development assistance should be allocated to population programmes. In 1991, however, the industrialised countries contributed an average of slightly more than one per cent of total foreign aid to population assistance. Overall, the share of development assistance allocated to population activities increased only marginally between 1982 and 1991.

Some donors did more than others. Norway had led the way by consistently committing four to five per cent of economic assistance to population. Finland, the United States, Denmark, Sweden and Canada had also contributed well above the donor average. Other countries making a significant effort included the Netherlands, the United Kingdom and Germany.

"Many rich countries, however" Population Action International commented, "are still not doing their fair share to make family planning more widely available in poorer countries." Japan, while a major donor in absolute terms, had consistently contributed under one per cent of official development assistance to population. France and Italy provided negligible levels of population assistance relative to their large aid programmes and to the effort made by the United Kingdom and Germany.

THE UN GENERAL ASSEMBLY, NOVEMBER 1993

On 4–5 November 1993, the UN General Assembly considered a number of documents relating to the ICPD, including the Report of the Secretary

46

General on the implementation of General Assembly resolution 47/167 and ECOSOC resolution 1991/93 (A/48/430) and the annotated outline of the final document of the conference (A/48/430/Add.1) which covered the main headings shown in the box overleaf.

The annotated outline was the focus of many statements during the Second Committee debate. These were summarised by Dr Sadik in her closing statement as follows:

- The "centrality of population" must be maintained in the deliberations and in the final document, while at the same time the interrelationships between population, sustained economic growth and sustainable development were to be stressed.
- The recommendations should be action-oriented, clear and concise.
- There should be an emphasis on implementable activities, not just recommendations.
- The interests and rights of the individual must be central in all population and development efforts.
- Personal integrity, the particular needs of women, and freedom of choice must be extended in all population programmes.
- The empowerment of women in society must be championed in its own right.
- The document should give more attention to sexuality and the family planning needs of youth and adolescents.

With regard to *goals*, Dr Sadik observed:

> "I am pleased to note your strong support for the inclusion of a set of 20-year goals in the draft Cairo document. I should like to reiterate here that we are *not* proposing the setting of demographic targets or quotas. The attainment of these goals, which focus on the needs of the individual and the responsibility of society to protect them, will result, in the opinion of the experts, in demographic consequences, that is, a decline in population growth rates. *The optimistic estimates indicate that population levels could stabilise at the low population projection level of the United Nations.* The goals we are proposing relate to infant, child and maternal mortality; universal access to and completion of primary school education; and *universal access to family planning information and services with emphasis on meeting all unmet demand.*" [author's emphasis]

This then was the skeleton of the new World Population Plan of Action as it was presented to the UN General Assembly in November 1993. With the Second Committee's debate on the International Conference on Population and Development at an end, the next step could begin. Delegates would meet in informal session to negotiate a resolution that would likely elevate the status of the ICPD Preparatory Committee to a subsidiary body of the General Assembly, and determine the 1994

Part One Preamble and Principles

I Preamble

II Principles

Part Two Choices and Responsibilities

III The Interrelationships between Population, Sustained Economic Growth and Sustainable Development
   A Population, sustained economic growth and sustainable development
   B Population, socio-economic development and poverty alleviation
   C Population and the environment

IV Gender Equality and Empowerment of Women
   A Empowerment and the status of women
   B Male responsibilities and participation
   C The girl child

V The Family, its Roles, Composition and Structure
   A Diversity of family structures and composition
   B Socio-economic support to the family

VI Population Growth and Structure
   A Diversity of fertility, mortality and population growth rates
   B Children and youth
   C Ageing populations
   D Disabled persons
   E Indigenous people

VII Reproductive Rights, Reproductive Health and Family Planning
   A Reproductive health
   B Family planning
   C Human sexuality and gender relations
   D Adolescents

VIII Health and Mortality
   A Maternal morbidity and mortality
   B Infant and child mortality
   C Sexually transmitted diseases and acquired immune deficiency syndrome
   D Primary health care and the health-care sector

IX Population Distribution, Urbanisation and Internal Migration
   A Population distribution, natural resources and the environment
   B Population distribution policies and sustainable development strategies
   C Population growth in large urban agglomerations
   D Displaced persons

X International Migration
   A International migration and development
   B Documented migrants
   C Undocumented migrants
   D Refugees

XI Population Information, Education and Communication
   A Public awareness
   B Information, education and communication

XII Capacity-Building
   A Management of programmes
   B Education and training of policy makers, managers and other personnel
   C Institutional development

XIII Technology, Research and Development
   A Basic data collection and analysis
   B Biomedical research and development
   C Social and economic research and development

XIV National Action
   A National policies and plans of action
   B Resource allocation

XV International Cooperation
   A Modalities
   B Resource mobilisation: bilateral and multilateral development assistance

XVI Partnerships with Non-Governmental Groups, Including Non-Governmental Organisations, the Private Sector and Local Community Groups

XVII Follow-Up
   A Implementation
   B Monitoring and review

budgetary implications for the Preparatory Committee and the conference. That resolution would be procedural in nature. It was expected to be adopted by the Second Committee in mid-December and then forwarded to the Plenary before the General Assembly concluded for the year.

As far as the *substance* was concerned — the business of putting flesh on the skeleton — the preparatory process would be pursued with ever-increasing intensity through the first half of 1994 with the third session of the PrepCom formally scheduled to take place at UN headquarters in New York from 4–22 April 1994. With the active participation of non-governmental organisations envisaged for every stage of the process (including at the Cairo conference itself where some 10,000 NGOs were anticipated), it would at the end of the day be up to the nations and peoples of the world to ensure that the document which finally went to, and emerged from, Cairo in September 1994 was the best that could possibly be achieved.

Chapter 3

The Third Meeting of ICPD's Preparatory Committee

On 24 January, 1994, the United Nations circulated to the Preparatory Committee for the International Conference on Population and Development (ICPD) a document for discussion at the Committee's third session, to be held in New York in April 1994. The document was called: "DRAFT FINAL DOCUMENT OF THE CONFERENCE: Draft Programme of Action."[1]

The ICPD PrepCom, like the forthcoming Cairo conference itself, would of course be sovereign in its deliberations and therefore not necessarily bound by the text prepared by the secretariat (even though that text followed closely the outline shown in the previous chapter); it is none the less worth looking fairly closely at the Draft Programme of Action in so far as it represented at that time the most comprehensive statement to date of a possible new international consensus on population and development.

The ICPD's Draft Programme of Action was not a short document. With its 83 pages, it exceeded in length the World Population Plan of Action adopted at the first World Population Conference held at Bucharest in August 1974 (23 pages),[2] as well the Recommendations for the Further Implementation of the World Population Plan of Action adopted at the International Conference on Population held in Mexico City in August 1984 (36 pages).[3] For *aficionados* of the international conference circuit, some comfort could be taken from the fact that the draft Cairo document was substantially shorter than the 600-page draft of Agenda 21 submitted to the United Nations Conference on Environment and Development (UNCED) held in Rio de Janeiro in June 1992.[4]

Within those 83 pages of the ICPD's Draft Programme of Action, what were the key elements of the possible new consensus? There is, inevitably, an element of subjectiveness in producing an answer to that question. People tend to look first for the things they expect or wish to see. Environmentalists may look for evidence that the Draft Programme has something new to say about the thorny issue of "changing consumption patterns". The priority according to the role of "indigenous peoples" will be a primary interest of several non-governmental organisations (NGOs). NGOs as a whole will probably focus on the way in which the Draft Programme recognises NGO concerns and provides for their active involvement and participation.

That said, given the particular perspectives of this book and given the limitations of space, what were the most noteworthy features of the draft programme?

POPULATION GROWTH

As we have seen,[5] the objective of *world population stabilisation* had not so far been formally retained by an official intergovernmental conference organised under the auspices of the UN. The Cairo draft programme pointed out that in 1985–1990, 44 per cent of the world's population were living in the 114 countries that had population growth rates of more than 2 per cent per annum. Those countries included nearly all countries in Africa, whose population doubling times average about 24 years, two-thirds of those in Asia and one-third of those in Latin America. On the other hand, 66 countries comprising 23 per cent of the world population, the majority of them in Europe, had growth rates of less than one per cent per annum. The first *objective* proposed in the draft programme's section on Population Growth and Structure,[6] was:

> "To reduce disparities in national and regional population growth and *achieve stabilisation of the world population as soon as possible*, fully respecting individual rights, aspirations and responsibilities, in order to create conditions for developmental sustainability at the community, national and global level." [author's emphasis].

The draft programme's section on The Interrelationships Between Population, Sustained Economic Growth and Sustainable Development,[7] argued that indiscriminate pursuit of economic growth in nearly all countries "with little or no regard for conserving natural resources or protecting the environment" was threatening or undermining the basis for progress by future generations. "Substantial research also indicates that demographic pressures often exacerbate problems of environmental degradation and resource depletion and thus inhibit sustainable development." The Draft Programme proposed as an *objective*:[8]

> "To achieve and maintain a *harmonious balance between population, resources, food supplies, the environment, and development*, in order not to constrain the prospects for future generations to attain a decent quality of life. This implies reassessing and changing agricultural, industrial and energy policies, reducing excessive resource consumption, and *curbing unsustainable population growth and distribution*." [author's emphasis]

How soon was population stabilisation to be achieved? The January 1994 draft programme did not tackle this issue head on but rather suggested that, if the measures proposed in the Programme were taken, the result would be world population growth "close to the United Nations low variant." Paragraph 1.20 of the draft programme is worth quoting in full.

> "During the remaining six years of this critical decade the world's nations by their actions or inactions will choose from among a range of alternative demographic futures. The most likely of these alternatives are foreseen in the low, medium and high variants of the United Nations populations projections. Looking ahead 20 years, these alternate projections range from a low of 7.27 billion people in 2015 to a high of 7.92 billion. The difference of 660 million people in the short span of 20 years is nearly equivalent to the current population of the African continent. By the year 2050, the United Nations low projection shows a world population of 7.8 billion, and the high projection a population of 12.5 billion. *Implementation of the goals and objectives contained in this 20-year Programme of Action, which address many of the fundamental population, health, education and development challenges facing the entire human community, would result in world population growth during this period and beyond at levels close to the United Nations low variant.*" [author's emphasis]

OTHER KEY ELEMENTS OF THE PROGRAMME OF ACTION

What were some of the specific elements of the proposed Programme of Action, which, if implemented, could result in the attainment of the "low variant" population levels (which would see world population peak at about 7.8 billion around the middle of the next century and decline thereafter)?

The January 1994 draft proposed that the Cairo conference should adopt quantitative goals in three areas that were described as "mutually supporting and of critical importance to the achievement of other population and development objectives". These areas are: education, especially for girls; infant, child and mortality reduction; and the provision of universal access to family planning and reproductive health services.

Education

The draft pointed out that in spite of notable efforts by countries around the globe that have appreciably expanded access to basic education, there were approximately 960 million illiterate adults in the world, of whom two-thirds were women. More than one-third of the world's adults, most of them women, had no access to printed knowledge, to new skills and technologies that would improve the quality of their lives and help them shape and adapt to social and economic change. Around 130 million children were not enrolled in primary school and 70 per cent were girls.

> "Beyond the achievement of the goal of universal primary education in all countries before 2015, all countries are urged to ensure the widest and earliest possible access by girls and women to secondary and higher levels of education, bearing in mind the need to improve the quality and relevance of that education."[9]

Infant and maternal mortality

In the last half century, expectation of life at birth in the world as a whole had increased by about 20 years and the risk of dying in the first year of life had been reduced by nearly two-thirds. The draft pointed out that there nevertheless remained entire national populations and sizeable population groups within many countries that were still subject to very high rates of morbidity and mortality, particularly among infants and young children and women in their childbearing years. The draft proposed that:

> "Countries should aim to achieve by 2015 a life expectancy at birth greater than 75 years; countries with the highest levels of mortality should aim to achieve by 2015 a life expectancy at birth greater than 70 years"[10]

The draft pointed out that the number of infant deaths per 1000 live births at the world level had declined from 92 in 1970–1975 to about 62 in 1990–1995. For developed regions, the decline was from 22 to 12 deaths of children under one per 1000 births, and for developing regions from 105 to 69 deaths per 1000 births. The draft proposed that, over the next 20 years, the gap between average infant and child mortality rates should be "substantially lowered", and major differences among socio-economic and ethnic groups should be eliminated.

> "Countries should strive to reduce their infant and under-five mortality rates by one-third or to 50 and 70 per 1000 live births, respectively, whichever is less, by 2000, with appropriate adaptation to the particular situation of each country: countries with the highest levels of mortality should aim in any case to achieve these levels by 2015. Countries with intermediate levels of mortality should aim to achieve by 2015 an infant mortality rate below 35 per 1000 live births and an under-five mortality rate below 45 per 1000. Countries which achieve these levels should strive to further lower them."

As far as maternal mortality was concerned, the draft pointed out that, at the global level, half a million women each year died from pregnancy-related causes, 99 per cent of them in developing countries. Rates of maternal mortality range from 700 per 100,000 live births in the least developed countries to about 26 per 100,000 live births in the developed regions. The draft proposed as an objective:

> "To achieve a rapid and substantial reduction of maternal morbidity and mortality, reducing the differences observed between developing and developed countries, and eliminate all deaths from unsafe abortion."

The draft proposed that countries with intermediate levels of mortality should aim to achieve by the year 2015 a maternal mortality rate below 60 per 100,000 live births. Countries with the highest levels of mortality should aim to achieve by 2015 a maternal mortality rate below 75 per 100,000 live births.

The draft's treatment of the still controversial issue of abortion was clear and concise. It was estimated[11] that 50 million abortions occurred each year, many of them unsafe. Mortality resulting from complications of poorly performed abortions accounted for a significant proportion of the annual 500,000 maternal deaths "particularly in countries where abortions are unsafe and illegal."[12]

> "All governments, intergovernmental and non-governmental organisations are urged to deal openly and forthrightly with unsafe abortion as a major health concern. Governments are urged to assess the health impact of unsafe abortion, to reduce the need for abortion through expanded and improved family planning services and to frame abortion laws and policies on the basis of a commitment to women's health and well-being rather than on criminal codes and punitive measures. Prevention of unwanted pregnancies must always be given the highest priority and all attempts should be made to eliminate the need for abortion. In the case of rape and incest, women should have access to safe abortion services. Women who wish to

terminate their pregnancies should have ready access to reliable information, compassionate counselling and services for the management of unsafe abortions."

Though the draft stopped short of calling for the general legalisation of abortion, there was no question that a new orientation, a new approach was being proposed, in particular with the reference to the need to frame abortion laws on the basis of a commitment to women's health rather than from a criminal or punitive perspective. It remained an open question whether this brave language would survive the April 1994 meeting of the ICPD's PrepCom and the subsequent debate during the Cairo conference itself.

Family planning

The draft Cairo document clearly stated that the aim of family planning programmes must be to establish the widest possible freedom of choice in matters of procreation.[13] About 55 per cent of couples in developing regions used some method of family planning, a figure which represents a nearly five-fold increase since the 1960s. However, the full range of modern family planning methods still remained unavailable to at least 350 million couples world-wide, many of whom said that they wished to space their children or prevent another pregnancy. Another 120 million additional women were potential users of a modern family planning method given better information or more supportive husbands. The draft proposed as an *objective*:

"To help couples and individuals meet their reproductive goals in a framework that promotes good health and respects the dignity of all persons and their right to bear and raise children. To eliminate unwanted pregnancies and reduce the incidence of high-risk pregnancies. To make family planning services available to all who need and want them. To improve the quality of family planning services. To increase the participation of men in family planning."

The draft proposed the target date of 2015 for all countries to provide "universal access to the full range of safe and reliable family planning methods and to related reproductive health services". The draft goes on to state:

"If all expressed unmet need for family planning were to be met over the next two decades, along with efforts to improve the status of women and reduce child mortality, it is expected that average contraceptive use would rise to an average of 69 per cent in the developing world, close to the levels seen in developed countries."[14]

Significant efforts would need to be made to improve the quality of care. Programmes should "recognise that no one method is appropriate for all individuals and couples and ensure that women and men have information on and access to the widest possible range of safe and effective family planning methods".

Population information, education and communication (IEC)

The draft proposed as an *objective*:

"To increase awareness, understanding and commitment at all levels of society so that individuals, groups, nations and the international community will take those actions necessary to address population issues within the context of sustainable development. To alter attitudes in favour of responsible behaviour in family life; to encourage individuals and couples to make informed choices and to take advantage of family planning and reproductive health services."[15]

Technology, research and development

The draft also called, predictably but — in this case — wholly justifiably, for more research. "The international community must mobilise the full spectrum of basic, biomedical, social and behavioural and programme related research on reproductive health and sexuality."

"Special priority should be given to the development and introduction of new fertility regulation methods that are safe, effective, affordable, suitable for different age groups and designed in response to users' needs. High priority should also be given to the development of new contraceptives for men."[16]

Resource mobilisation and allocation

The draft programme spelt out in some detail the resource implications of implementing the measures outlined above.

"• Meeting unmet needs for family planning information and services implies that the number of couples using contraceptives in the developing countries and countries in economic transition (countries of Eastern Europe and the former Soviet Union) will rise from some 550 million in 1995 to nearly 640 million in the year 2000 and 880 million in 2015. In 1993 US dollars, this would cost 10.2 billion in 2000, 11.5 billion in 2005, 12.6 billion in 2010 and 13.8 billion in 2105.

• Adding an expanded package of activities for reproductive health care going beyond the usual components of family planning programmes but still executable in a primary health care setting would cost an additional 1.2 billion in 2000, approximately 1.3

billion in both 2005 and 2010 and 1.4 billion in 2015. Similar amounts would be needed for a package of activities relating to the prevention of sexually transmitted diseases (including HIV infection).

- An additional package of activities to meet expanded population data collection, analysis and dissemination, and policy formulation needs would add between 220 million and 670 million per year."[17]

Overall, the Cairo Draft Programme of Action estimated that the projected resource requirements of national population programmes (in 1993 US dollars) would total: $13.2 billion in 2000, $14.4 billion in 2005, $16.1 billion in 2010 and $17.0 billion in 2015. The draft indicated: "The savings in other sectoral costs and the benefits to be derived from these programmes far exceed these modest investments."

The draft submitted to the April 1994 meeting of the ICPD's PrepCom confidently expected that two-thirds of the costs of national population programmes will continue to be met by the countries themselves. But it also recognised that developing countries were faced with increasing difficulties in allocating sufficient funds for their population programmes. Additional resources were urgently required, not only to satisfy the already large unmet need for reproductive health care including family planning information and services, but also to respond to future increases in demand, to keep pace with the growing populations that needed to be served, and to improve the quality and scope of the programmes. The draft estimated that the need for "complementary" resource flows from donor countries would be (in 1993 US dollars): 4.4 billion in 2000, 4.8 billion in 2005, 5.3 billion in 2010 and 5.7 billion in 2015.

A BOLD, VISIONARY DOCUMENT

In sum, the Draft Programme of Action circulated in early 1994 was a bold, even visionary document, setting out clear goals and commitments in a number of fields and stressing consistently two main themes: the need to integrate population and development issues and the need to emphasise what Dr Nafis Sadik, UNFPA's Executive Director and the Secretary General of the ICPD, frequently referred to as the "centrality of the individual".

These two main themes were themselves increasingly interrelated, the intellectual synthesis being attained in phrases such as "people-centred development" or the "human development index" (first devised by the United Nations Development Programme) which, in addition to the classical macro-economic indicators such as GNP, GNP per capita and so on, included social factors such as education, health and other forms of social infrastructure.

Development programmes which emphasised health and education, especially female education, might not only be a useful adjunct to family planning programmes; they might actually be *the vital concomitant* if such programmes were to be successful quite apart from the other objectives which they were designed to meet.

Equally, stressing the "centrality of the individual" was much more than a slogan. The emphasis placed in the Draft Programme of Action on individual rights and choices, particularly on what have come to be referred to as "gender issues", was an increasingly important feature of the "Cairo process" and, as much as any other factor, was serving to distinguish the preparations for Cairo, 1994 from the previous world population conferences.

As delegates met in New York in April 1994 at the final meeting of the ICPD's Preparatory Committee (PrepCom) they had before them a detailed analysis which made it clear that, despite many expected modifications, the draft that would be sent to Cairo was certain to contain dozens of issues, actions and approaches never approved by earlier population conferences. That analysis, compiled by the ICPD secretariat, cross-referenced sections of the current draft of the Programme of Action with the World Population Plan of Action approved in Bucharest in 1974 and the recommendations of the Mexico City population conference in 1984. According to the secretariat's own count, the current draft contained 40 "new issues" and 22 "new specific actions" that had no precedent in the Bucharest or Mexico City documents. In addition, the current draft contained 78 "new approaches" that "bring a distinctly innovative perspective" to issues previously considered.

In the introduction to the document, the secretariat said it was compiled in response to requests for highlighting what was described as "the value added" of the ICPD Draft Programme of Action. Most of the "new issues" cited dealt with gender issues, including: exploitation of and violence against women (paragraph 4.7); women's time (4.8); preference for sons (4.14); female genital mutilation (4.19, 7.33); responsibility of men in sexual behaviour and family life (4.24); high-risk sexual behaviour of men (8.23).

Many of the "new issues" in the ICPD draft expanded on the question of violence and exploitation of women and children. They dealt specifically with: domestic violence, drugs and alcohol, sexual and child abuse and neglect (5.9); child exploitation and abuse, prostitution and child labour (6.8); protecting women and children from sexual exploitation and violence (7.32).

Related "new specific actions" called for by the ICPD draft included: meeting the nutritional, reproductive health, educational and social needs of girls and young women (4.17); and ensuring that fathers meet their financial responsibilities (4.25). Most of the remaining "new issues" raised in the ICPD draft deal with sustainable development and the environment, reproductive health issues, and the needs of specific groups such as migrants, adolescents, the urban poor, indigenous peoples and people with disabilities.

New issues covered by the draft in the area of health care included: reproductive health needs of countries in transition (7.8); reproductive health care needs of migrants (7.9); sexually transmitted diseases (7.24, 7.25, 7.26); the need to base policies on a better understanding of sexuality and sexual behaviour (7.30); the reproductive health care needs of adolescents (7.38); the role of women as primary custodians of family health (8.6); HIV/AIDS (8.26, 8.27, 8.28); the need for ethical and technical standards in reproductive health research (12.12); and the need to involve the for-profit sector in contraceptive research (15.15, 15.16, 15.17).

Many of the "new specific actions" called for in the ICPD draft also dealt with research. They include: research on specific population and environmental issues (3.33); monitoring the impact of governmental policies on families (5.8); compiling comprehensive statistical data-bases (12.5); research on the linkages between population, the environment and economic development (12.16); research on eco-systems beset by population pressures (12.18); research on specific aspects of sexuality and gender (12.21); research on the causes of differentials in mortality rates of various groups (12.22).

The secretariat's analysis of the Cairo draft also showed dramatically increased emphasis on education, on the equitable representation of women in population policy-making, the elimination of gender stereo-types in society, and strict enforcement of laws setting a minimum age for marriage. New approaches in the current draft also called for focusing on the poorest families and increasing the earning power of poor women, and enforcing laws against child labour and child abuse. The draft called for establishment of a global facility for the procure-ment of contraceptives, for considering unsafe abortion as a major public health concern, and for making condoms more widely available.

CHILDREN BY CHOICE NOT CHANCE

By any yardstick this was an impressive inventory. It was a demon-stration, in very practical terms, of what "putting people first" or the "centrality of the individual" could mean. All of these were, moreover, "win-win" or "no regret" actions or activities in the sense that they were not only of outstanding value and importance in and of themselves and likely to enhance the potential and capabilities of the individual and of his or her position in society; they were also likely to improve dramatically the prospects for achieving the goals of safe motherhood, responsible parenthood, family planning, fertility regulation, population stabilization or whatever. The point was made perhaps most succinctly by Baroness Chalker of Wallasey, the British Minister for Overseas Development, when she stressed that the underlying philosophy of the British aid programme in the field of population was "children by choice not chance". The achievement of demographic goals, whatever they might be, was inextricably linked to issues of gender empowerment, personal responsibility and expanded freedom of choice by individuals and couples. "Countries whose governments establish a climate within which couples can exercise reproductive choice should eventually attain population growth rates that are in balance with their economic and natural resources."[18]

THE THIRD PREPCOM

Looking back at the third PrepCom, it is fair to say that many of the programmes and activities and actions put forward in the January Draft Programme of Action survived more or less intact after discussion in the April PrepCom. Take, for example, Section IV. As submitted to PrepCom, this section was entitled: Gender Equity and Empowerment of Women. It contained three sub-sections on (A) Empowerment and status of women; (B) The girl child; and (C) Male responsibilities and participation. Each of these sub-sections contained a range of commitments. Under sub-section A, paragraph 4.4 read:

> "countries should empower women and close the gender gap as soon as possible by:
> * encouraging women's participation at all levels of the political process in each community and society;
> * promoting the fulfilment of their potential through education and skill development, paying urgent attention to the elimination of illiteracy among adult women;
> * eliminating all legal, political and social barriers against women; assisting women to establish and realise their rights, particularly those that relate to sexual and reproductive health;
> * adopting concrete measures to improve women's ability to earn income, achieve economic self-reliance, inherit, own and dispose of property and have access to credit."[19]

There then followed a number of specific actions to be undertaken by those concerned (governments, employers and so on) to meet those objectives. A similar pattern was followed for the other programme areas in Section IV.

It might have been supposed, given the fact that in many countries women are as far from "empowerment" as they ever were, that this section of the draft programme would emerge from the PrepCom, if it emerged at all, littered with square brackets denoting serious disagreements to be resolved (hopefully) at a later date. In practice this was not the case. The *Earth Negotiations Bulletin* of 7 April 1994 gave an illuminating summary of the debate which took place in PrepCom's Working Group II, the previous day. (The *Earth Negotiations Bulletin* appeared at regular intervals during the meetings of the Preparatory Committee for the ICPD both in written form and on various electronic information exchange networks. Though not an official publication of the United Nations, the *Bulletin*'s concise and prompt summaries of debates were much appreciated by delegates — all the more so since United Nations verbatim records had long since been curtailed for budgetary reasons.)

"**IV   Gender Equality, Equity and Empowerment of Women:**

"**A   Empowerment and status of women:** In the paragraph on objectives, Australia suggested making explicit reference to women's decision-making. In paragraph 4.4 (gender gap), New Zealand, the US and Australia called for a stronger statement on closing the gender gap. Indonesia suggested that literacy and development of skills are imperative for both men and women. Norway asked to make the issue of child care more central. The Holy See objected because of problems in the French and Spanish translations. Peru agreed with the text itself, but asked that translation problems be dealt with separately. Benin disagreed. Peru and US asked to strengthen the sub-paragraph on women's property rights.

"In 4.5 (discrimination and sexual harassment), Australia suggested a more encompassing definition of sexual harassment. Switzerland called for an exclusive section on disaggregated gender data. Senegal asked for reference to the enforcement of anti-discrimination laws. Sweden proposed deleting the unrealistic deadline of 2015. Bolivia and Peru asked for a statement against discrimination based on proof of pregnancy. In 4.7 (violence against women), the US, Australia, Peru, New Zealand and Malaysia asked for stronger wording, including domestic violence against women, girls and boys. Croatia, Pakistan and Norway called for a phrase on war violence against women. In 4.8 (burden of women's work), Mexico and Australia wanted a statement on men's responsibility in domestic labour. In 4.9 (grassroots support for women), Nigeria and Mexico asked for clarity on the role of government.

"B The girl child: Venezuela objected to the title and asked that it include women. In paragraph 4.13 (objectives), the US called for more emphasis on the role of poverty in gender discrimination. Norway said that poverty does not always lead to gender preference. In 4.14 (gender discrimination), Switzerland, the US and Egypt added "inheritance" to the list of gender inequalities. In 4.15 (education for girls), Switzerland and Sweden asked to delete the target date for education for all. Bangladesh asked to include vocational training for women. In 4.16 (school stereotypes), Switzerland and Norway asked to include sex selection as a form of discrimination. The US asked for a statement on change in teachers' attitudes and curricula. In 4.18 (minimum age of consent), the US, Madagascar and Switzerland asked for an increase in the minimum age of marriage. Norway and Cuba asked for reference to child pornography. In 4.19 (female genital mutilation), Indonesia and India objected to forcing any policy on a country. Bolivia called for a statement on the active prevention of genital mutilation. In 4.20 (education for girls), Sweden, Norway, Bangladesh and Bolivia called for reference opposing expulsion of pregnant girls from school. Burkina Faso and Morocco asked for international financial contribution to building schools.

"C Male Responsibilities and participation: In the objectives (4.22), Australia and Holy See asked to include women in the section on fertility and parental responsibility. In 4.23 (family responsibility), Bangladesh and India asked for a more emphatic statement on men's participation. In 4.25 (child support), numerous countries asked for mechanisms to enforce child support payments."

The above extract gives something of the flavour of the debate on this Section. The generally positive tone was on the whole maintained during later discussions. On 13 April, for example, at a further meeting of Working Group II, Malaysia and most Muslim delegations objected to "equal inheritance for women". However, after informal deliberation with the Vice Chair of Working Group II, they eventually agreed that women could "receive" property on an equal basis with men.[20]

In the final outcome, Section IV was renamed "Gender Equality, Equity and Empowerment of Women." At the request of the European Union (formerly the European Community), the reference to the goal of achieving universal primary education for all by the year 2015 (para 4.15) remained in square brackets (for discussion at Cairo) pending the discussion of goals. The only other brackets in this chapter were around the terms "reproductive and sexual health", at the request of the Holy See. This particular difficulty, as we shall see, was part of the Vatican's general concern with the preparations for the ICPD and should not be construed as an attack on the overall objectives of Section IV on Gender Equality and so on, which the Vatican, as most other delegations, appeared to endorse warmly.

A funny thing happened on the way to Cairo

The *Earth Times*, a newspaper produced by some of the NGOs attending the PrepCom, ran the following editorial by Robert S Hirschfield on 21 April as the PrepCom finally wound down after a long and exhausting session.

> "A funny thing has happened on the way to Cairo. During PrepCom III for the International Conference on Population and Development, the scope of this world meeting has metamorphosed to include the subject of women's rights. The addition of this third element was unplanned but not accidental. It has come about quite naturally, indeed inevitably, as the PrepCom's mostly female participants have gotten more deeply involved in fashioning an Action Programme. For in this process it has become increasingly apparent that the way to attain population stabilisation is not just providing more information, services and devices related to family planning. What is needed, rather, is a basic global change in the status of women. Thus issues like guaranteeing that girls are accorded the same educational opportunities as boys, that legal or cultural barriers to female ownership of property are removed, and that other similar areas of inequity which relegate women to an inferior position are addressed, become matters of world attention.
>
> "Interestingly, the initial stimulus for this new approach at PrepCom III came from a man — the head of the American delegation, State Department Counsellor Timothy Wirth — who outlined a seven-point agenda designed to achieve the empowerment, employment and involvement of women, at the beginning of the session. With women present in unprecedented numbers at the PrepCom, serving on national delegations, as well as representing a record number of non-governmental organisations, this call for change has been answered enthusiastically. Moreover, it has been aided by the actions of Secretary General Nafis Sadik and Chairman Fred Sai in opening PrepCom proceedings to allow for significant participation by eager NGOs. The result has been an expansion of scope and a change of focus that has had the effect of relating population problems to both women's rights and social development, thus linking the Cairo conference to last year's Vienna meeting on Human Rights and to next year's Copenhagen Social Summit. It also sets the stage for making Cairo itself an historic event.
>
> "How much of this new approach to the way the world works will be reflected in the final document for ICPD remains to be seen."

The *Earth Times* editorial cited went on to say: "If family planning and population stabilisation are placed in the context of achieving gender equality, and if effective programmes to attain that goal can be approved in Cairo, the International Conference on Population and Development will be a landmark in global affairs."

HOW IMPORTANT WERE THE "IFS"?

Just how big and important were the "ifs?'

On the positive side, it was clear from the meetings of the Preparatory Committee that the United States was once again ready to play a leading role in the population field and that it had firmly put behind it the doldrums of the "Mexico" years. Over the two previous years the United States had increased its overseas population budget by US $152 million to a total of $502 million. The Clinton administration had asked Congress for $585 million for population assistance in 1995 and plans to reach $1.2 billion by the year 2000. Japan had announced that it would expand its funding of population and AIDS-related programmes to US $3 billion over the next seven years, seven times the current Japanese contribution to such programmes. Germany had also announced a substantial increase in its population assistance and other nations, such as Norway — a traditional high donor of development aid, including population assistance — had indicated that they would maintain the priority accorded to such programmes.

The fact that "new and additional money" was clearly on the table was psychologically extremely important. Though the bulk of the resources for population, family planning and related activities would continue to come from the developing countries themselves, the perceived readiness of donor nations to contribute to this effort — *and to announce this in good time* — would hopefully make a major difference to the climate in which the final Cairo text was negotiated. And while for some countries, such as China, external assistance might be a very small proportion of total spending (in China's case, some $15 million out of an annual total of $1.1 billion), for others the question of extra financial resources could be crucial. As the delegate of Bangladesh put it in his statement to the PrepCom on 5 April:

> "Mobilisation of new and additional resources at international level is crucial in order to achieve the goals set forth in the Programme of Action. The less-developed countries (LDCs) should receive increased technical and financial support. The seriousness with which we approach the Programme of Action will have to be matched by equal seriousness for new and additional resources mobilisation and its allocation."

It remained to be seen whether other donor nations, particularly those of the European Union, would be ready to match the United States, Japan, Germany, Norway, and so on, with a clear commitment to increased funding. Judging by the performance of the European Union at PrepCom, where EU delegates sprinkled square brackets like confetti whenever the question of financial resources was discussed, there was still some way to go before this issue is resolved. This is all the more disappointing — and ironic — in view of the fact that it was often EU delegations who had pushed for a steady expansion in the very concept of population activities to include the wider notions of reproductive health, female education and even women's rights in general. Seen from the perspective of the developing countries, this was a situation where either the existing butter would be spread more thinly or there would have to be more butter.

THE POSITION OF THE VATICAN

At the end of April 1994, one other major question mark hung over the forthcoming Cairo conference: the position of the Vatican.

Two weeks before PrepCom III began Dr Nafis Sadik had an interview with Pope John Paul II in the Vatican. Unusually, the Vatican issued a statement on that occasion recapitulating the message which His Holiness had conveyed to his visitor. Ironically, the points of departure for the Vatican on the one hand and for UNFPA on the other seemed to be not a million miles apart. The Pope told Dr Sadik:

"Today, the duty to safeguard the family demands that particular attention be given to securing for husband and wife the liberty to decide responsibly, free from all social or legal coercion, the number of children they will have and the spacing of their births. It should not be the intent of governments or other agencies to decide for couples but, rather, to create the social conditions which will enable them to make appropriate decisions in the light of their responsibilities to God, to themselves, to the society of which they are a part, and to the objective moral order. What the Church calls "responsible parenthood" is not a question of unlimited procreation or lack of awareness of what is involved in rearing children, but rather the empowerment of couples to use their inviolable liberty wisely and responsibly, taking into account social and demographic realities as well as their own situation and legitimate desires, in the light of objective moral criteria. All propaganda and misinformation directed at persuading couples that they must limit their family to one or two children should be steadfastly avoided, and couples that generously choose to have large families are to be supported."

Give or take a nuance here or there it was not impossible to imagine such a paragraph being penned in the offices of the International Planned Parenthood Federation. However, though the starting points might be more or less the same, the tracks soon began to differ. The Pope went on to tell Dr Sadik:

> "In defence of the human person, the Church stands opposed to the imposition of limits on family size, and to the promotion of methods of limiting births which separate the unitive and procreative dimensions of marital intercourse, which are contrary to the moral law inscribed in the human heart, or which constitute an assault on the sacredness of life. Thus, sterilisation, which is more and more promoted as a method of family planning, because of its finality and its potential for the violation of human rights, especially of women, is clearly unacceptable; it poses a most grave threat to human dignity and liberty when promoted as part of a population policy. Abortion, which destroys existing human life, is a heinous evil, and it is never an acceptable method of family planning, as was recognised by consensus at the Mexico City United Nations International Conference on Population (1984)."

The Pope emphasised his unease with regard to the preparations for Cairo. It was not just a question of the references to abortion and to fertility regulation. "Marriage is ignored, as if it were something of the past. An institution as natural, universal and fundamental as the family cannot be manipulated without causing serious damage to the fabric and stability of society."

HOW MANY DIVISIONS HAS THE POPE?

The Pope's powerful restatement of his position just before PrepCom was not the most auspicious sign — hardly a benediction — though those who knew the man and his record probably expected no less. Pope John Paul II had never been afraid to stand up for what he saw as the truth. What did, however, take many people by surprise was the energy, even the ferocity, with which the Vatican defended its position at PrepCom III. Nor was the Holy See alone. Honduras, Nicaragua, Malta, Benin, Morocco, Guatemala and Argentina all lined up at various times and in various ways in support of the Vatican's stance. Terms like "family planning" and "reproductive health" which few thought were still contentious given national and international developments over the past 20 or 30 years were suddenly questioned, challenged and — when disagreement persisted — placed in square brackets. Though it is true that the Vatican had officially dissociated itself from the Bucharest and

Mexico consensus, other Catholic countries had not. It began to seem possible, even probable, that not only would the Holy See refuse to sign up to the Cairo Final Document; this time round at least a handful of other countries might join it in abstaining.

In UN terms, a consensus exists as long as countries do not oppose and abstention does not count as opposition. But a consensus document with only one abstention certainly carries more weight than a document with half a dozen or more abstentions. Worse still, it is highly probable that in the process of trying to reach agreement, to avoid abstentions (or outright opposition), the texts themselves may be significantly weakened.

When PrepCom III finished, the preparations for the ICPD appeared to face precisely this danger. So far from Cairo advancing the international consensus on population, there seemed to be the real prospect that at least in some areas it might be rolled back.

The phrase "couples and individuals", for example, had been negotiated with great difficulty at Bucharest in 1974.[21] Paragraph 14(f) of the World Population Plan of Action stated that "All couples and individuals have the basic right to decide freely and responsibly the number and spacing of their children and to have the information, education and the means to do so .. ".[22] This language, including the term "couples and individuals" was repeated in Recommendation 30 of the Mexico City consensus document.[23] The Draft Programme of Action as submitted to PrepCom III referred to both "couples and individuals" (paragraph 7.12) and "individuals and couples" (paragraph 7.15).

This was not just a semantic issue. It could affect the well-being of hundreds of millions. As Dr Halfdan Mahler, the Secretary General of the International Planned Parenthood Federation, put it in his speech to PrepCom III:

> "In meeting the unmet demand we must recognise that the term unmet need is a broad one that means different things to different people at different times. Women's perspectives and realities, when attempting to quantify and qualify unmet needs and demands in so-called family planning, have too often been ignored. For example, surveys have traditionally addressed only married women of reproductive age, leaving out the unmet needs of hundreds of millions who are active, or potentially so, but are not covered by these surveys. *For IPPF, unmet needs and demands refer not only to the hundreds of millions of couples, most of them poor and marginalised, living in urban slums and remote rural areas, who do not presently have access to acceptable and affordable quality family planning as an integral part of sexual and reproductive health care. It also refers to the hundreds of millions of young women and men who, at present, are*

excluded from such sexual and reproductive health care." [author's emphasis]

Globally, there were about 500 million adolescents aged 15 to 19, most of whom would become sexually active before the age of 20. The evidence appeared to indicate that young people (who would be included in the term "individuals") seldom use contraceptives and were at high risk of pregnancy, AIDS and other sexually transmitted diseases (STDs). Yet in most countries, youth were not reached by existing reproductive health services. The World Health Organisation (WHO) had recently reviewed 35 studies in several countries, concluding that appropriate sexuality education did not encourage earlier initiation of intercourse, but often delayed sexual activity and led to safer sexual practices. WHO and other studies also show that access to contraceptive services was not associated with earlier sexual activity.[24]

Seen in this perspective, the Holy See's attempts to remove the word "individuals" or Honduras' effort to replace the term "couples and individuals" with the term "men and women" appeared bizarre, even grotesque. And though these delegations appeared finally to have agreed to let the phrase stand unbracketed for the time being, their reservations had been expressed for the record and there was no guarantee that the controversy would not be revived at Cairo.

ABORTION

As far as the question of abortion was concerned, no such spirit of compromise — if such it can be called — was on offer. When Section VII on Reproductive Rights, Sexual and Reproductive Health and Family Planning was considered by the plenary on the final day of the PrepCom, Costa Rica, Argentina, Malta, Venezuela, Morocco and Ecuador argued passionately that they could not agree to any terms unless these were clearly defined so as to exclude abortion. That blanket reservation therefore extended to many of the expressions currently to be found in the population and family planning lexicon, including abortion, safe abortion, legal abortion, unsafe abortion, illegal abortion, fertility regulation, reproductive health, sexual health, safe motherhood, reproductive rights and even the phrase "family planning" itself.

On 22 April 1994, the day PrepCom III ended, a revealing article by Susan Chira appeared in the *New York Times*.

"Pope John Paul II has campaigned vigorously against the United Nations plan" Chira wrote. "The Vatican is particularly troubled by the United States' shift on abortion since the last major population conference, in Mexico City in 1984, when Washington declared it would not give aid to family planning programmes that offered abortion. President Clinton reversed that policy when he was elected."

Susan Chira went on to write:

> " 'It would be very sad if this were to become a conference about abortion', said Monsignor Diarmuid Martin, the Vatican delegate. 'The United States wants the question of abortion as a fundamental dimension of population policy throughout the world to be a major theme of the conference.'
>
> "Timothy E. Wirth, the United States representative to the conference, said: 'I think it is unfair that any group would say the US is out promoting abortion. That simply is not true. The US has been a wonderfully moderating influence. Clearly we will not get agreement on our position, which is that abortion should be safe, legal and rare.'
>
> "Dr Sadik defended the United States. 'I think the tirade against the US is being used to whip up emotion against the Programme of Action', she said about the United Nations plan."

At this point, of course, the International Conference on Population and Development was still in the future. Four months later, the final gavel would descend in Cairo and it would be clear at that moment just how much of the Draft Programme of Action had been retained as presented and how much had suffered significant modification as a result of the laborious intergovernmental process.

On the whole, at the end of April 1994, a sense of optimism prevailed among the organisers of the Cairo conference. Though there were still some major disagreements to be resolved (particularly as far as the Vatican and its supporters are concerned), there had already been a great deal of progress towards an agreed text. If Chairman Fred Sai of Ghana could work his customary magic to ensure that the text was finally adopted more or less in the form it had emerged from PrepCom III, then it would be fair to say that the international community had at last (and not before time) reached that definitive consensus on population which had so far eluded it. Most important of all, if the commitments as far as the allocation of resources — both external and domestic — were concerned, were actually firm and "bankable", if in other words the Cairo Programme was given the political and material backing to put it into effect, there must be every prospect of attaining the goals which were proposed, both quantitative and qualitative (including, therefore, the goals relating to infant and maternal mortality, female education, reproductive health, family planning and, ultimately, population stabilisation).

The challenge was great, but not insuperable. The mood in the Conference secretariat in UNFPA's New York offices was definitely upbeat. A few weeks later, however, as the Vatican's campaign against the Cairo draft gathered momentum — and as new allies seemed ready to join the Holy See's banner — the prospects for worthwhile agreement at Cairo seemed suddenly to be thrown into doubt and confusion.

Chapter 4
The Guns of August, 1994

There can have been few international conferences where the opening barrages have been quite so ominous. With only a few weeks to go before the opening of the Cairo meeting, the Islamic world appeared set to join the Vatican in open hostility to the concepts set out in the draft programme and indeed to the very idea of holding such a conference in a predominantly Muslim country.

OBJECTIONS FROM THE ISLAMIC STATES

On Wednesday 10 August 1994, al-Azhar, the Islamic institution at the heart of Egypt's religious establishment, sharply condemned the Programme of Action as being counter to Islamic Sharia (law). Al-Azhar's Islamic Research Academy met under Grand Sheikh Gad ul Haq and issued a statement:

> "The draft's loose language indicates it aims to adopt the opposite of Islam's basic postulates for families, to legitimise abortion and to protect sexual relationships between members of the same sex or of opposite sexes outside of marriage."[1]

Al-Azhar criticised the document for "asking parents to overlook sexual activity by teenagers", insisting that abortion would be illegitimate, even in the case of rape or adultery while emphasising that Islam "orders the harshest of penalties for adultery and homosexuality", including stoning to death (in the case of adultery) and being thrown to death off the top of a mountain (in the case of homosexuality).

> "If we single out these issues it does not mean the draft is innocent from violating Sharia elsewhere, for instance in insinuating unacceptable things such as equating males and females in inheritance and demanding that the minimum age of marriage be raised while providing alternative outlets. ... which may be understood as a call for facilitating prostitution"

As the al-Azhar statement was being issued, Adel Hussein, Deputy Chairman of the pro-fundamentalist opposition Labour Party claimed: "This is a Satanic plot ... under the cloak of the United Nations and the World Bank ... to de-populate the Islamic world by the year 2020." He wrote in the party's organ *al Shaab* that the rich nations were "terrified" by the exponential growth in the number of Muslims and planned to spend billions of dollars to abort it over the next two decades.

Abdul Sabur Shaheen, a reputed fundamentalist and a senior faculty member at Cairo University did not hesitate to stir the pot. "Israel is trying by all means to stop us from getting what is more devastating than the atomic bomb, namely increased offspring which is in the interest of Muslims by any criteria".

The arguments were not all on one side, however. On 22 August, Egypt's Grand Mufti joined the dispute and publicly rejected criticism of the meeting by al-Azhar theologians.

"The draft recommendations do not contain anything counter to Islamic teachings, and I found no encouragement for free sexual relations outside of matrimony nor for abortion as a means of birth control", Sheikh Mohamed Sayid Tantawi said in statements published by the Cairo daily *al-Ahram*. He said al-Azhar had apparently assailed the draft on the basis of a faulty Arabic-language translation which had many "loosely defined words that allowed free rein to those given to interpretations".

Sheikh Tantawi differed explicitly with al-Azhar on the issue of abortion, which he said could be legitimate where a woman had been raped or a parent was a carrier of serious genetic defects or even is a victim of poverty.

For Egypt's President Hosni Mubarak, this outbreak of hostility from Islamic activists was alarming. He had invested a great deal of personal and political capital in having a successful outcome to the Cairo conference and he did not wish to see the train derailed before it had even left the station. Three days after al-Azhar had pronounced, the President forcefully criticised what he described as a "sandstorm" kicked around the conference by fundamentalist groups. He said the event was geared to the welfare of mankind and that Muslim countries would not subscribe to any plans of action that run counter to Islamic teachings.[2]

He reiterated that development was the major issue that preoccupied officials in Egypt, who were concentrating on providing a proper standard of living for citizens, maintaining stability and supporting and facilitating investment. He warned in an interview with the London-based *Al-Sharq al-Awsat* newspaper that overlooking development could bring about catastrophes as a result of the constant population increase and the high rate of unemployment.[3]

President Mubarak explained that the recommendations to be discussed by the International Conference on Population and Development (ICPD) did not constitute binding resolutions or agreements. It was necessary to seize this opportunity to explain Islam's viewpoint on population issues and show its respect for mankind and the attention it gave to women and children.

It might, as President Mubarak suggested, have been a sandstorm in the desert, but his intervention appeared to be less than totally successful in calming it.

"Al-Azhar's position is firm and we are not responsible for the Mufti's views", a spokesman for al-Azhar was quoted as telling the Nasserite Cairo weekly *al-Arabi*. "Islam sanctions abortion only if the mother's life is threatened."

Al-Azhar's representative indicated that he was encouraged by Mubarak's statement that Muslim countries would not subscribe to doctrines they opposed. Nevertheless he urged Muslims to rally against the conference, which he described as "an evil passing through our country".

As the days passed, it became clear that al-Azhar's call had not gone unheeded. The Mecca-based Moslem World League in Saudi Arabia urged all Muslim nations to "renounce everything in the draft which is completely against religious values, human ideals and Nature itself".

Islamic groups campaigning against the conference in Cairo received a major boost when, towards the end of the month, Bangladeshi Prime Minister Khaleda Zia decided not to attend.

"The prime minister will not be able to attend the International Conference on Population and Development, as she will be extremely busy at home", said a Foreign Ministry statement released through the government-controlled Bangladesh News Agency late Saturday night, 27 August.[4]

This was undoubtedly a blow. The hope of the conference organisers had been that Prime Minister Zia, as a woman and as the leader of a populous Muslim nation would (like her next-door neighbour, Benazir Bhutto) be one of the star performers at the conference. Her influence could have been crucial in winning over wavering delegates, not only because of who she was but also because of what she would have to say. With 115 million people crammed on to 55,600 square miles (144,000 sq km) of land, Bangladesh was one of the world's most densely populated states. Those with long memories could remember the heart-wrenching plea made 20 years earlier by the Bangladesh representative at the Bucharest conference, a plea which had been instrumental in saving that earlier meeting from breaking up in disarray. Since then, Bangladesh had earned global acclaim by reducing its fertility rate from seven children per woman in 1972, to 4.2 in 1994. The birth rate among Bangladesh's 115 million people had been reduced to 2.1 per cent, from nearly 4 per cent in 1972. This success was attributed to national family planning programmes which had provided contraceptives to nearly 45 per cent of married couples, up from 10 per cent in 1972.

Prime Minister Zia's decision to pull out of the ICPD left conference observers in Dhaka in a state of shock. Many of those observers were expecting the Cairo conference to become a watershed in Bangladesh's battle against overpopulation and widespread poverty. "I can't believe she is not going. Bangladesh is supposed to be a showcase of family planning success, and Zia was going to be the star at Cairo", said the population programme officer of a Western funding agency, who wished to remain anonymous.[5] "The Cairo conference is on the verge of collapse as a result of the storm of protests in Muslim and Christian countries", crowed the daily newspaper *Inquilab*, Bangladesh's top-selling Islamic paper, on Sunday 28 August. The paper said the ICPD was "falling apart" because it represented "a despicable conspiracy to encourage homosexuality, to legalise abortion, spread free pre-marital sex and sex among young people".

Major Bangladeshi fundamentalist parties went so far as to describe the conference as "anti-Islam". "This conference is a challenge to all religions, humanity, morality and civilisation. It is a deep conspiracy", said top Bangladeshi Islamic scholar Mufti Fazlul Huq Amini. Amini had risen to prominence in recent months by leading a campaign against Bangladesh's feminist author Taslima Nasrin, whom he had accused of being a "proponent of free sex".

Further shocks in store

On the last Thursday in August, Saudi Arabia's top theologians were reported to have unanimously branded the forthcoming UN Conference on Population and Development as "heresy" and to have warned that any Muslim who attended would be guilty of violating Sharia religious law. The position was pronounced in a lengthy and sharply worded statement published in the London-based, Saudi-owned Arabic daily *al Hayat* after an emergency meeting in Taif by the 21-member Council of Senior Ulemmas (theologians) of Saudi Arabia.

The next Monday Saudi Arabia was reported to have decided to boycott the conference. The Kuwaiti News Agency quoted Ayman al Amir, the official spokesman for the conference, as saying that the Saudis had indicated they would not be attending. No reason was given.

Turkish Prime Minister Tansu Ciller, who was to have attended the opening of the conference on 5 September, also announced that she had had to cancel that visit on the grounds that she was too busy preparing for the opening of parliament in early September.

The lengthening list of no-shows was worrying. Most Muslim states, like the Vatican, had already made it clear that they did not approve of the conference's draft "program of action", especially those parts of it that appeared to promote abortion and accept extramarital sex and homosexual relationships. But this was the first time Muslim states had said they would boycott the conference in protest.

Sudan's decision was announced on Tuesday by that country's state radio, which called on other nations not to attend the conference and demanded the formation of an international forum to counter the recommendations of the conference. In Jordan, meanwhile, the influential Islamic Action Front Party, the political arm of the Muslim Brotherhood, issued a statement urging all Arab and Islamic states to boycott the conference. Those countries should reject the conference's resolutions and activate their media and educational institutions to shield their people, the Jordanian fundamentalists said.

On 1 September, Foreign Minister Aseff Ahmed Ali of Pakistan said Pakistan would challenge items on the agenda of the forthcoming United Nations Population Conference which it considered contrary to Islamic teachings and values. "It is an intellectual challenge from the West. We will face it", the minister told the National Assembly, the lower house of parliament.[6]

Ali made the statement amid speculation that Prime Minister Benazir Bhutto would drop her plans to attend the conference in the face of growing criticism of the conference by Moslem fundamentalists at home and abroad. It was announced on the national radio that Pakistan would strongly oppose the "anti-Islamic clauses" in the final draft of the International Conference on Population and Development Programme of Action in Cairo and would ensure that the recommendations conformed to Islamic values and teaching of the Holy Koran.

This was reiterated by the special assistant to the Prime Minister, Begum Shahnaz Wazir Ali, at a briefing in Islamabad as the conference opened. She categorically stated that a very strong statement would be made by the Prime Minister, Mohtarma Benazir Bhutto, in the conference, rejecting in totality all those documents which were opposed to Islam.

A ray of light

There were none the less some rays of light.[7] To the surprise of some whose vision of Iranian foreign policy had been formed in the days when Ayatollah Homeini was launching incessant broadsides "against the great Satan", namely the United States of America, the government of Iran took a more moderate line on the population conference than that adopted by some other Islamic states.

Mr Ali Reza Marandi, Iran's health minister, said that the draft document seemed to have "disregarded the religious views of the Islamic world and formulated the text with a sense of sexual liberty". Criticism of the Cairo conference centred on the pragmatic approach taken towards issues such as extramarital and adolescent sex. But Iranian opposition to the UN population conference was not so great that it would join Saudi Arabia and Sudan in boycotting it. On the contrary, Iran was sending a delegation which it hoped would "adapt the final document to incorporate religious ethics".

This emollient line on the part of Iran probably reflected the change in official attitudes towards Iran's own population situation. When the Islamic government took over after the 1979 revolution, the average population growth rate of 3.9 per cent a year was among the highest in the world. The Islamic government welcomed the growth in population, clearly seeing it in terms of increased resources to build the country into an Islamic model. It laid greater emphasis than before on early marriage and the woman's role as wife and mother and saw no reason to encourage birth control.

By the mid-1980s, however, concerns about the economy led to fears that the high population growth was a threat rather than an aid to economic development. Iran's population grew from just over 37 million at the beginning of the revolution in 1979 to 57 million by 1986, an increase attributed to the lack of a family planning programme combined with improved health care since the 1960s. In 1994, Iran's population was believed to stand at more than 60 million.

Implementation of a family planning programme in 1988 had witnessed a drop in the annual average growth rate from the 3.9 per cent peak to 2.3 per cent in 1993 and down further to 1.8 per cent in 1994, according to government figures quoted in the *Financial Times*.

Demographic experts, while acknowledging that Iran had been successful in controlling its population growth, were sceptical of these figures. They argued that such a rapid population decrease was impossible in such a short period of time and cited the need for strengthened data collection and statistical analysis. The most reliable figures were those of the country's census, taken every five years. This showed an annual average growth rate of 2.9 per cent in 1991, well above the current 2 per cent growth rate for developing countries as a whole. Subsequent figures, demographic experts argued, could have been based on less reliable samples.

Whatever the true figures were, the evidence was that Iran's family planning programme had been a considerable success, partly because of the strength of the government's commitment. It had been supportive of all contraceptive methods, including male sterilisation. Only abortion was not allowed.

The main thrust of the government's population programme had been based on an increased supply of contraceptives, the training of rural midwives and counselling in family planning techniques. The Ministry of Health, which established a Fertility Regulation Council in 1988 to implement the programme, reported a decline in total fertility from 6.4 children per woman in 1988 to 4.25 in 1993. Increased use of contraceptives had been partly fuelled by the lack of family planning services for almost a decade. An active family planning programme had been launched under the Shah's regime, so the implementation of the current programme had been relatively easy given the public's existing awareness.

Another reason for the success of the family planning programme had been a relatively good health infrastructure which, according to UNFPA experts working in Iran, reached 60 per cent of those living in the countryside and 90 per cent of the majority urban population. The primary health care network was good especially in rural areas and the infrastructure was much better than for many Asian countries. Iran had a relatively high literacy rate of 74 per cent and girls' enrolment in primary school was nearly as high as that of boys. The spread of education and literacy had increased a widespread desire for smaller families.

Despite the success of the programme to date, the tasks ahead were still formidable. A relatively large number of Iranians, born in the baby boom of 1976–1986, would be of childbearing age from 1996 onwards, so fertility rates would increase. Since 65 per cent of the population was under the age of 25, there was a need for even more emphasis to be placed on education.

A combination of all of these factors was probably behind Iran's more positive pre-Cairo stance. And during the Cairo meeting itself, as we shall see, Iran was generally judged to have played a fair and constructive role, helping rather than hindering the solutions which finally emerged.

ISLAM AND THE VATICAN

The rumblings in the Islamic world, during the weeks which preceded the conference, inevitably sparked frenzied interest in the world's media. Meanwhile speculation mounted in the world's press that the Vatican, seeking to head off approval of abortion rights or greater sexual freedom at the forthcoming Cairo conference, was reaching out for support to some radical and fundamentalist governments and groups in Islamic countries, including Iran and Libya.

News reports from Teheran quoted a senior Iranian government official as saying the Vatican had Iran's "full endorsement" on the issue. The British newspaper, the *Guardian*, said the Pope's envoy met on 1 August with Deputy Foreign Minister Mohammad Hashemi Rafsanjani, the brother of President Hashemi Rafsanjani. It said the Iranian newspaper *Abrar* reported that the Deputy Minister had "announced Iran's full endorsement of this (Islam–Vatican) collaboration and said there were many avenues for co-operation between religious states which were not confined to the prohibition of abortion". The Teheran newspaper quoted him as adding: "The future war is between the religious and the materialists. Collaboration between religious governments in support of outlawing abortion is a fine beginning for the conception of collaboration in other fields."[8]

The *Guardian* quoted the Vatican spokesman, Joaquin Navarro Valls, as saying, on 8 August, "The positions of some of the delegations going to Cairo, coming from different countries, different backgrounds, and certainly not from a Catholic and even Christian background, are now closer to the position of the Holy See."

Even more striking was the report by the Libyan news agency, Jana, that Vatican diplomats were supporting Libya in efforts to resolve differences with Western governments over the bombing of the Pan Am jetliner over Lockerbie, Scotland, in 1988. The Libyan agency linked this supposed Vatican assistance to what it said was an identity of views with the Vatican condemning the Cairo document.

For its part, the Vatican insisted that it had appealed to leaders of all religions for backing in the struggle against what it saw as an assault on traditional sexual morality. Vatican officials said the papal envoy in Teheran, Monsignor Romeo Panciroli, had met recently with Iranian officials, but they denied that there was any pact with Iran's radical Islamic leaders to oppose the adoption of the Cairo programme. The Vatican also acknowledged that there had been discussions with Libyan officials but denied that there was any deal over the Cairo document.

Whatever the truth may have been about the "alliance" between the Vatican and Islam, there is no doubt that in the weeks before Cairo, the Vatican looked for — and to some extent found — support from its traditional allies.

Speaking in Calcutta on 1 September, 1994, Mother Teresa added her voice to the Vatican's. She criticised the Cairo conference on population, which she would be unable to attend in person, for allegedly sanctioning abortion, which she called the greatest destroyer of peace.

"I have said often and I am sure of it, that the greatest destroyer of peace today in the world is abortion", she told reporters called to her residence in central Calcutta. "If a mother can kill her own child, what is there to stop you and me from killing each other?" she asked.

ANTI-US FEELINGS

An increasingly anti-US flavour emerged in some of the pre-Cairo statements. On 9 August, a Filipino senator denounced the Clinton administration for planning to use the Cairo conference to promote "abortion, destruction and death". In a speech to the Senate, Senator Francisco Tatad, a lay member of the Roman Catholic Church's ultra-conservative Opus Dei, said the United States was marshalling a coalition "bigger than the one assembled for Desert Storm" to promote abortion and "extinguish the right to life of the unborn".

"We must stand in fear of the United States", Tatad said. "For thanks to the Clinton agenda for the unborn children, women and families around the globe, the US has become one of the most frightening countries in the world." Tatad said that in its 200-year history, the United States had been transformed from "a country founded under God" to "a country where the most offensive and violent language qualifies as a constitutionally protected speech, while praying in school and on campus invites arrest, prison and penalties." "Today, the Clinton administration seems determined to make the US the spearhead of global decadence, destruction and death", Tatad said.[9]

The Church in the Philippines, Asia's only predominately Catholic country, had been especially active in promoting the Vatican's opposition to abortion and artificial birth control. Cardinal Jaime L Sin, Archbishop of Manila, had urged the Philippines to boycott the Cairo conference and had called on Catholics to rally against the government's population programme which included counselling and free condoms for the poor although abortion was banned by the constitution. Parents of children attending Catholic schools received letters urging them to attend the rally to "make known to the President and his cabinet our indignation and outrage at the abuses being allowed by government against the family and our children".

Cardinal Sin's alarm — in his terms — was understandable since the Catholic Church in the Philippines was engaged in a bitter struggle to defend its position. About 85 per cent of the 65 million Filipinos were nominally Catholic. But surveys showed a majority practised some form of artificial birth control. The Catholic hierarchy had shown little support for President Fidel Ramos, a Protestant. In 1992, Sin lobbied strongly with President Corazon Aquino against endorsing him. Although a devout Catholic, Corazon Aquino ignored the cardinal's advice, and Ramos won in a seven-way election in May 1992. Though denouncing abortion, Ramos remained firmly committed to holding the line on family planning and the status of women.

As the leaders of the Catholic Church in the Philippines were urging the faithful to rally to their cause, the Italian government announced that it would reject approving abortion as a form of birth control at the Cairo conference. "If the UN document says abortion can be used as a means of population control, we will not agree," said Antonio Guidi, Minister for the Family and head of Italy's delegation to Cairo. Guidi, speaking to reporters after Italy's position paper was approved during a cabinet meeting, also said he would raise a discussion on the dangers of genetic engineering and research using foetal tissue. Giudi said that no ministers voiced their objections to the position paper during the cabinet meeting.

Earlier in the month members of the government of Prime Minister Silvio Berlusconi had clashed over abortion. Environment Minister Altero Matteoli, a member of the neo-Fascist-led National Alliance, called it murder and his comments drew criticism from colleagues in the coalition. Abortion on demand during the first three months of pregnancy had been legal in the largely Roman Catholic country since 1978, a policy strongly endorsed by a 1981 referendum.[10]

VIEWS WITHIN THE US

Even more significantly there were signs in the United States itself that some Catholics were beginning to resent the high-profile line taken by the US administration in the months preceding the Cairo conference.

The Washington-based Catholic Campaign for America denounced the US government's backing of the UN's proposals for the Cairo meeting. "By advocating abortion on demand, sterilisation, and the distribution of contraceptives, [the conference organisers] seem preoccupied with the notion that people are the problem rather than economic development being the answer," said Thomas Wykes, Executive Director of the campaign. "Policies that redefine the family, that undermine the rights of parents to determine family size, and that encourage quantitative population goals, which is the worst kind of imperialism, interfere with the rights of developing countries to shape their own economic destiny", Wykes said. "It is irresponsible to claim that the United States has all the answers to world population when the greatest threat to the environment comes from the high consumption level of resources by Western countries like our own. . . . It is not in the best interest of the developing world to be reflective of a United States with abortion on demand, [where] one in two marriages ends in divorce, [a United States] with epidemic levels of sexually transmitted diseases, high teenage pregnancy and suicide rates, sexual promiscuity and numerous broken families." As a consequence of his policies on population, President Bill Clinton "runs the risk of alienating the Catholic vote, which is the most important swing vote in the United States", Wykes said.[11]

Patricia Scalia, who was to represent the Catholic Campaign for America in Cairo, said that the conference document "marginalises marriage and denies motherhood the recognition and respect it deserves ... As Americans, we should be cautious in pressuring other nations to accept policies that undermine the stability of the family", she said. "In our country, we are concerned as never before with the welfare of our families, and we have become all too familiar with the unfortunate results that a value-neutral approach to sexuality and reproduction brings."

Mercedes Arzu Wilson, President of Maryland-based Family of the Americas, said the United States is going along with a "kind of dictatorship imposed by international agencies such as the World Bank", by conditioning foreign aid to the implementation of family planning programmes that include contraceptives, abortion, and sterilisation. "The best aid would be that developed nations pay fair prices for developing countries's products", she said. At the Cairo conference "it is expected that all countries support the radical proposals put forward in the United Nations' document, imposed by the United States", Arzu said. US bishops, who had accused Washington of being the driving force behind attempts to support abortion, told President Bill Clinton the Cairo gathering was an attempt to promote "a self-centred and casual view of human sexuality, an approach so destructive of family life and the moral fibre of society." And the six US cardinals told Clinton, a Baptist, that his policy was "trampling the rights and religious values of people around the world".

By the end of August it appeared that the White House was concerned that the Catholic voter support for President Clinton might be softening and that Clinton might be headed for trouble in 1996 with Catholics, the nation's largest group of swing voters and the group that gave him his winning margin in 1992. The first move to head off a potentially damaging public clash with Pope John Paul II at the Cairo conference came when Vice President Al Gore went out of his way to praise Pope John Paul and to express a willingness to amend the Cairo document so it did not declare a world-wide right to abortion. Under Secretary of State Timothy Wirth, who had led the US delegation and the meetings of the Cairo conference's preparatory committee, and who would act as President Clinton's No 2 in Cairo, confirmed the new more conciliatory line. He said the United States was not seeking universal adoption of abortion as a "right" but supported the notion of "access to the full range of reproductive health care services". Timothy Wirth sought to clarify an earlier statement in which he had said that the United States believed "access to safe, legal, and voluntary abortion is a fundamental right of all women". "We were talking about access, and other people thought it was a capital 'R', a universal human right", Wirth said at a State Department briefing for reporters a few days before the Cairo meeting. "It was a matter of just sort of not understanding what kind of perception there would be of that language."[12]

This was followed by the tacit admission by White House Chief of Staff Leon Panetta that some in the administration had been guilty of anti-Catholic comments, requiring White House discipline. Panetta, noting he was "speaking as a Catholic", insisted that anti-Catholic remarks are not tolerated. "You shouldn't assume that there haven't been discussions with [administration members] about those remarks", he said. A case in point was US Surgeon General Jocelyn Elders who was reported to have said that the Catholic Church was made up of "celibate old men" who were in love with the foetus. Elders, Panetta suggested, had been taken to "a modified woodshed."[13]

Panetta, the administration's highest-ranking Catholic, said the White House was trying to shift the Cairo focus onto "population control ... and not get into a fight over abortion, which ought to be left to the sovereignty of different countries". That, he said, was Clinton's position, and "I think, very frankly, that Catholics are in line with that position."

Tony Coelho, a former California congressman recently installed as senior adviser to the Democratic National Committee, urged the White House to build "better ties, more communication with the Catholic hierarchy". Concerned by some of the attacks on the administration from bishops, Coelho — who once studied for the priesthood — said the White House needed to understand that "it is important to talk to the bishops, negotiate with them, work with them, make them understand where we are coming from".

Coelho argued that Clinton "may be more in line with the Catholic parishioners than he is with the Catholic hierarchy". But author Michael Novak, who had written extensively about Catholics in America, warned that Clinton was in trouble with this key constituency, which routinely made up 28 per cent of the electorate and held disproportionate sway in the ten largest states. "There is a shakiness in the Catholic support for Mr Clinton", he said. "There are worrisome signs that the percentages aren't as high and the fervour isn't as great as a Democrat normally needs in key states."

The importance of the Catholic vote was clear from the 1992 election, in which Clinton and George Bush evenly split the Protestant vote. But Clinton beat Bush by 9 percentage points among Catholics, easily the best showing for any Democrat since 1964. In late June 1994, the most recent Gallup Poll in which questions about religious affiliation had been asked, 50 per cent of Catholics had said they approved of Clinton's job as president and 44 per cent said they disapproved. But even though Clinton was faring far better with Catholics than with white Protestants — of which 56 per cent disapproved of his job, to only 26 per cent approving — the support was thin. Novak said: "In a number of states, the Catholic vote has to be over 55 per cent for a Democrat to win. Fifty per cent isn't so good." Despite the diversity in rank-and-file Catholic opinion on issues such as abortion and birth control, an administration clash with the Vatican in Cairo could be devastating to Clinton, Novak said. "Seldom does anyone get into direct conflict with the Pope", he said. "But that is what seems to be shaping up at the Cairo conference. It's a very dicey situation for the president." A clash with the Pope would force American Catholics "to divide their sense of loyalty and esteem", he said.

Novak, in trying to steer Clinton toward a more Catholic-friendly policy, found himself making the same arguments he used 22 years previously when he was writing memos to then Democratic presidential nominee George McGovern, the first Democrat to chase a majority of Catholics into the GOP camp. At the same time, Republican Richard Nixon was getting peppered by similar memos from young aide Patrick J Buchanan. As the Cairo conference approached, Buchanan returned once more to his theme. "It's still true — if Clinton loses the Catholic vote, he is done for", said Buchanan, who was considering a run for the presidency in 1996 built around a strong appeal to Catholics.

FURTHER SHENANIGANS

As in the great battles of the First World War, salvos fired by one side were returned with interest by the other. Though the Vatican might take comfort from the strength of its support in the Philippines, and from the fact that countries like Argentina and Nicaragua appeared to be rallying to its flag, Brazil — the largest nation in Latin America — and the country with the greatest number of Catholics in the world, indicated that it would be one of the Vatican's main opponents in the debates at the Cairo conference. Brazilian Foreign Ministry representative Marcia Coutinho Adorno admitted at a seminar in Sao Paulo on 19 August that the Brazilian delegation would not endorse the Holy See's restrictions regarding women's reproductive rights, sexual education for teenagers, and different forms of family organisation.

"Together with other countries of the region, Brazil is following a line definitively in favour of women's reproductive rights, with a realistic perception of the needs of teenagers and a flexible vision regarding the family", said Adorno. This did not mean that Brazilians would defend abortion as a family planning method. "We do not support that idea under any condition", she added. "That is not contemplated by our laws, which we cannot go beyond or ignore."

The Foreign Ministry representative said that the Brazilian position was that of the Latin America and Caribbean Consensus. In March 1994, representatives from the countries of the region met in Mexico and arrived at a consensus. Later on, the Vatican began to discuss with each government separately the terms of the document. Some countries, like Argentina and Nicaragua, had accepted the impositions of the Vatican, and had broken away from the consensus they had signed. The Brazilian government, however, had not changed its position. In a letter to Pope John Paul II, President Itamar Franco said that the Brazilian position was based on the constitution and on the terms of the international documents signed by consensus.[14]

Brazil's stance could not be ignored. If the Clinton administration was wondering — as the month of August came to an end — about the wisdom of having allowed its dispute with the Vatican to escalate into a full-scale confrontation, there were — by the same token — many who wondered whether the real interests of the Catholic church were being served by encouraging public debate to focus on abortion and contraception to the exclusion of some of the wider issues on the table at Cairo.

An article in the UK's *Guardian* entitled "The Pope's Last Stand" put it thus:

"So why, Vatican watchers are asking, is John Paul treading what any half-way sensible politician would realise is a *via dolorosa* at Cairo? For behind all his bluster about the evils of contraception and how these lead to abortion, he is setting himself up as the fall guy of the conference, someone to blame for the world's problems.

"While Catholic teaching certainly does not help efforts in Africa or Asia to curb an unsustainable birth rate, it is not the real cause, many secular experts will concede, of the population problem. Rather than letting the Pope offer himself up as a sacrificial lamb at Cairo, there is a substantial body of opinion which says that he is being used as a stool pigeon by western governments whose tiny — and shrinking — aid budgets fail to tackle the real cause of population growth in Africa, namely poverty. And he has become the punchbag for western consumers reluctant to accept that their desire for mahogany toilet seats has a much more profound impact on the Brazilian rain forests than the Catholic family in the slums of Rio with six children."[15]

With hindsight August's shenanigans served only to increase world interest in the ICPD. At the time, they seemed more threatening. There was a palpable sense of relief in many quarters when last minute legal challenges by fundamentalists in the Cairo courts to try to prevent the conference from taking place at all were thrown out by the judges and the premises of the Cairo International Conference Centre, constructed by Egypt with Chinese assistance, were officially handed over to the UN.[16] On 25 August, the UN flag was hoisted over the centre, along with the Egyptian national flag. A number of Egyptian officials, including Population Minister Maher Mahran and Tourism Minister Mamdouh al-Beltagui, attended the ceremony. Mahran said in his speech that everything in the conference centre had been made ready for the ICPD and Cairo international airport would render round-the-clock service to participants. He also said that he had coordinated with the ministry of defence so that military helicopters would be available for any emergency or rescue operation covering the Greater Cairo area and some tourist resorts.

Mamdouh al-Beltagui said that all of the facilities and equipment in the Cairo International Conference Centre would be at the UN's disposal during the conference period. In addition, all the hotels in Cairo were ready to receive the estimated 15,000 participants to the conference. The tourism minister expressed the hope that the participants, including some heads of state and government, would seize the chance to tour some of Egypt's most brilliant attractions and resorts. A series of tourism-related exhibitions would be held to enhance the interest of the participants in the splendid civilisation of Egypt.

Confirming that there would be no unseemly disruptions, the Governor of Cairo was quoted as vowing forcibly to stop any demonstrations by homosexuals during the conference. "I shall not allow any marches by these deviates even if I have to resort to force", the opposition Cairo daily *al Ahrar* quoted Governor Omar Abdel Akher as saying at a meeting with youths. "These things are against our Sharia [Islamic laws] and public morals."[17]

The same warning was echoed by Interior Minister Hassan el Alfi who said that police "will not allow any marches or excesses which may do harm to the Egyptian people, their values and traditions". The minister, in statements circulated by the Egyptian Middle East News Agency, also directed a stern warning to Muslim fundamentalist groups against trying to stir trouble during the conference. "Security organs are monitoring all suspect movements which are trying to incite public opinion for ulterior motives", the minister said, apparently referring to the Muslim Brothers and other fundamentalist groups which had been campaigning against the conference. "We shall not allow any infringements of law and order," said the minister, announcing cancellation of all police leave and a state of heightened security alert until the end of the conference.

A less ominous note was struck when, from Chiba, east of Tokyo, Seiko Instruments Inc announced that the United Nations' new clocks showing the growth of the world population had been completed and were ready for delivery to UN member countries. UNFPA Executive Director Nafis Sadik would present the clocks in Cairo to countries participating in the ICPD.

The latest model population clock was the second revision of the original, which had been created in 1987 when the world population topped five billion. The clock showed the total population of the world body's 223 member countries and the entire population on Earth in a digital display, renewing the figures every minute on the basis of UN population data announced in 1993. The clock would show the world population figure of 6,272,927,873 on 1 January, 2001, the first day of the twenty-first century, up from some 5.66 billion on 1 July, 1994, as estimated by the UN.

The company had manufactured 1350 specimens of the clock, which was 14.5 cm high, 17 cm wide and 11.8 cm deep, and weighed 1.7 kilograms. The clocks were not for sale.[18]

Chapter 5

The Opening of the Cairo Conference

More than four years after it was first authorised by the UN, the International Conference on Population and Development (ICPD) opened in an atmosphere of considerable excitement. It is not often that a UN meeting manages to grab the attention of the world's media but the Cairo conference, largely thanks to the heated controversies that had developed over the previous weeks, certainly managed to do that. Egyptian officials indicated that 20,000 people were expected. Others suggested that as many as 25,000 would attend the conference and related activities. Among them would be diplomats from 180 nations, representatives of 2000 non-governmental organisations, as well as some 3000 journalists and other media representatives.

On the whole, those who expected fireworks from the opening session were not disappointed. Compared with the official openings of the Bucharest and Mexico population conferences, held respectively 20 and 10 years previously, the inaugural session of the International Conference on Population and Development which took place in the Cheops Hall of Cairo's International Conference Centre (CICC) in the morning of Monday 5 September, 1994, was a tumultuous affair full of fire and passion.

BRUNDTLAND AND BHUTTO

As far as the world's press and media coverage was concerned, women dominated the opening session: Gro Harlem Brundtland, the Prime Minister of Norway and Benazir Bhutto, Prime Minister of Pakistan.

Gro Harlem Brundtland was, of course, a familiar face on the international circuit. Besides being a long-serving prime minister, she had in the mid-1980s chaired the World Commission on Environment and Development which had produced the so-called "Brundtland Report", a document which, even if it did not actually coin the phrase "sustainable development", was certainly responsible for giving it wide currency. She had given one of the keynote speeches at the Earth Summit in Rio and had remained active in the post-UNCED follow-up.

Yet Benazir Bhutto was in her own way just as remarkable. Whereas Norway's population was around 4.3 million, Pakistan's was around 125 million, 29 times larger, making it one of the nine most populous countries in the world. Though the Indian sub-continent had a habit of throwing up female leaders — Gandhi of India, Bandaranaike of Sri Lanka come to mind — Benazir Bhutto's achievements as a leader of her country, her success in conciliating warring factions within her country, and her personal courage in making the journey to Cairo in the face of fierce opposition gave her a special stature among the delegates.

Division over the abortion issue

Inevitably, the media focused more on what divided the two women than on what united them. Some observers used the language of the boxing-ring to describe the scene. In the red corner, Brundtland ... in the blue corner, Bhutto .... Equally inevitably, the issue of abortion was the area where the confrontation between the two women could be shown to be at its most acute. Gro Harlem Brundtland called in the clearest possible language for abortion to be "decriminalised".

She said she was pleased by the emerging consensus that everyone should have access to the whole range of family planning services at an affordable price. Sometimes religion was a major obstacle. But morality could not only be a question of controlling sexuality and protecting unborn life. Morality was also a question of giving individuals the opportunity of choice.

> "Morality becomes hypocrisy if it means accepting mothers suffering or dying in connection with unwanted pregnancies and illegal abortions, and unwanted children living in misery."

She went on to say that nobody could disregard the fact that abortions occur, and that where they were illegal, or heavily restricted, the life and health of the woman were often at risk.

> "Decriminalising abortions should therefore be a minimal response to this reality, and a necessary means of protecting the life and health of women."

Brundtland argued that in a forward-looking plan of action it seemed sensible to combine health concerns that dealt with human sexuality under the heading "reproductive health care". She said she had "tried, in vain, to understand how that term can possibly be read as promoting abortions or qualifying abortion as a means of family planning. Rarely — if ever — have so many misrepresentations been used to imply meaning that was never there in the first place."

The total number of abortions in Norway, she added, had stayed the same after abortion was legalised, while illegal abortions sank to zero. Norway's experience was similar to that of other countries, namely that the law had an impact on the decision-making process and with the safety of abortion — but not on the numbers. Norway's abortion rate was one of the lowest in the world. She added:

> "Unsafe abortion is a major public health problem, in most corners of the globe. We know full well, all of us, that wealthy people often manage to pay their way to safe abortion regardless of the law. A conference of this status and importance should not accept attempts to distort facts or neglect the agony to millions of women who are risking their lives and health. I simply refuse to believe that the stalemate reached over this crucial question will be allowed to block a serious and forward-looking outcome of the Cairo conference — hopefully based on full consensus and adopted in good faith."

Brundtland received a standing ovation at the end of her speech. But Benazir Bhutto, who followed Mrs Brundtland to the podium, made a no less spirited defence of Islamic and family values.

> "Regrettably, the conference document contains serious flaws striking at the heart of a great many cultural values, in the North and in the South, in the mosque and in the church. In Pakistan, our response will doubtless be shaped by our belief in the eternal teachings of Islam, a dynamic religion committed to human progress. The Holy Qur'ān says: 'Allah wishes you ease, and wishes not hardship for you.'
>
> "Again, the Holy Book says: 'He has chosen you, and has not laid on you any hardship in religion.'"

Benazir Bhutto said the followers of Islam had no conceptual difficulty in addressing questions of regulating population in the light of available resources. The only constraint was that the process must be consistent with abiding moral principles.

> "Islam lays a great deal of stress on the sanctity of life. The Holy Book tells us: 'Kill not your children on a plea of want. We provide sustenance for them and for you.'"

Islam, therefore, except in exceptional circumstances, rejected abortion as a method of population control. There was little compromise on

Islam's emphasis on the family unit. "The traditional family", she said, "is the basic unit on which any society rests. It is the anchor on which the individual relies."

Islam aimed at harmonious lives built upon a bedrock of conjugal fidelity and parental responsibility. Muslims, with their overriding commitment to knowledge, would have no difficulty with dissemination of information about reproductive health, so long as its modalities remained compatible with their religious and spiritual heritage. Lack of an adequate infrastructure of services, not ideology, was the basic problem.

United on the issue of empowerment of women

In reality, there was much more uniting the two women leaders than dividing them. Bhutto received the warmest applause when, in perhaps the most moving statement of the whole meeting, she said:

> "I dream of a Pakistan, of an Asia, of a world, where every pregnancy is planned and every child conceived is nurtured, loved, educated and supported. I dream of a Pakistan, of an Asia, of a world, where we can commit our social resources to the development of human life and not to its destruction. That dream is far from the reality we endure. We are a planet in crisis, a planet moving towards catastrophe. The question is whether we have the will to do something about it. I say we do. We must."

The conference should not be viewed "as a universal social charter seeking to impose adultery, abortion, sex education and other such matters on individuals, societies and religions which have their own social ethos". By convening this conference, the international community had reaffirmed its resolve that problems of a global nature would be solved through global efforts.

> "How do we tackle population growth in a country like Pakistan? By tackling infant mortality, by providing villages with electrification, by raising an army of women, 33,000 strong, to educate our mothers, sisters, daughters in child welfare and population control. By setting up a bank run by women for women, to help women achieve economic independence, and to have the wherewithal to make independent choices."

Benazir Bhutto pointed out that in Pakistan, in a period of 30 years from 1951 to 1981, the population rose by 50 million. As she spoke, it was 126 million. By the year 2020 Pakistan's population might be 243 million.

> "Pakistan cannot progress if it cannot check its rapid population growth. Check it we must, for it is not the destiny of the people of Pakistan to live in squalor and poverty."

91

For Benazir Bhutto, the goal of controlling population — an unfashionable term which she did not hesitate to use — was not in doubt. Nor was she in doubt about the means. Leaders were elected to lead nations. Leaders were not elected to "let a vocal narrow-minded minority dictate an agenda of backwardness".

> "We are committed to an agenda for change, to take our mothers and infants into the twenty-first century with the hope of a better future, free from diseases that rack and ruin. These are the battles that we must fight, not only as a nation but as a global community. These are the battles on which history — and our people — will judge us. These are the battles to which the mosque and the church must contribute, along with governments and other organisations and families.
>
> "Empowerment of women is one part of this battle. Today women pilots fly planes in Pakistan, women serve as judges in the superior judiciary, women work in police stations, women work in our civil service, our foreign service and our media. Our working women uphold the Islamic principle that all individuals are equal in the eyes of God. By empowering our women, we work for our goal of population stabilisation and, with it, promotion of human dignity."

When Benazir Bhutto talked in these forthright terms about the empowerment of women she was echoing, not contradicting, Gro Harlem Brundtland's earlier remarks. The agreement between the two leaders on this aspect of the Cairo draft was at the end of the day far more significant than any disagreements they might have had over abortion.

Brundtland's remarks did not perhaps have the poetry of Bhutto's. Nevertheless, they cut to the heart of the debate and set the tone and the context for much of what was to follow.

Gro Harlem Brundtland had told the Conference:

> "It is encouraging that there is already so much common ground between us. The final programme of action must embody irreversible commitments towards strengthening the role and status of women. We must all be prepared to be held accountable. That is how democracy works."

It could not be repeated often enough that there were few investments that could bring greater rewards than investment in women. But still women were being patronised and discriminated against in terms of access to education, productive assets, credit, income and services, decision-making, working conditions and pay. For too many women in too many countries, real development had only been an illusion.

Women's education was the single most important path to higher productivity, lower infant mortality and lower fertility. The economic returns on investment in women's education were generally comparable to those for men, but the social returns in terms of health and fertility by far exceeded what was gained from men's education.

Gro Harlem Brundtland had appealed to the meeting:

"So let us pledge to watch over the numbers of school-enrolment for girls. Let us watch also the numbers of girls that complete their education and ask why if the numbers differ."

And one of the reasons for asking why, she added in one of the conference's most memorable phrases, was "because the girl who receives her diploma will have fewer babies than her sister who does not".

The "empowerment of women" theme had also been touched on in the addresses made on the opening day by President Hosni Mubarak and by UN Secretary General Boutros Boutros-Ghali. Both signalled the shift in perspective that had occurred in the way the population problem was seen and, more important, in the means now envisaged for dealing with that problem.

Boutros-Ghali had said:

"The population problem facing our present world cannot be correctly solved on the basis of handling the demographic dimensions only .... The honest translation of this integrated vision of the dimensions of the population problem necessitates intensifying the efforts we exert to upgrade educational and health services and pay more attention to women who play a major role in forming a family, raising children and also bear a bigger responsibility in implementing the programmes relevant to population.

"The cornerstone and starting point in any successful demographic policies aiming at establishing a society capable of waging the battle of development with efficiency, is working on improving women's conditions, especially, in the developing countries, raising awareness of the gravity of the problem and revealing to them all the various dimensions."

He went on to say that states must be supported in their efforts to control population increase. "The purpose of a conference such as ours is not only to measure the progress achieved over a decade, but also to devise better ways of combining population and development, as the very title of our Conference urges us to do."

"We must also consider population and family-planning policies from the broadest and most global perspective so as to address not only the immediate problem, but also its underlying causes. Indeed, population policies are inseparable from health, nutrition and education policies.

"In this connection, I should like to stress the role that such policies must assign to women. Educating and mobilising women are goals essential to the success of all population and development policies throughout the world."[1]

Like Boutros Ghali, like Gro Harlem Brundtland and Benazir Bhutto, the Vice President of the United States, Al Gore, stressed in his opening remarks to the Cairo conference the new perspective on the population problem. Forced as a result of a recent leg injury to hobble to the podium on crutches, he was the first, though certainly not the only speaker, to use the word "holistic" in describing the new approach.

He said that a real change had occurred during the last several years in the way most people in the world looked at and understood the population problem. The change was part of a larger philosophical shift in the way most people had begun to think about many large problems. There used to be an automatic tendency — especially in the developed world — to think about the process of change in terms of single causes producing single effects. And thus, when searching for the way to solve a particular problem, however large, it seemed natural enough to search for the single most prominent "cause" of the problem and then address it forcefully. Many divisive arguments resulted between groups advocating the selection of different causes as the "primary" culprit deserving of full attention.

> "Thus, when it became clear that new medical technologies were bringing dramatic declines in death rates but not in birth rates, many pioneers in the effort to address the population question settled on the notion that the lack of contraceptives was the primary problem and argued that making them widely available everywhere would produce the effect we desired — the completion of the demographic transition with the achievement of low birth rates as well as low death rates."

But as it became clear that contraception alone seldom led to the change nations were seeking to bring about, other single causes were afforded primary attention.

> "But here, at Cairo, there is a new and very widely shared consensus that no single one of these solutions is likely to be sufficient by itself to produce the pattern of change we are seeking. However, we also now agree that all of them together, when simultaneously present for a sufficient length of time, will reliably bring about a systemic change to low birth and death rates and a stabilised population. In this new consensus, equitable and sustainable development and population stabilisation go together. The education and empowerment of women, high levels of literacy, the availability of contraception and quality health care: these factors are all crucial."

Al Gore possibly lacked the media appeal of Brundtland and Bhutto, and his analysis of the problem and his outline of the required solutions was

94

possibly too abstract for many of the delegates present. Vice President Gore's holistic solution went beyond family planning, reproductive rights and the empowerment of women to become a universal, almost mystical force.

> "Personally, I am convinced that the holistic solution we must seek is one that is rooted in faith and a commitment to basic human values of the kind enshrined in all of our major religious traditions and principles increasingly shared by men and women all around the world."

THE "THIRD WOMAN": DR NAFIS SADIK

If there was one single person who deserved the credit for steering the conference between the Scylla of total generality and the Charybdis of a too-narrowly-focused-family-planning-oriented document it was the ICPD's Secretary General Nafis Sadik.

A spate of articles appeared in the press as the conference opened describing the "third woman" in the opening session's celebrity line-up. One article, which appeared in the *Los Angeles Times* on Sunday 4 September, 1995, seemed to capture the essential.

> "Born in Jaunpur, India, on Aug. 18, 1929, Sadik spent much of her childhood in Calcutta, where her father, Mohammed Shoaib, was a government finance officer. In school, she loved engineering, medicine and Indian classical music. She was a top-ranked badminton player, good at tennis and a tournament bridge player.
>
> " 'I used to tell my mother sometimes I wished I could live two lives at once', she said. 'She used to say, "You're mad. Nobody can live two lives." '
>
> " 'At that time, I wanted to change everything . . . I said, "I want to do something in which I'll be known and I'll contribute to society." ' "

Sadik chose medicine, but feared opposition from her father, who later became Minister of Finance in Pakistan and vice president of the World Bank. But instead of insisting she get married, he supported her and went along for her interview at Calcutta Medical College.

Her mother was more reluctant. Until her last year of medical school, Sadik said, her mother would say: "I don't know why you're doing all this medicine. You're not going to work. Why don't you get married, and I'll give you lots of jewelry and clothes?"

She married Azhar Sadik, a Pakistani army officer, in Washington, DC, after finishing medical school and an internship and residency at City Hospital in Baltimore. He encouraged her to work, and when they returned to Pakistan she became a civilian doctor in army hospitals.

Working with women in rural villages, part of the army's community service programme, sparked her interest in family planning.

When she would tell new mothers they shouldn't get pregnant again for two years, the women would say their husbands or mothers-in-law had other ideas — especially if the baby was a girl.

> " 'Then it started to come home to me that these poor women really had no control over their lives', she said."

In Pakistan in the 1950s, there were no family planning services. Sadik decided to start a programme and asked her commanding officer for money to buy contraceptives.

> " 'He nearly fell off his chair', she said, but finally gave her some money with a warning that if there were any complaints, 'I'm going to say you're doing it all on your own.' "
>
> "Sadik bought condoms, took them to villages and talked to husbands about family planning.
>
> " 'I think first they were a bit shocked, because I looked very young', she said. 'But I think they got convinced that I was quite firm, and I was very determined. I don't think I got anyone who said, "No, I'm not going to listen." '
>
> "When one woman became pregnant, Sadik was so angry with the husband that she made all the men sign pledges not to make their wives pregnant. She now says, with a laugh, that it was a "brash" and "stupid" thing to do."

After a three-month break in 1963 to try life without work, Sadik decided on a new career and went to Johns Hopkins University to study public health and health planning. By that time, she had three children of her own and two adopted daughters.

Back in Pakistan the next year, she helped design the country's five-year family planning programme and spent the next three years helping make it work.

She joined the UN Population Fund as an adviser in 1971 and was appointed Executive Director in 1987, becoming one of the first women to head a major UN organisation.

The *Los Angeles Times* article ended by pointing out that her contract as Executive Director of UNFPA would end in April, 1995, and that Dr Sadik hoped that Boutros Boutros-Ghali, the current Secretary General, would renew it so she could help implement the programme agreed upon in Cairo.

> " 'When I ultimately retire, I feel I still have a lot of things that I can do in Pakistan', she said. 'The rights for women and the empowerment of women is very poor there.' "[2]

Dr Sadik in fact made two speeches to the ICPD on the opening day. The first was of a formal nature; the second set the scene in a comprehensive manner for the debates of the next ten days.

> "The antecedents of this conference go back at least to 1974, to the World Population Conference in Bucharest, where the World Population Plan of Action was adopted. From the perspective of international population policies, the world looked very different then. Only 27 countries had explicit population policies. Only a handful more provided significant support to national family-planning programmes. For most people in 1974, population issues seemed to be quite overwhelming; they seemed either too complex or too controversial, or both."[3]

In the 20 years which had passed since the Bucharest conference, developing countries had made very dramatic progress in their population and development policies. Birth and death rates had both fallen substantially. Over one hundred countries had national population policies, and all but a handful of the world's governments provided support for family-planning services. More than 55 per cent of couples now used family planning. The 1994 projections showed lower rates of population growth and substantial reductions in the numbers added each year. Sadik went on to say:

> "Many of today's developing countries will accomplish in less than a single generation a transformation which took 100 years in many parts of Europe."

The experience of many countries showed that population programmes and other investments in human development — especially investments which made women more equal partners in development — interact in powerful ways. The results showed themselves in smaller, healthier and better educated families, and in a generation of women and men who could think for themselves, decide for themselves and take their full part in family, community and national life.

Dr Sadik paid a special tribute to her predecessor, Rafael Salas, who had spoken about the "empowerment of women" long before that term gained general currency.

> "As my predecessor and first executive director of UNFPA Rafael M Salas said 19 years ago: 'Equality for women does more than contribute to development. Equality for women is development'."

Dr Sadik pointed out emphatically that the empowerment of women not only contributed to the goal of population stabilisation; it was the vital underpinning of sustainable development.

> "As each of the regional preparatory conferences emphasised, women's role in the family is only part of their contribution to

development. On the grounds of social justice alone, there is the strongest possible case for emphasising investment in health, education and special programmes for women. As many countries have now demonstrated, higher literacy, better health and slower population growth are the best basis for economic development. None of these aims can be achieved without involving women as actors and agents, as well as beneficiaries."

She told the conference that the Draft Programme of Action called on countries to facilitate equal participation of women in community life, just as it recognised the necessity for the full involvement of men in family life, family planning and child-rearing from the earliest ages. It also called on countries to promote women's education and employment, and to eliminate violence against women.

"Many people regard the draft chapter on these subjects, Chapter IV, as one of the most comprehensive chapters on this subject ever to come out of a major United Nations conference. Apart from references to sexual and reproductive health and family planning, you have agreed this chapter in its entirety."

Dr Sadik went on to say that the Draft Programme of Action was the fruit of years of inclusive and exhaustive discussion, involving at one time or another 170 countries, 4000 non-governmental organisations, all walks of life and all value systems. It must be one of the most thoroughly discussed documents in United Nations history.

"It is certainly one of the most specific documents that international consultation has ever brought forth on such a subject. It is a measure of our agreement on what was once a most controversial topic, that such a broad document can also be so precise. It is a measure of the ambition of the framers of the Draft Programme of Action that they can come here expecting it to be accepted ...

"You have laboured mightily, and your labours have already brought forth fruit. You have already adopted the great bulk of the Draft Programme of Action's 16 chapters. Only about 10 per cent of the Draft Programme of Action remains to be negotiated."

Dr Sadik continued with three specific points concerning the document and how it should be read.

"First, the principle of sovereignty underlies the whole text. Nothing in the document can or should be interpreted as interfering in any way with a nation's sovereign right to make and carry out policy according to its own laws, precepts, culture and moral codes. That is fundamental, and dates from the earliest days of discussion on population. It is, in fact, the principle that makes all international discussion on population possible. The formulation and implementation of population policies, including those of reproductive health, are the sovereign right of each nation, consistent with national laws and in conformity with international human rights standards . . . .

"Second, the language of the document is framed so as to be acceptable to the widest possible spectrum of approaches to population. In this room are representatives of countries with over a billion people, and some with populations of under 100,000. Some modes of government draw on traditions spanning many centuries, others benefit from constitutions and legal systems framed in the last generation. All religions and systems of belief are represented here. The language of each part of the document should be acceptable to all. If it is not, then it will be changed. If no phrasing acceptable to all can be found on a particular matter, then other means will be taken. One way or another, we will leave here with a document that all can accept, with goals that we all believe in and feel are realistic . . . .

"Third, we are all hoping for full agreement among all the countries represented here, so the terms of agreement will necessarily be quite broad. At the same time, we are looking for a basis for firm and determined action in the next 20 years. This demands some definite and precise terminology . . . ."

Dr Sadik pointed out that a main theme throughout the Draft Programme of Action was partnership at all levels, in particular, between governments, non-governmental organisations and the private sector. Non-governmental organisation participation during the entire period of preparation for this conference had been unprecedented. And the role of non-governmental organisations would be critically important in the implementation of the programme of action. Over the next two decades, an effective partnership at all levels between governments and non-governmental organisations in the implementation, monitoring and evaluation of the programme of action would be vital.

Finally Dr Sadik turned to the question of the resources necessary to implement the programme.

"There is strong consensus on the need for additional financial resources for national population programmes in support of sustainable development. Several countries have already indicated the intention to increase their population assistance in the near future. Developing countries now provide about 75 per cent of the total cost of population programmes, and the Draft Programme of Action suggests that external donors should raise their contribution to one third of the total. The cost appears modest, compared to the potential results. The estimates set out in the Draft Programme of Action are for discussion here: I am sure the conference will arrive at a satisfactory conclusion."

The historical significance of the conference would depend on the effectiveness with which commitment was translated into action. The most effective population and development programmes reflected the determination of leaders at all levels to make them work. The same would be true of the measures adopted in Cairo. Nafis Sadik told her audience that at the end of their deliberations, "you will have the satisfaction of knowing that you have made a historic contribution to the health and well-being of every person, every family and every country on our planet."

Dr Sadik's enthusiasm was infectious and the applause which greeted her speech testified to the high esteem in which she was held by the delegations present. Few — and Dr Sadik herself least of all — underestimated the difficulties which lay ahead. Over the coming ten days, Cairo would witness a clash of ideas, of attitudes, of ideologies. Though — as Dr Sadik pointed out — much had already been agreed at the meetings of the preparatory committee, it seemed possible that the conference could actually founder over these hard-fought issues — abortion, contraception, homosexuality, women's rights — where agreement was not yet in sight. Either the text would be fatally weakened in the attempt to reach consensus, or else there would be so many reservations — on parts of the text or on the whole thing — that the document would lose all authority.

Chapter 6

The Controversy over Abortion

If the Cairo conference has passed into history as one of the most widely reported conferences ever held under UN auspices, the Earth Summit included, the reason was the controversy over abortion. This controversy, as we have seen, not only dominated the run-up to the conference; it dominated much of the nine-day meeting.

When, on Monday 5 September, Dr Nafis Sadik, Secretary General of the ICPD, walked into the hall for her first press briefing, a horde of photographers materialised as she took her seat, and video and still cameras jostled frantically for positions. But not for long. Grim-faced security men rushed up to distance the popping flashguns from the dais — a telling reflection of security concerns emanating from the controversy surrounding the population conference that Dr Sadik was piloting.

Countering criticism that the draft threatened the family institution, Dr Sadik stressed that the Programme of Action supported and sought to strengthen the family, the vulnerable members of society, and the weakest of the international community. "Above all, it is a document based on moral grounds. The Programme of Action is not laying down the moral law, but it includes the moral dimension."

She emphasised that the final Programme of Action would be designed by all the nations represented at the conference, and in the tradition of the UN system each nation could air its problems, as well as its suggestions. Touching on the issues of reproductive health and personal choice, which were also at the centre of the criticisms against the draft document, Dr Sadik said a key objective was to meet the needs of families and individuals, especially women.

"On the grounds of social justice alone, I believe there is the strongest possible cause for emphasising equality for women. But the case is even stronger than that. As many countries have now demonstrated, higher literacy, better health and slower population growth are the best basis for economic development. And the fact is that none of these aims can be achieved without involving women as actors, and agents, as well as beneficiaries."

Dr Sadik said the measures called for in the Programme of Action were simple and undramatic, and called for no great strides in technology or vast transfers of resources from North to South. However, implementation would call for commitment to change and dynamism. "Based on the highest of moral and ethical principles, it is a reminder to every country that they are responsible for the quality of life of every individual." That, she said, was the real challenge of the programme.

This was the context in which the draft's more controversial language had to be seen. "We must not allow poor health care in pregnancy to take the lives of 500,000 women, and to destroy the health of ten times that number, to say nothing of the 3 million infants' lives lost in the first week of life as a result of poor pregnancy management. That is morally unacceptable."

On the issue of abortion, which had been the focus of criticisms of the draft, Dr Sadik said the facts should be faced squarely. There are some 50–60 million abortions each year, and between 70,000 and 200,000 women died annually from unsafe abortions. Dr Sadik expressed confidence that by the end of the conference the Programme of Action would be approved. Asked to comment on the effect of the seeming alliance between the Vatican and some Muslim leaders against the objectives of the ICPD, Dr Sadik quipped: "Well, the controversy has been successful in creating a lot of international interest in the conference."[1]

Dr Sadik was not alone in calling for action on abortion. As we have seen, in her speech at the opening session of the ICPD Gro Harlem Brundtland had pleaded:

"Let us turn from the dramatising of this conference which has been going on in the media, and focus on the main issues. We are gathered here to answer a moral call to action. Solidarity with present and future generations has its price. But if we do not pay it in full, we will be faced with global bankruptcy."

In making this appeal, she was of course referring to the way in which the abortion issue had dominated the world's press and media in the months, weeks and days before the conference opened. In practice, as we have seen in a previous chapter, her own challenging remarks on the subject of abortion effectively ensured that the spotlight remained firmly fixed on this question. When Gro Harlem Brundtland called for "decriminalising abortion", she meant, or at least she implied, that she wanted abortion to be legal and that she wanted the conference to endorse that position. Though Al Gore in his own speech to the plenary denied that the United States was seeking to "establish a new international right to abortion" or was encouraging resort to abortion as a method of family planning, he was emphatic that unsafe abortion was an issue that must be addressed.

> "For example, we are all well aware that views about abortion are as diverse among nations as among individuals. I want to be clear about the US position on abortion so that there is no misunderstanding. We believe that making available the highest quality family-planning and health care services will simultaneously respect women's own desires to prevent unintended pregnancies, reduce population growth and the rate of abortion."
>
> "The United States Constitution guarantees every woman within our borders a right to choose an abortion, subject to limited and specific exceptions. We are committed to that principle. But let us take a false issue off the table: the United States does not seek to establish a new international right to abortion, and we do not believe that abortion should be encouraged as a method of family planning."

Though Al Gore's remarks were less categorical than some of the "pro-abortion" statements that had emanated from the United States administration over the previous months, the language he used was hardly non-contentious. He might reject abortion as a means of family planning; he might no longer insist on general legalisation.

> "We also believe that policy making in these matters should be the province of each government, within the context of its own laws and national circumstances, and consistent with previously agreed human rights standards. In this context, we abhor and condemn coercion related to abortion or any other matters of reproduction."

But still he and the US government believed in the concept of "safe" abortion. "We believe that where abortion is permitted, it should be medically safe and that unsafe abortion is a matter of women's health that must be addressed."

But as far as the opponents of abortion were concerned, there could be no such thing as a "safe" abortion. From the point of view of the foetus at least, all abortions had to be considered unsafe.

Faced with these kinds of challenges small wonder that Benazir Bhutto had felt moved to quote from the Koran: "Kill not your children

. . . . We provide sustenance for them and for you." She had categorically rejected abortion as a means of birth control and had branded certain clauses in the ICPD draft declaration as being offensive to the feelings of the faithful.

THE SPEECHES OF THE PLENARY DEBATE

As the plenary debate got under way, speaker after speaker set out his or her point of view on the abortion issue. Because these statements would later be reflected to a greater or lesser extent in the positions taken by delegates in the conference's committees and working groups, it is worth looking at a few of them.

The developed world, on the whole, took a "liberal" approach though the balance and emphasis varied. The Scandinavian countries tended to follow what could be referred to as the Brundtland approach, that is that abortion should be decriminalised everywhere and that the conference should endorse that option.

Denmark's Minister for Development Cooperation, Helle Degn, said:

"Half a million women — and most of them in developing countries — die every year as a result of pregnancy and birth-related causes. And out of that number 200,000 women die due to unsafe abortions. Many more suffer serious health implications. This figure — 500,000 — is not acceptable. We can change the situation. All it takes is determination to do something about it — and an open mind as to the necessary means.

"Most important amongst these means are improved health services, information and education. This also includes the free and affordable access to quality contraceptives for all segments of the population.

"We also have to address the painful issue of unsafe abortions which threaten the life and health of so many women. I would like to emphasise that I fully support the notion that abortion should not be promoted as a method of family planning. But, when a woman herself has made the very difficult decision to have an abortion, she must be given access to safe and legal abortion services. Otherwise, she risks to pay with her life."

Elizabeth Regn, Finland's Minister of Equality Affairs, stated:

"The present high levels of unsafe and illegal abortions must also be properly addressed. Every nation must decide how it deals with these problems. Women's health is of course a priority, which affects the well-being of their children and families as well. Unless we address these matters now we endanger the health and lives of millions of women. Abortion should not be a family-planning method. Our national experience suggests that given the availability of information and services on reproductive health the number of abortions continues to decrease even though abortion is allowed on medical and social grounds. Finland is also the only country in Europe where the number of abortions among those under 19 years of age has decreased."

Inger Davidson, Sweden's Minister of Public Administration and Youth, said:

"Experience shows that abortions take place whether the national legislation permits them or not. Making abortions illegal hence does not solve the problem of unsafe abortion; on the contrary it increases maternal morbidity and deaths and removes the issue from the national statistics.

"In Sweden we agonized over this question for decades, but in the 70s came to the conclusion that the abortion option in the early stages of a pregnancy should be open to the choice of the woman when she sees no other possibility. One main objective in our policy in this field has however been and continues to be a strong emphasis on preventive measures. Availability of services, information and education can reduce the abortion rate significantly."

Johanna Dohnal, Austria's Federal Minister for Women's Affairs, took a similar line.

"Austria emphasises the importance of this problem. Women should be provided with a legal framework which would allow them to terminate unwanted pregnancies without resort to dangerous methods."

Ukraine, where family planning services were still largely inadequate and where abortion was indeed used as a means of family planning on a large scale, was even more emphatic.

"Abortion does great harm to the woman's health and results in other negative population consequences. *But its prohibition now, in the conditions of insufficient supply of effective contraceptives, would evoke more negative consequences in connection with the inevitable growth of illegal abortions.* We believe that an access to contraceptives, adequate medical assistance and information, as it is envisaged by the draft Programme of Action of our conference, is an alternative to the abortion." [author's emphasis]

If the Scandinavian countries, Austria, New Zealand and so on were forthright in their support of safe legal abortion, others were more hesitant or downright hostile.

Brendan Howlin, Ireland's Minister for Health, pointed out that, in Ireland, as in very many other countries, there were deeply held convictions on this matter. The Irish Constitution provided that the State acknowledged the right to life of the unborn and, with due regard to the equal right to life of the mother, guaranteed in its laws to respect and, as far as practicable, by its laws to defend and vindicate that right. This constitutional provision had been ruled by the Irish Supreme Court to prohibit abortion except in circumstances where a real and substantial risk to the life of the mother could not be averted by any other means.

"It is, therefore," he said, "of great importance to Ireland, as it clearly is also to many other countries, that the document would recognise that policy and legislation in relation to the circumstances in which the termination of pregnancy may be permitted is a matter for each country to determine for itself."

In the opposing camp, the Holy See was uncompromising. Two days after the conference opened, the Vatican and its supporters launched a counter-attack against liberals campaigning for "safe abortion" and provisions for birth control services to teenagers.

"There have been efforts by some to foster the concept of a 'right to abortion' ", delegates were told by Archbishop Renato R Martino, permanent observer of the Holy See to the UN.

He said texts under consideration at the three-day-old conference "ask that countries re-examine their legislation on abortion" and "provide in the coming years services of 'pregnancy termination' for persons 'of all ages' ".

This in effect might lead to elevating "unrestricted access to abortion" to the status of a right, something which he said "would be contrary to the constitutional and legislative positions of many states as well as being alien to the sensitivities of vast numbers of persons, believers and unbelievers alike".

The Archbishop's statement drew the loudest applause from the delegates since the previous Monday's speech by Norway's Prime Minister Gro Harlem Brundtland. He said:

> "The Holy See is particularly concerned about the manner in which the question of abortion has been treated in the preparation of this conference.
>
> "International consensus language urges governments to 'take appropriate steps to help women to avoid abortion, which in no case should be promoted as a method of family planning, and whenever possible, to provide for the humane treatment and counselling of women who have had recourse to abortion'. The Holy See is hopeful that the conference will reaffirm this principle.

"While there are many texts in the document which would clearly infer a desire of nations to reduce the number of abortions and to remove the conditions which lead women to have recourse to abortions, there have been efforts by some to foster the concept of 'a right to abortion' and to establish abortion as an essential component of population policy. Texts under negotiation ask that countries re-examine their legislation on abortion and countries are urged, in similar texts, to provide in the coming years, services of 'pregnancy termination' for persons 'of all ages'. Should current bracketed texts be approved they would endorse 'pregnancy termination' without setting any limits, any criteria or any restrictions on such practices as integral parts of reproductive health services. Through the possible approval of other bracketed language addressed to the entire international community such unrestricted access to abortion might be elevated to the level of a right.

"None of these new tendencies emerged during the regional preparatory conferences. The concept of a 'right to abortion' would be entirely innovative in the international community and would be contrary to the constitutional and legislative positions of many states as well as being alien to the sensitivities of vast numbers of persons, believers and unbelievers alike."

The Vatican unquestionably had hard-line allies.

For Argentina, His Excellency, Senor Canciller Guido de Tella said:

"La aceptacion del aborto o la esterilizacion como metodos de control poblacional para aquellos sectores privados de todo bienestar material abre la puerta para otro tipo de causalidades como pueden ser la seleccion del sexo, la presuncion o constatacion de discapacidades y otros.

"La practica del aborto compromete y vulnera una vida humana plena de dignidad y derechos, distinta de la vida de la madre, y constituye en si misma, por lo menos, el fracaso de la planificacion familiar."

For Chile, Minister Maria J Bilbao Mendoza said:

"Nuestro pais tiene una politica de planificacion familiar basada en razones de salud y de derechos humanos, que ha sido pionera en America Latina y que ha permitido promover el concepto de paternidad responsable. Los servicios otorgados por el estado respetan el derecho de las parejas a decidir libremente el numero de hijos, espaciamiento y oportunidad del nacimiento de sus hijos y ponen a su disposicion, los metodos anticonceptivos que sean mas aceptables para ellas.

"Suscribimos el concepto de salud reproductiva sobre el cual trabaja la organizacion mundial de la salud. Este concepto ha inspirado las actividades de planificacion familiar dentro del pais, sin embargo, entiende que, en dicha definicion, el termino regulacion de la fecundidad no incluye el uso del aborto, el cual mi gobierno rechaza como metodo de planificacion familiar."

On the other hand, Brazil was ready to take a constructive look at the texts which were before the meeting, thus maintaining the generally supportive attitude which we have already remarked.

The church had lobbied hard to keep abortion illegal in Brazil, yet as many illegal abortions were performed in Brazil as legal ones in the US. Only 10,000 American women were hospitalised for complications of abortion each year, while in Brazil the number was 400,000. Brazil had the world's largest Catholic population; yet two-thirds of married women practised birth control. In 1970 the average Brazilian family had close to six children; in 1994 the number was slightly over two. Though the Vatican won partial support from a dozen heavily Catholic countries in Latin America, Brazil, the largest Roman Catholic state, refused to back the Vatican's anti-abortion stand unreservedly.

The leader of the Brazilian delegation, Minister Leonor Franco, said:

> "In our view, nothing in the proposed Programme of Action — the text of which can of course still be improved upon — deviates from commitments agreed upon in existing international instruments. In particular, we see nothing that would suggest that abortion be a method of family planning. This is an issue of great concern in our society. Brazilian law on this point is clear: abortion is illegal, except in cases in which it is necessary to save the mother's life or in which pregnancy is due to rape."

As far as the Muslim countries were concerned, the abortion issue was possibly less central to their objections than other issues, such as the role of the family and the treatment of adolescent sex.

Dr Haryono Haryono Suyono, Indonesia's State Minister for Population and Chairman of the National Family Planning Coordinating Board, said:

> "Regarding the issue of abortion, I wish to make unmistakably clear to this distinguished forum that in Indonesia abortion is essentially prohibited and permitted only for health reasons and strictly regulated by law. Obviously, Indonesian family planning programmes have never been and will never be promoted through abortion using it as one of its methods. If there are treatments given to solve complications of unsafe abortion then these treatments are purely out of humanitarian and health considerations."

For Malaysia, Minister Dato' Napsiah Bte Omar said:

> "Malaysia would like to reiterate its stand from PrepCom II for the need to incorporate ethical and moral perspectives in dealing with this document and related issues. While we recognise the need to

respect basic human and individual rights in dealing with issues such as the centrality of the individual, reproductive and sexual rights and freedom of choice, we believe that values and responsibilities cannot be sacrificed on the altar of human and social development. We would need to maintain a just balance between the demand for rights and the fulfilling of individual and societal responsibilities.

"As an example, Malaysia's Constitution and legal provisions would not allow the provision of abortion services as a reproductive health service."

However, Malaysia went on to add:

"We maintain that prevention and not interruption of pregnancy be the method of choice. Hence it is our duty to enlighten especially women, to empower them, take them out of the dark, as we must remember that developing countries still face problems of unsafe abortions leading to maternal deaths among married women with high fertility. The humane management of complications of abortions, as is the management of any other reproductive tract diseases, infection or disorder must be a component of reproductive health services."

Detailed negotiations were not of course carried out in the plenary. The relevant texts were to be found in Chapters VII and VIII of the draft and the conference organisers had scheduled early discussions in the Main Committee of these two chapters in the hope that early agreement would permit the conference to devote its time to other matters.

Two passages in the draft in particular had attracted the attention of delegates and the media. Paragraph 8.25 from the chapter dealing with Health, Morbidity and Mortality, and paragraphs 7.1 and 7.2 from the draft chapter dealing with Reproductive Rights, [Sexual and Reproductive Health] and Family Planning.

Both passages were fundamentally concerned with the abortion issue. For practical reasons, the full debate on Chapter VII only took place after the debate on Chapter VIII was largely concluded and the outlines of a solution to the abortion controversy already in place.

THE BATTLE OVER PARAGRAPH 8.25

The outcome of PrepCom III had been two alternative texts.

Alternative A

8.25.   [All Governments, intergovernmental organisations and relevant non-governmental organisations are urged to deal openly and forthrightly with [unsafe abortion] as a major public health concern. Particular efforts should be made to obtain objective and reliable information on the policies on, incidence of and consequences of abortion in every country. Unwanted pregnancies should be prevented through sexual health education and through expanded and improved family planning services, including proper counselling to reduce the rate of abortion. Governments are urged to assess the health and social impact of induced abortion, to address the situations that cause women to have recourse to abortion and to provide adequate medical care and counselling. [Governments are urged to evaluate and review laws and policies on abortion so that they take into account the commitment to women's health and well-being in accordance with local situations, rather than relying on criminal codes or punitive measures. Although the main objective of public policy is to prevent unwanted pregnancies and reduce the rate of abortion, women should have ready access to quality health care services that include reliable information, counselling and medical care to enable them to terminate pregnancies in those cases where it is allowed by law, if they so decide, and that provide for the management of complications and sequelae of unsafe abortion. Post-abortion counselling, education and family planning services should be offered promptly so as to prevent repeat abortions.]"

Alternative B

"[ALTERNATIVE 8.25 All Governments and intergovernmental and non-governmental organisations are urged to deal openly and forthrightly with unsafe abortion as a major public health concern.

"Governments are urged to assess the health impact of unsafe abortion and to reduce the need for abortion through expanded and improved family planning services. Prevention of unwanted pregnancies must always be given the highest priority and all attempts should be made to eliminate the need for abortion. In no case should abortion be promoted as a method of family planning. In circumstances where abortion is legal, women who wish to terminate their pregnancies should have ready access to reliable information and compassionate counselling and such abortion should be safe. In all cases, women should have access to services for the management of complications arising from unsafe abortions. Any measures to provide for safe and legal abortion within the health system can only be determined at national level through policy changes and legislative processes which reflect the diversity of views on the issue of abortion.]"

The first text could be seen as the one going the furthest in the direction of the "liberal" position. Urging governments to deal "openly and forthrightly with unsafe abortion" was the kind of language Gro Harlem

Brundtland and her Scandinavian colleagues would approve. And even though the text stopped short of asking for the decriminalisation of abortion, the bracketed language in the middle of the paragraph went in that direction by inviting governments to "review and evaluate" their laws and policies on abortion. The text also stated that women should "have ready access to quality health care services that include reliable information, counselling and medical care to enable them to terminate pregnancies in those cases where it is allowed by law."

Alternative B was somewhat more restrictive. There was no invitation to governments to review their legislation on abortion. On the contrary there was a specific reference at the end of the paragraph to national prerogatives and the diversity of views.

Alternative B had been tabled by the European Union at the final PrepCom in April 1994 and as the controversy over abortion deepened in the weeks before the conference it was seized upon by many as offering a likely or at least a possible way out of the impasse.

"The European Union has come up with a draft language which we think is very promising as a compromise", the US Under Secretary of State for Global Affairs, Timothy Wirth, said on 4 September.

The first negotiating session on the abortion issue took place on the second day of the conference, Tuesday 6 September, and is captured well by the *Earth Negotiations Bulletin* in its report of the following day (vol 6, no 33, 7 September 1994):

"Main Committee Vice Chair Nicolaas Biegman chaired the day's discussions on Chapters VII and VIII.

"CHAPTER VIII — HEALTH, MORBIDITY AND MORTALITY: Biegman opened discussion on paragraph 8.25 (abortion) and urged delegates to move swiftly on this issue to show the world and the media that this conference is not about abortion, but population. He added that the media has highlighted the issue of abortion because it can be grasped by the public, is easy to write about and is a very emotional matter. The purpose here, he said, is not to delve on the ethical or moral dimensions of the question but, rather, to concentrate on the medical aspects of unsafe abortion. Delegates addressed most of their comments on the alternative version of paragraph 8.25, which was originally proposed by the EU at PrepCom III.

"Over 85 delegations took the floor to comment on this paragraph, and their views were quite divergent. Three general positions emerged. Norway opened the debate by saying that his delegation's position had been to keep the original version of paragraph 8.25, but that he would listen carefully to what the other delegates had to say before electing to support the new version or to uphold the earlier draft. Many other delegates, including South Africa, Canada, Finland, the US, the Former Yugoslav Republic of Macedonia and Estonia said that they preferred the original 8.25, but would agree to the new one in order to reach consensus. Among those who indicated support for the alternative paragraph 8.25 were the EU, Australia, Japan, Paraguay, Cote d'Ivoire, the Philippines, Burkina Faso, Brazil, India, Cape Verde, Malawi, Mali, Bolivia, Panama, Austria, Cuba, Kazakhstan, Slovenia, Mexico, Malaysia, Costa Rica, China, Liberia, Kenya, Peru, Solomon Islands (on behalf of the Pacific Island States), Papua New Guinea, Niger, Vietnam,Tunisia, Tanzania, Cyprus, Nepal, Chad, Colombia, Venezuela, Senegal, Guinea and Guinea-Bissau. Some of these delegates suggested minor modifications in terminology.

"Substantive amendments to the alternative paragraph 8.25 were suggested by several delegations. Barbados tabled an amended version, which said that governments should not have recourse to punitive measures and access to reliable health care services should be provided. This amendment was supported by the Caribbean States, Benin, Zambia, Canada, the US, Nigeria, Swaziland, Kenya, Bangladesh and others. Suriname, on behalf of the Caribbean States, indicated that the amendment would be withdrawn if there was consensus on the alternative draft for paragraph 8.25.

"Pakistan suggested opening the paragraph by stating that in no case should abortion be promoted as a family planning method and to urge governments, IGOs (intergovernmental organisations), and NGOs to work for the reduction of the incidence of abortion through expanded and improved family planning services. He suggested deleting the last two sentences of alternative paragraph 8.25. This amendment was supported by Iran, Malaysia, Indonesia and Egypt.

"Zimbabwe suggested that the last sentence of the original 8.25, which deals with post-abortion counselling, education and family planning, be retained in the alternative draft. This position was supported by a number of countries, including Cyprus, Zambia, Zaire, Nigeria, Bangladesh and Vietnam.

"Ecuador rejected the new draft altogether, arguing that, in essence, it still favoured and granted a stamp of approval to abortion. The Chair noted that neither this paragraph nor the whole text is in favour of abortion; however, illegal abortions are carried out and this is a medical problem that must be faced. The Holy See said that it could only accept the alternative draft as a basis for reaching consensus, but that it still had a problem with endorsing a situation with which it, and other delegations, still have fundamental difficulties. Malta accepted alternative 8.25 as a basis for discussion, but had reservations regarding the terms 'safe' versus 'unsafe' abortion and wanted to delete the last sentence. The latter point was supported by Honduras and Argentina. El Salvador, supported by Nicaragua and the Dominican Republic, suggested removing the qualifiers before the term 'abortion' and replacing 'legal' with 'permitted or allowed'. The EU reported that, after consultations, it could accept the amendment made by Zimbabwe."

After this unpromising start to its consideration of Chapter VIII, the Main Committee moved on to Chapter VII. However, on Tuesday evening, 6 September, Ambassador Biegman interrupted the debate on Chapter VII to introduce a new text for the controversial paragraph 8.25. The text read as follows:

> "In no case should abortion be promoted as a method of family planning. All governments and relevant inter-governmental and non-governmental organisations are urged to strengthen their commitment to women's health, to deal with the health impact of unsafe abortion as a major public health concern and to reduce the recourse to abortion through expanded and improved family planning services. Women who have unwanted pregnancies should have ready access to reliable information and compassionate counselling. Prevention of unwanted pregnancies must always be given the highest priority and all attempts should be made to eliminate the need for abortion. In circumstances in which abortion is legal, such abortion should be safe. Any measures or changes related to abortion within the health system can only be determined at the national or local level according to the national legislative process. In all cases women should have access to quality services for the management of complications arising from abortion. Post-abortion counselling, education and family planning services should be offered promptly which will also help to avoid repeat abortions."

The Chair asked countries to comment. Pakistan, Norway, Benin, Barbados (on behalf of the Caribbean Group), Sweden, Iran, Bangladesh, the US, Germany (on behalf of the EU) and Zimbabwe indicated various reservations about the proposal but were willing to accept it in the spirit of compromise. The Holy See stated that while the text was much improved, they were not prepared to accept it and found the phrase, "In circumstances in which abortion is legal", difficult. According to the report of the *Earth Negotiations Bulletin*, there were cries of "no" throughout the room. The Chair suggested replacing "legal" with "permitted," but the Holy See asked to postpone further discussion. Benin took the floor and said that this was an international conference and no delegation should prevent others from speaking freely. Delegates responded with applause. The Chair announced that there was no point in continuing at this stage and adjourned the meeting at 9 pm.

The apparent breakdown of negotiations caused major consternation. Clinton administration officials who briefed reporters after the closed session adjourned cited support for the compromise from Iran as well as

African and Latin American countries that were traditional allies of the Vatican and said that the Vatican appeared to be the principal holdout.

"It is a surprise. Muslim countries, Nicaragua, Latin American countries agreed", said one dejected US official. "It's striking, in any case."

Most of the 180 nations represented in Cairo were ready to agree on the formulation sought by the Vatican, namely that "in no case should abortion be promoted as a method of family planning" and that governments should do their best to reduce its widespread use.

But the proposed compromise also made it clear that in countries where abortion was legal, women should have access to safe abortion services and "reliable information and compassionate counselling". That guarantee apparently was unacceptable to the Vatican, according to participants in Tuesday night's sessions.

As the meeting broke up there were fears that other countries would reflect overnight and join the Vatican in objecting to Biegman's latest draft and that deadlock would ensue.

The following morning, Wednesday 7 September, Egypt — exercising its prerogatives as host country — accused the Vatican of trying to dictate to the world and questioned its good faith.

Egyptian Population Minister Maher Mahran, in an outburst at a news conference, said the Vatican should bow to the will of states:

"Does the Vatican rule the world? If the Vatican rules the world, if the world is one country and the Vatican is the boss, then fair enough. But we are equal partners", he said.

Mahran went on to say: "We respect the Vatican, we respect the Pope, but we don't accept anyone to impose his ideas. If they are not going to negotiate, why did they come?

> "My definition of a conference is that people meet to discuss an issue, to go in dialogue .... The world is not here to be dictated to. And let me tell you, the people here represent more than five billion people in the world, and not only 190 (at the Vatican)."[2]

Speaking the same day, the American film star Jane Fonda, who was also a United Nations goodwill ambassador, pleaded with governments to invest in women and their education. She said the world's future depended on it.

"Sustainable development begins and ends with women", Fonda said in her lecture entitled "Cairo: A Citizen's View", which drew on her roles as an activist and environmental campaigner.

"It makes economic sense to invest in women ... women in developing countries are agents of change", she added.

Fonda argued that educating women, providing them with financial security and allowing them to make their own choices would mean fewer unwanted pregnancies.

"If this conference succeeds, abortion is no longer necessary", she added. At a lecture which drew a bigger audience than the plenary session in the adjoining conference hall, she argued that "Women with access to money would gain status and would want and need less children. The environment, women's empowerment and fertility issues are all integrated . . . if we do not adjust now, adjustment will be made by nature and it will be brutal."[3]

Meanwhile the Main Committee was once again considering the text that Ambassador Biegman had tabled the previous evening.

Slovakia, supported by Malta and El Salvador, expressed difficulty with the "need for abortion" and suggested it be replaced with "to address situations which cause women to have recourse to abortion". Malta suggested that the reference to unsafe abortion be retained if a footnote was attached, containing the WHO (World Health Organisation) definition of unsafe abortions. Afghanistan, Tanzania, Indonesia and El Salvador asked that the reference to unsafe abortion be deleted. Several delegates said that abortion should be referred to as an "important" rather than "major" public health concern.

As the *Earth Negotiations Bulletin* (ENB) reported (vol 6, no 34 of 8 September 1995), the reference to "legal abortion" was one that also gave rise to heated debate. Malta expressed difficulties since a state could not be expected to legalise something it considered illegal. Afghanistan, Guam and Honduras asked that reference to legal abortion be deleted. Guatemala said that to have legal abortion was tantamount to having legal robbery or legal rape. On the other hand, Zambia said that keeping the reference to legal abortion was their rock bottom position. Brazil offered compromise language by referring to "cases and circumstances where abortion is not penalised". Ecuador could not go along with the new draft and Argentina said that it should reflect on the fundamental right to life as a human right.

At the opposite end of the spectrum, the delegate from Cyprus, supported by Canada, highlighted some of the amendments he had made on pre- and post-abortion counselling that had not been taken into account. Canada said that if the text was open to comments by those countries who oppose abortion, the views of others should also be reflected. Cyprus suggested an amendment calling on national governments and relevant IGOs and NGOs to deal with the health impact of unsafe abortion and to address women's health issues. Norway said that the text was carefully crafted and balanced.

The ENB went on to report: "The Holy See said the text has taken into account ethical considerations and the sensitivities of others." However, in an official statement issued earlier in the day, the Vatican reiterated its stand against abortion and artificial contraception. The Vatican acknowledged that the draft plan contained "many positive points", lauding its focus on education and health care services for women and children. But it said the church could not give "explicit or implicit support to those points of the document regarding abortion, the weakening of several family-related terminologies, the effective encouragement among adolescents of a liberal sexual lifestyle free of parental rights, with no reference to ethical values — all of which in the long term can only bring damage to individuals and society".

Separately, the Holy See implied it was prepared to quietly agree to disagree on the issue of contraception as long as it was specifically stated that family planning programmes did not include abortion.

SOME SIGNS OF AGREEMENT

The first important signs of an overall agreement came early on Wednesday when Benin, Malta and Ivory Coast, which earlier had backed the Vatican's opposition to the abortion provisions, signed on to the compromise along with several Muslim states.

A small working group, chaired by Pakistan, was established to negotiate a compromise on paragraph 8.25. The group, which met late Wednesday afternoon and into the evening, included: Iran, Egypt, the US, Norway, Indonesia, the EU, the Russian Federation, Barbados, South Africa, Nicaragua, Trinidad and Tobago, El Salvador, Benin and Malta. This group was expected to produce a consensus text that could be accepted by the Main Committee (with reservations, if necessary) on Friday.

Later, when an informal working group met to finalise the details, ten additional nations, including Norway and Pakistan, endorsed the wording. The ENB commented:

> "Norway, with one of the most liberal abortion policies in the world, has endorsed world-wide decriminalisation of abortion, while Pakistan, a predominantly Muslim nation, has shared the Islamic bloc's reservations on the issue. Thus their endorsement was seen as something of a bellwether, indicating the Vatican may be left nearly alone in its opposition."[4]

Outside the conference halls, liberal voices were expressing reservations about the emerging compromise, arguing that it did not go far enough to protect women against the dangers of unsafe illegal abortions.

"We still view it as a compromise", said Jacqueline Jackson, for the International Planned Parenthood Federation. She said Planned Parenthood, which operated family planning clinics around the world and was an observer at the Cairo meeting, was of the view that the abortion language as it was emerging Tuesday did not provide enough focus on women, did not adequately address the quality of care for women, was not "proactive enough" and still provided "the opportunity for people to view abortion as a legal issue, rather than a health care issue".

However, she said most opposition to the abortion issue had been overcome even from Muslim nations, many of which had initially shared the Vatican's concerns.[5]

Tim Wirth, in a meeting with reporters, reiterated the US position that abortion should be "safe, legal and rare", adding that as far as the Vatican and its allies were concerned, "We're at a time of respectful disagreement."

That crucial Wednesday, the dominant feeling outside the hall was certainly one of frustration. "I think the Vatican is behaving outrageously", said Joan Dunlop, president of the International Women's Health Coalition, one of the many women's groups represented in Cairo. "We have gone a long, long way to compromise, far further than we would have preferred."

Many activists sported a lapel button that seemed to epitomize the frustration on the abortion issue: "I'm poped out".

An American Catholic theologian took advantage of his allotted speaking time on the morning of Thursday 8 September to blast the Vatican for holding up agreement: "Due to the Vatican's idiosyncratic fixation [on abortion] the moral triumph of this document has been overshadowed ...", said Daniel Maguire, a professor of Marquette University in Milwaukee, Wisconsin. "Once again religions have been made to look like obstructive icebergs in the shipping lanes of progress."

By the Thursday, even some Muslim delegates at the world population conference seemed to think that the Vatican was holding up progress with its intense focus on abortion.

"We are drowning in these issues ... let's move on to others", Mohammed Ali Tashkiri, head of the Islamic Republic of Iran's delegation, said in an interview. Tashkiri appeared before the conference in the white turban of a "mullah", or religious leader, and said the meeting could constitute a "positive step" toward world cooperation on family planning.

Tashkiri said Iran agreed to compromise language on abortion that the Vatican is fighting, a stance that conference officials say had been joined by Pakistan and other Muslim-majority states.

Opponents of abortion tended to quote, as Benazir Bhutto had in her speech to the plenary, the Koran's Sura of the Cattle, verse 151, which says, in part: "Ye slay not your children because of penury. We provide for you and for them." But some with a more liberal view argued that a saying by Prophet Mohammed leaves a time for ending pregnancies. The prophet is quoted as saying the soul does not enter the foetus prompted by an angel until the fourth month.

In essence Tashkiri's concern with the conference document was not so much what it said about abortion or contraception, but rather that the text should to nothing to undermine the family, the life of the unborn child should not be "compromised", and "sexual health education"' should be limited to adults.

"One should not overlook the dangerous implications ... of expanding this education to children and teenagers", he said. "We reject this very strongly."

He also said the conference "should not be exploited for the recognition of immoral behaviour and homosexuality or measures which undermine religion."

He listed some objections to the conference's draft plan setting 20-year guidelines for population policy. But his speech did not echo outraged cries by other Muslim politicians that the meeting would encourage promiscuity and homosexuality.

Meanwhile, in the Main Committee consultations on paragraph 8.25 continued. At 6 pm, Ambassador Biegman distributed new text in English, announcing that the text would be available in all languages on Friday and that it would be discussed in the Main Committee. The WHO definition for "unsafe abortion" was now in a footnote: "a procedure for terminating an unwanted pregnancy either by persons lacking the necessary skills or in an environment lacking the minimal medical standards or both." In addition, the word "legal" no longer appeared and the sentence read: "In circumstances in which abortion is not against the law, such abortion should be safe."

Notwithstanding the high hopes that Biegman obviously had for the new draft, the delegate of Malta immediately stated that although a lot of work had been put into the text, his delegation could not be party to it.

At 6 pm on Friday 9 September, an informal session of the Main Committee turned its attention once again to the text of paragraph 8.25 which Ambassador Biegman had distributed the previous evening. As the ENB reported:

> "At 6 pm, the Chair asked delegates to put this matter to rest so that media attention could focus on the issues of population and development. He said the paragraph in its present form will be

118

submitted to the plenary without prejudice to the position of Governments until the final Programme of Action is adopted. He asked if there were any delegations who wished to reserve their judgement before the final adoption of Chapter VIII. The only change was that the sequence of sentences three and four in the earlier version of the text is reversed. Several delegations noted translation problems and Biegman said that the English version of the text was the one that was negotiated by the working group and, if there are minor translations problems, they would be addressed. El Salvador, Costa Rica (on behalf of the Central American States) and Guatemala said they could support the text, but expressed concern about the Spanish translation.

"The Holy See stated that it attaches great importance to the question of maternal death and endorses those aims of paragraph 8.25 that address women's health, but for moral reasons it does not endorse legal abortion and will withhold its assent until the end of discussions on Chapters VII and VIII. The following delegations indicated similar reservations: Argentina, Peru, Malta and the Dominican Republic.

"The following delegations supported the text in the interest of consensus: Benin, the US, Senegal, Cameroon, Turkey, Turkmenistan, the Philippines, France, Uruguay, Zambia, Bolivia, Tunisia, China, Panama, Tanzania, Burkina Faso, Guinea, Cape Verde, Mali, the Central African Republic, India, Austria, Paraguay, Nicaragua, Israel, Mexico, Barbados (on behalf of the Caribbean States), Spain, Germany (on behalf of the EU), The Gambia, Venezuela, Congo, Norway, the Solomon Islands (on behalf of the Pacific Island States), Japan, South Africa, Colombia, Chile, Indonesia, Jordan and Brazil. Egypt and Bahrain accepted the text, but noted that it would be interpreted in accordance with national and religious laws."

The above paragraphs illustrate dramatically how the (putative) alliance between the Vatican and the Islamic countries had effectively crumbled by the end of the first week of the conference. No Islamic country backed the Vatican in opposing the final version of paragraph 8.25 that Friday evening, though Egypt and Bahrain noted that it "would be interpreted in accordance with national and religious laws". Indeed, the large majority of Catholic countries also accepted the text, leaving only a handful supporting the Vatican.

THE FINAL TEXT

The formal meeting of the Main Committee to discuss the final text of Chapter VIII took place on the morning of Saturday 10 September.

With the minor amendments introduced by the working group, Paragraph 8.25 now read:

"In no case should abortion be promoted as a method of family planning. All governments and relevant intergovernmental and non-governmental organisations are urged to strengthen their commitment to women's health, to deal with the health impact of unsafe abortion* as a major public health concern and to reduce the recourse to abortion through expanded and improved family planning services. Prevention of unwanted pregnancies must always be given the highest priority and all attempts should be made to eliminate the need for abortion. Women who have unwanted pregnancies should have ready access to reliable information and compassionate counselling. Any measures or changes related to abortion within the health system can only be determined at the national or local level according to the national legislative process. In circumstances in which abortion is not against the law, such abortion should be safe. In all cases, women should have access to quality services for the management of complications arising from abortion. Post-abortion counselling, education and family planning services should be offered promptly which will also help to avoid repeat abortions."

*The footnote read: "Unsafe abortion is defined as a procedure for terminating an unwanted pregnancy either by persons lacking necessary skills or in an environment lacking the minimal medical standards or both."

The Holy See, supported by Malta and Ecuador, said that it did not endorse legalised abortion and withheld assent until discussion in plenary. Jordan, supported by Libya, said that it would interpret this paragraph according to Islamic Law. The Central American States said that they were working on the Spanish text and would reserve their position, pending the translation. Benin said that the Francophone countries had agreed on acceptable text. The text was adopted *ad referendum* and the reservations were noted.

Thus ended one of the most remarkable episodes in the history of international negotiations. Barbara Crosette in a special dispatch to the *New York Times* captured the mood (10 September, 1994, Late Edition — Final):

"The Vatican gave up its struggle today to significantly weaken language on abortion in a United Nations plan to stabilize population growth, clearing the way for conference delegates to declare next week that abortion should be safe in countries where it is legal.

"After a five-day standoff, delegates to the International Conference on Population and Development approved a paragraph urging nations to 'strengthen their commitment' to 'deal with the impact of unsafe abortion'.

"It was a significant setback for the Vatican, which had argued that there is no such thing as a 'safe' abortion because it results in the death of a human life.

"In a statement read by a spokesman, Joaquin Navarro-Valls, the Vatican delegation said it was abandoning its manoeuvres over the paragraph's wording because 'it does not wish to prolong the present discussion.' It said the church would formally register its objections to parts of the passage when the document is adopted by the full conference on Tuesday."

DEFINITION OF REPRODUCTIVE HEALTH: ANOTHER HARD-FOUGHT ISSUE

If the battle over paragraph 8.25 was the most public, in the sense that it began early and lasted for the whole of the first week, the clash over reproductive health as defined in Chapter VII of the draft was still of immense significance — and in some ways just as hardly fought.

The key passages as contained in the Draft Programme of Action were as follows:

"7.1 Reproductive health is a state of complete physical, mental and social well-being and not merely the absence of disease or infirmity, in all matters relating to the reproductive system and to its functions and processes. Reproductive health therefore implies that people are able to have a satisfying and safe sex life and that they have the capability to reproduce and the freedom to decide if, when and how often to do so. Implicit in this last condition are the right of men and women to be informed and to have access to safe, effective, affordable and acceptable methods of [fertility regulation] of their choice, and the right of access to appropriate health care services that will enable women to go safely through pregnancy and childbirth and provide couples with the best chance of having a healthy infant. In line with the above definition of reproductive health, reproductive health care is defined as the constellation of methods, techniques and services that contribute to reproductive health and well-being through preventing and solving reproductive health problems. Sexual health is the integration of somatic, emotional, intellectual and social aspects of sexual being, in ways that are positively enriching and that enhance personality, communication and love, and thus the notion of sexual health implies a positive approach to human sexuality, and the purpose of sexual health care should be the enhancement of life and personal relations, and not merely counselling and care related to reproduction and sexually transmitted diseases.

"7.2 [Sexual and reproductive rights embrace certain human rights that are already recognised in various international human rights documents and in other documents reflecting international consensus.] The cornerstone of [sexual and reproductive health] rests on the recognition of the basic right of all couples and individuals to decide freely and responsibly the number, spacing and timing of their children and to have the information and means to do so, [and the right to the enjoyment of the highest attainable standard of sexual and reproductive health]. It also includes respect for [security of the person and] physical integrity of the human body as expressed in human rights documents, [and the right of couples and individuals to make decisions concerning reproduction free of discrimination, coercion and violence]. In the exercise of this right, couples and individuals should take into account the needs of their living and future children and their responsibilities towards the community. The promotion of the responsible exercise of these rights for all people should be the fundamental basis for government- and community-supported policies and programmes in the area of [sexual and reproductive health], including family planning. As part of their commitment, full attention should be given to the promotion of mutually respectful and equitable gender relations and particularly to meeting the educational and service needs of adolescents to enable them to deal in a positive and responsible way with their sexuality. [Reproductive and sexual health] eludes many of the world's people because of such factors as: inadequate levels of knowledge about human sexuality and inappropriate or poor-quality [reproductive health] information and services; the prevalence of high-risk sexual behaviour; discriminatory social practices; negative attitudes towards women and girls; the limited power many women and girls have over their sexual and reproductive lives. Adolescents are particularly vulnerable because of their lack of information and access to services in most countries. Older women and men have distinct [reproductive and sexual health] issues which are often inadequately addressed."

The crucial point in the above text lay in the definition of "fertility regulation". A number of delegations at the Preparatory Committee meetings had found it hard to accept this expression and the idea that men and women had a "right of access" to methods of fertility regulation if the term "fertility regulation" could be interpreted to include abortion. When consulted, the WHO confirmed that according to its working definition, fertility regulation includes family planning, delayed childbearing, the use of contraception, treatment of infertility, interruption of unwanted pregnancies and breastfeeding.

The phrase "interruption of unwanted pregnancies" was clear enough. Taking the paragraph as a whole, including the bracketed text, it could indeed be seen as going a long way towards establishing an "international right to abortion".

A new working group, established to address the outstanding issues in Chapter VII, held its first meeting Thursday afternoon, 8 September, and began with consideration of paragraph 7.1. The group was chaired by Colombia and other members included: Benin, Brazil, El Salvador, Egypt, Germany (EU), the Holy See, Indonesia, Iran, Sweden, South Africa, the US, Canada, Pakistan and Poland. The working group worked late on the Thursday evening and met again the next day, Friday, 9 September.

The *Earth Negotiations Bulletin* summarised the discussions thus: Since the working group was supposed to finish all its work Friday night, many delegates were expecting a late night.

"PARAGRAPH 7.2: More than 70 delegates commented on this paragraph on sexual and reproductive rights. Canada pointed out that the text in the second set of brackets was misprinted and should read "sexual and reproductive rights" rather than "health".

"Numerous delegates suggested removing all of the brackets in the paragraph, including: Albania, Barbados (on behalf of the Caribbean countries), Bolivia, Brazil, Bulgaria, Burkina Faso, Cape Verde, Chile, China, Cote d'Ivoire, Cuba, Finland, Germany (on behalf of the EU), Guinea, Israel, Japan, Mexico, Nepal, New Zealand, Papua New Guinea, Slovenia, the Solomon Islands (on behalf of the Pacific Island States), Sweden, Tanzania, Turkey, Venezuela, Vietnam and Zimbabwe.

"Chad, The Gambia and Liberia agreed to delete the brackets if various ambiguities in the text are clarified. Benin, Libya, Algeria, the Holy See, Honduras, Nigeria, Cameroon, Peru, the Dominican Republic, Ecuador and Malta also asked for clarification of these ambiguities. Particular emphasis was given to the need to clarify the types of international human rights referred to in the first sentence."

There were a variety of positions on the first bracketed sentence, which read: "Sexual and reproductive rights embrace certain human rights . . . ." Iran, Argentina and Malta called for its deletion. Canada, Switzerland, the Holy See and Papua New Guinea stressed that this sentence did not or could not create new rights. Egypt, Burkina Faso, Indonesia, Uganda, Peru, Sri Lanka and Costa Rica called for reference to national laws and legislation.

Switzerland and Pakistan proposed deleting the term "sexual rights", since it was encompassed in "reproductive rights". Austria, the Solomon Islands (on behalf of the Pacific Island States) and Zambia wanted to retain "sexual rights". The Central African Republic, the Holy See, Poland, Argentina, Ecuador and Malta indicated that they could agree, if sexual and reproductive rights did not include abortion.

Another area of controversy was the right of "couples and individuals" to decide freely and responsibly the number, spacing and timing of their children, as well as the right to make decisions concerning reproduction free of discrimination, coercion and violence. Egypt, the Central African Republic, Libya, Iran, Jordan, and the Dominican

Republic called for deletion of the reference to "individuals". The delegate from Zimbabwe pointed out that if the term "individuals" was removed, it would remove the right of individuals to remain celibate and he did not think the Holy See would be happy about that. Furthermore, individuals should have the right to reject sexual advances because of AIDS, STDs or unwanted pregnancy. The Chair responded that the phrase "couples and individuals" had been accepted language since the 1974 Conference in Bucharest. He agreed that the individual right was as much about saying "no" as saying "yes". Austria, India, the Solomon Islands, Nigeria, Haiti and South Africa also supported this position. Iran, supported by Belize, suggested that Australia's proposal in the Friends of the Chair meeting on the principles, which would replace "individuals and couples" with "people", might provide a way out.

The discussions of Paragraph 7.3 were equally vigorous. ENB reported:

> "PARAGRAPH 7.3: The Chair said that the brackets around "fertility regulation" should not be considered since this is under consideration in the working group. Nevertheless, delegates debated at length on replacing "fertility regulation" with "family planning". Zambia proposed "fertility decisions" as an alternative, while Mali suggested "health relating to reproduction" and Zambia mentioned "regulation of fertility" or "programme on the desirable number of births". Over a dozen more delegates took the floor to reiterate their position and the Chair twice commented that they were taxing his patience. Benin said that the positions of developed and developing countries were diametrically opposed and that a North-South divide was becoming apparent, since this issue is related to development. The Chair answered that, on the contrary, this conference is unique as it is not a North-South confrontation. He then concluded the debate on this paragraph."

In the morning of Monday 12 September, Vice Chair Nicolaas Biegman convened an informal session of the Main Committee to distribute the revised text of Chapter VII. He then adjourned the session for 20 minutes to give delegates time to review the text. Biegman informed delegates that the working group chaired by Hernando Clavijo (Colombia) had agreed on text with the exception of two sections in brackets. Since the working group was supposed to remove all brackets, he asked Clavijo to reconvene his group and reach consensus in an hour. This was not the case, and the working group continued to meet through the lunch break, while other delegates and observers waited in the corridors and Chefren Hall.

At 3 pm, Biegman reconvened the informal session of the Main Committee to address Chapter VII. Clavijo introduced oral amendments to the paragraphs that had been discussed during the morning's consultations.

In paragraphs 7.1 and 7.3(b), the phrase "methods of fertility regulation of their choice" was replaced by "methods of their choice for regulation of fertility". In paragraph 7.2, reference to "security of the person and physical integrity of the human body" was deleted and the sentence now read: "It also includes the right of all to make decisions concerning reproduction free of discrimination, coercion and violence, as expressed in human rights documents."

Before the informal meeting was adjourned, Ecuador said that without a clear definition of the right to life from the moment of conception, all other rights were meaningless. Pakistan said their concerns had been addressed in this text. The delegate from Egypt asked for confirmation that the definitions in this chapter apply throughout the text. The Chair assured her that this was the case.

A few minutes later, Ambassador Biegman convened a formal session, where Chapter VII was adopted *ad referendum*. Argentina, the Holy See, Malta and Nicaragua announced their intention to express reservations on various paragraphs in plenary on Tuesday.

Jordan and Syria expressed concern about the use of the term "individuals" in paragraph 7.2. Jordan and Libya also said that they would interpret this paragraph in accordance with Islamic Law. Egypt noted that the chapter was guided by the principles in Chapter II, especially the chapeau which referred to the sovereign rights of countries to implement the action programme in a manner consistent with their own national laws and development priorities. Although the chapter contained words and concepts that revealed certain tendencies in Western and Eastern cultures, Egypt's understanding of the text would be based on its own national, religious and cultural values. Sweden, on behalf of the Nordic States, said that although this text was not ideal, it was negotiated in good faith and the difficult and delicate compromise represented a good balance. The chapter, when implemented, would give men, women and children a strong instrument for leading a richer and healthier life.

As adopted by the Main Committee, the text of paragraphs 7.2 and 7.3 relating to reproductive rights and reproductive health read as follows:

> "7.2   Reproductive health is a state of complete physical, mental and social well-being and not merely the absence of disease or infirmity, in all matters relating to the reproductive system and to its functions and processes. Reproductive health therefore implies that people are able to have a satisfying and safe sex life and that they have the capability to reproduce and the freedom to decide if, when and how often to do so. Implicit in this last condition are the right of men and

women to be informed and to have access to safe, effective, affordable and acceptable methods of family planning of their choice, as well as other methods of their choice for regulation of fertility which are not against the law, and the right of access to appropriate health care services that will enable women to go safely through pregnancy and childbirth and provide couples with the best chance of having a healthy infant. In line with the above definition of reproductive health, reproductive health care is defined as the constellation of methods, techniques and services that contribute to reproductive health and well-being by preventing and solving reproductive health problems. It also includes sexual health, the purpose of which is the enhancement of life and personal relations, and not merely counselling and care related to reproduction and sexually transmitted diseases.

"7.3 Bearing in mind the above definition, reproductive rights embrace certain human rights that are already recognised in national laws, international human rights documents and other consensus documents. These rights rest on the recognition of the basic right of all couples and individuals to decide freely and responsibly the number, spacing and timing of their children and to have the information and means to do so, and the right to attain the highest standard of sexual and reproductive health. It also includes their right to make decisions concerning reproduction free of discrimination, coercion and violence, as expressed in human rights documents. In the exercise of this right, they should take into account the needs of their living and future children and their responsibilities towards the community. The promotion of the responsible exercise of these rights for all people should be the fundamental basis for government- and community-supported policies and programmes in the area of reproductive health, including family planning. As part of their commitment, full attention should be given to the promotion of mutually respectful and equitable gender relations and particularly to meeting the educational and service needs of adolescents to enable them to deal in a positive and responsible way with their sexuality. Reproductive health eludes many of the world's people because of such factors as: inadequate levels of knowledge about human sexuality and inappropriate or poor-quality reproductive health information and services; the prevalence of high-risk sexual behaviour; discriminatory social practices; negative attitudes towards women and girls; and the limited power many women and girls have over their sexual and reproductive lives. Adolescents are particularly vulnerable because of their lack of information and access to relevant services in most countries. Older women and men have distinct reproductive and sexual health issues which are often inadequately addressed."

In summary, the text approved by the Main Committee stopped short of including explicitly access to safe abortion as part of the overall package of reproductive health measures in the sense that it backed away from using the WHO-approved term "fertility regulation" which included abortion in favour of the phrase "regulation of fertility". This was possibly one of the nicest terminological distinctions ever to preoccupy an international gathering for the best part of a week.

Western liberals had also tried to include "sexual rights" but the text approved by the Main Committee on Monday did not include the expression because of opposition from Muslim and other religiously conservative delegations.

One Western delegation said it was worth abandoning sexual rights to obtain the broad definition of reproductive rights.

CONCLUDING BUSINESS

On Tuesday morning, 13 September 1994, the plenary convened at 11 am to adopt the Programme of Action and formally conclude its business. The ENB reported:

"On Chapter VII (Reproductive rights and reproductive health), Libya, Yemen, Afghanistan, Kuwait and Djibouti expressed their reservations on terminology that is in contradiction with Islamic Law, particularly the basic rights of couples and individuals. El Salvador also expressed reservations on the rights of individuals. Egypt made an observation that they had also called for deletion of the word "individuals". Algeria pointed out that the rights of individuals cannot be interpreted outside marriage. Syria said they would address these concepts according to the ethical, cultural and religious convictions of their society. Jordan said that they would interpret the document according to Islamic and national laws. Fred Sai, Chairman of the Main Committee, pointed out that, according to the chapeau in Chapter II, nothing in this Programme of Action must be implemented if it was outside of national laws and religious values.

"After the chapter was adopted, Malta expressed reservations on the chapter's title, the terms "reproductive health", "reproductive rights" and the "regulation of fertility". Iran expressed reservations with the language that addressed sexual relations outside of marriage. Malaysia and the Maldives said they would interpret the chapter according to Islamic law.

"On Chapter VIII (Health, morbidity and mortality), Libya expressed reservations on the term "unwanted pregnancies". El Salvador pointed out that there were still problems with the Spanish translation. Yemen registered its reservations with a number of terms that were not in accordance with Islamic law. After the chapter was adopted, Malta noted its reservations with the portion of paragraph 8.25 which referred to circumstances when abortion was not against the law."[6]

With the adoption of Chapters VII and VIII the main debate on abortion and the definition of reproductive rights was over. It remained to be seen to what extent the reservations expressed on the individual chapters or paragraphs would in turn be reflected by reservations on the Cairo programme as a whole. The UN for the most part operates under the rules of consensus and the Cairo conference was no exception. How many countries felt so strongly about what was said or not said in the programme that they would abstain from the consensus?

If more than a handful abstained, would not the document be fatally weakened and deprived of authority? The tension in the Conference Hall that final Tuesday morning, 13 September, was palpable. The final statements made by delegations, which are considered in the last chapter, reveal what a closely run affair it had been and how the abortion issue, as much and possibly more than any other factor, was until the very end a dominant consideration. One could almost argue that in Cairo in September 1994, the politics of population was at times reduced to the politics of abortion.

Chapter 7

The Empowerment of Women

How did the issue of female "empowerment" come to be the main theme of the Cairo conference?

It would be wrong to suggest that previous population conferences ignored the issue of women's rights. They did not. The World Population Plan of Action (WPPA) adopted in Bucharest in August 1984 in paragraph 32 (b) called for:

> "The full integration of women into the development process, particularly by means of their greater participation in educational, social, economic and political opportunities, and especially by means of the removal of obstacles to their employment in the non-agricultural sector wherever possible. In this context, national laws and policies, as well as relevant international recommendations, should be reviewed in order to eliminate discrimination in, and remove obstacles to, the education, training, employment and career advancement opportunities for women;"

Though this certainly did not go far enough for those early luminaries of the women's rights movement who were present at Bucharest, such as Betty Friedan and Germaine Greer, it was a start. Ten years later, the Mexico City conference undoubtedly represented a net advance on Bucharest in the treatment it gave to the status and role of women.

On the opening day of the conference, Queen Noor of Jordan had set the tone.

> " 'The woman of the family', she said, is 'the single most effective agent for improving the socio-economic welfare of a community'. Improving

129

women's status might be 'the most cost-effective and efficient investment possible in the long run'."

Queen Noor pointed out that of the 700 million illiterate people in the world, two-thirds were female; that women were generally in poorer health than men and that wage-earning women in industrialised countries worked longer hours, earned less money, had less free time and enjoyed fewer hours of sleep than men. If women's lot was improved, women would pass on their knowledge to their families, dramatically improve their welfare with an awareness of family planning and nutrition, and increase the family's standards of living with their extra income from work.

In its own conclusions, the Mexico City conference recalled that the World Population Plan of Action as well as other important international instruments — in particular the 1975 Mexico City Plan of Action, the 1980 Copenhagen Programme of Action for the United Nations Decade for Women and the Convention on the Elimination of all Forms of Discrimination Against Women (CEDAW) stressed the urgency of achieving the full integration of women in society on an equal basis with men and of abolishing any form of discrimination against women. The conference observed that the ability of women to control their own fertility formed an important basis for the enjoyment of other rights; likewise, the assurance of socio-economic opportunities on an equal basis with men and the provision of the necessary services and facilities enabled women to take greater responsibility for their reproductive lives. The conference therefore made several recommendations aimed at ensuring that women could effectively exercise rights equal to those of men and in all spheres of economic, social, cultural and political life, and in particular those rights which pertained most directly to population concerns.

These recommendations were also reflected in the Mexico City Declaration on Population and Development which stated:

> "Improving the status of women and enhancing their role is an important goal in itself and will also influence family life and size in a positive way. Community support is essential to bring about the full integration and participation of women into all phases and functions of the development process. Institutional, economic and cultural barriers must be removed and broad and swift action taken to assist women in attaining full equality with men in the social, political and economic life of their communities. To achieve this goal, it is necessary for men and women to share jointly responsibilities in areas such as family life, child-caring and family planning. Governments should formulate and implement concrete policies which would enhance the status and role of women."

The Mexico City conference noted that comprehensive strategies to address the above concerns would be formulated at the 1985 Nairobi conference which was being convened to review and appraise the achievements of the United Nations Decade for Women. In due course the Nairobi meeting proclaimed, *inter alia*, that "the ability of women to control their own fertility forms an important basis for enjoyment of other rights".

Notwithstanding such declarations, there was at the beginning of the 1990s a growing sense among some politically articulate women, in particular those associated with feminist groupings, that the population debate was largely taking place over their heads. Men, not women, were determining population policies; men, not women, were working out family planning targets and quotas; devising rewards and penalties for good or bad performance. Yet it was women's bodies which were, as it were, the delivery mechanisms of all population and family planning programmes. On them, and on their willingness to cooperate, hung all prospects of success. How could women not be the primary decision-takers where their reproductive rights, powers and duties were concerned? The feminists were, moreover, growing increasingly cynical at all this talk of women's rights to family planning. Were not other rights equally, or more, important — such as the right to health, to education, to jobs, to full participation in whatever social and economic framework they happened to live?

The rumblings of discontent had grown louder as preparations for the Rio Earth Summit continued. At a World Women's Congress held in Miami, Florida, in November 1991 four days of workshop discussion led to a Declaration for a Healthy Planet which included the following statement:

> "III **Empowerment of Women** The women's perspective, which recognises that meeting human social needs is a goal of higher importance than economic progress for its own sake, must be brought to bear on global problems of environmental destruction and poverty arising from inequitable access to necessary survival resources. Women must be empowered at all levels to contribute to the achievement of the principles of equity, social justice and ethics."

The meeting adopted a number of specific proposals on the subject of "the empowerment of women":

1 Governments should recognise women's role as managers and conservers of natural resources and should involve women in the decision-making process as equal partners.

2 Governments should act positively to implement fully Articles 7 and 9 of the Convention on the Elimination of Discrimination Against

131

Women (political participation, international representation). They should act immediately to increase the number of women decision-makers at all levels and especially in relation to sustainable development.

3 Governments should act positively to implement fully Article 14 of the Convention (Rural Women) to ensure that women participate in and benefit from rural development on the basis of equality of men and women, and in particular, that they have access to agricultural credit and loans, marketing facilities, appropriate technology and equal treatment in land and agrarian reform as well as in land resettlement schemes. They must also be assured of access to land use and ownership, education and health services.

4 Development and aid funding should be allocated to women's projects. Women should participate in equal terms and at all levels in decisions relating to development.

5 Article 16.1 (e) of CEDAW (recognising the equal right to decide freely and responsibly on the number and spacing of children and to have access to the information, education and means to exercise these rights) should be fully implemented.

6 Women in positions of power and influence should not lose a woman's perspective on development and environmental issues.

7 Women by acting together, by organising cooperatives and by managing credit and financial institutions can help change policy, protect the environment, improve their standards of living and challenge current economic analysis.

This was all a far cry from a narrowly focused concern on family planning or even "reproductive rights". And at the meeting of UNCED's preparatory committee in March 1992, the final negotiating round before the Rio meeting to be held in June of that year, representatives of the non-governmental women's caucus protested that "delegates are using references to women and issues of direct concern to women as pawns in the negotiating process. We protest at women being used in this manner."

The statement added: "We will take whatever steps are necessary to prevent this self-defeating negotiating tactic in which governments are playing dangerous games at the expense of women and the earth."

The redoubtable Bella Abzug led a delegation to meet ambassador Leon Mazairac of the Netherlands to discuss the role of women in the UNCED process. (Mazairac was coordinating negotiations on the subject of how governments should involve "major groups" in implementing Agenda 21. In addition to women, the other groups include young people, indigenous people and farmers.) At the meeting, Abzug reminded Mazairac that the third UNCED preparatory meeting held in

Geneva in August 1991 adopted a proposal designed to ensure the participation of women in all stages of the "Earth Summit".

Abzug and several other women's caucus members complained that some government delegations were proposing that women's concerns, including those on population and reproduction issues, be dropped in order to gain leverage on financial and other issues.

According to Abzug, among those guilty of deleting references to women from UNCED documents, were delegates of the 128-member 'group of 77' developing countries.

Abzug's charges hit their target. Jamsheed Marker, Pakistan's ambassador to the United Nations and chairman of the 'group of 77' was forced to admit that references to women had been deleted — "not because they weren't supported, but because certain delegates had difficulties with certain phrases", and that "unanimity had to be the rule" among the group's members. In making the deletions, Marker said that the group was aiming for "the lowest common denominator". To this Abzug had pithily responded: "nobody wants to be part of the lowest common denominator".

Dr Nafis Sadik had been quickly summoned from across the street to pour oil on troubled waters. She told her audience that unless women were given the freedom and means to manage their fertility, their effective participation in all spheres of life would be limited. "A woman's control over her own fertility is basic to her freedom. It is the source from which other freedoms flow".

Sadik said it was critical that all UN delegates and NGO representatives participating in the Earth Summit talks include recommendations for women and effective reproductive health care in the UNCED documents. She added that "all international fora must respond to this challenge, and address the central role which women have in any system of sustainable development". Sadik said "talk about empowering women will remain merely talk if women are not, at the same time, provided with the freedom and means to manage their fertility, and if their health needs are not adequately addressed". While population growth and distribution, poverty, consumption patterns, and the state of the environment could be addressed at a global level, it was important to recognise that "population issues are a matter of welfare and health and the right to make informed life choices".

Dr Sadik's remarks, concentrating as they did on questions of fertility and reproduction, were less than totally reassuring to those who had drafted or supported the demands set out in the Miami declaration. And when it came to the Earth Summit itself, many women's groups felt that Agenda 21's chapter 5 on "demographic dynamics and sustainability" failed adequately to reflect their concerns. They looked in at the debates in the heavily guarded conference centre some 20 kilometres from Rio and what did they see? A lot of men in suits talking about their bodies, their lives. At least that was how it felt. This was not what they wanted. Not at all.

AFTER THE EARTH SUMMIT

After Rio there was considerable debate as to whether the language actually agreed at UNCED as far as population and family planning was concerned was in any sense to be considered an advance when set against previously agreed texts, or whether on the contrary it was to be seen as a set-back. Take, for example, Rio's language on the subject of family planning programmes which are at the core of efforts to control fertility. Paragraph 5.50 of Agenda 21 talks about "women and men" having "the same right to decide freely and responsibly on the number and spacing of their children". This appears at first sight to echo the language of the World Population Plan of Action (WPPA) agreed at the World Population Conference, 1974. There are clear references in the WPPA to the right of couples to decide "in a free, informed and responsible manner, the number and spacing of their children".[1]

However, paragraph 5.50 also talks about "freedom, dignity and personally held values taking into account ethical and cultural considerations". This phraseology resulted from a controversial discussion which had taken place in New York during the final meeting of the UNCED Preparatory Committee in April 1992, and in particular from a set of amendments introduced by the Holy See both in Chapter 5 of Agenda 21 on Demographic Dynamics and Sustainability and in Chapter 6 of Agenda 21 which dealt with the Protection and Promotion of Human Health.

Though the language of the "Recommendations for the further implementation of the World Population Plan of Action" which were adopted at Mexico City in August 1984, ten years after the Bucharest meeting, on the occasion of the International Conference on Population, nuanced to some extent the Bucharest affirmation by referring to "changing individual and cultural values" (Recommendation 25), the victory which the Vatican gained at PrepCom 4 was seen by many as introducing an unnecessary qualification to a previously unambiguous statement.

Equally, Agenda 21's paragraph 5.51 talked about "responsible planning of family size" and the Vatican gloss was added "in keeping with freedom, dignity and personally held values and taking into account ethical and cultural considerations". After UNCED was over, Dr Nafis Sadik,[2] among others, pointed out that Agenda 21 did not mention family planning as such. She added: "The phrase used in Agenda 21, 'responsible planning of family size', is less comprehensive than the language we are used to; family planning refers to the well-being of the whole family, not just the question of size."

While the delegates to UNCED were trying, and failing, to say something definitive about population and its relationship to environment and development, another debate of considerable significance was taking place not in the Conference centre but in the Global Forum (a non-governmental event held in down-town Rio, some 20 or 30 miles from the UNCED proceedings). Discussions on population at the women's tent *Planeta Femea* were marked by harsh criticism of "top down" population control programmes which in the opinion of many speakers put an emphasis on demographic targets which "too often lead to insensitive and coercive services".

THE NGO TREATY ON POPULATION, ENVIRONMENT AND DEVELOPMENT

An Alternative Treaty on Population, Environment, and Development, negotiated and agreed by a wide and representative selection of NGOs present in Rio for the Earth Summit, stressed that women's empowerment to control their own lives is a foundation for all action linking these areas. The Alternative Treaty denounced "abusive population control programmes and called for 'women-centred, women-managed and women-controlled' comprehensive reproductive health care ... including safe and legal voluntary contraceptives and abortion facilities".[3]

This was strong stuff, stirring language which — though it made little or no impact on the official UNCED proceedings — was certainly noted by those whose task it was to prepare the first drafts of the documents which two years later would be on the table at Cairo.

A few months after the Earth Summit, in January 1993, 19 women's health advocates representing women from Africa, Asia, Latin America and the Caribbean, the US and Western Europe met to discuss how women's voices might best be heard before and after the 1994 Cairo conference.

THE WOMEN'S DECLARATION ON POPULATION POLICIES

The group initiated a "Women's Declaration on Population Policies", and a Women's Voices '94 Alliance to promote it, and asked the

NGO Treaty on Population

Preamble:

Women's empowerment to control their own lives is the foundation for all action linking population, environment and development.

We reject and denounce the concept of control of women's bodies by governments and international institutions. We reject and denounce forced sterilisation, the misuse of women as subjects for experimental contraceptives, and the denial of women's free choice.

We affirm and support women's health and reproductive rights and their freedom to control their own bodies. We demand the empowerment of women, half of the world's population, to exercise free choice and the right to control their fertility and to plan their families.

The international community must address problems arising from the relationship between population, environment and development within the framework and boundaries set by ethics, human rights, and democratic principles, and in recognition of the fact that one-quarter of the world's population — predominantly in the industrialised nations — consumes over 70 per cent of Earth's resources and is responsible for most of the global environmental degradation.

Demands and Commitments:

Birth rates decline when women's social, economic and health status improves and general living standards rise. The political and economic mechanisms operating within the prevailing world order and within each country, which create and perpetuate poverty, inequality and marginalisation of people in the South — and increasingly in the North — must be transformed.

Militarism, debt and structural adjustment and trade policies being promoted by corporations and international financial and trade institutions such as the International Monetary Fund, the World Bank and the General Agreement on Tariffs and Trade, are degrading the environment, impoverishing the majority of the world's people and perpetuating the inequity of the existing world order. We condemn these policies and call for the immediate adoption of alternative policies and call for the immediate adoption of alternative policies based on principles of justice, equity and sustainability.

Nuclear testing and toxic waste dumping are poisoning the environment, threatening food security and causing sterility, birth defects and disease. We demand an end to environmental hazards that deprive women and men of their right to health and healthy children.

Patterns of consumption and production in the North and among the privileged of the South, which are the main threat to the survival of life on Earth, must be changed in order to halt the squandering of natural resources and the exploitation of human beings.

We condemn and call for an immediate end to policies and programmes, whether by governments, institutions, organisations or employers, that attempt to deprive women of their freedom of choice or the full knowledge or means to exercise their reproductive rights, including the right to interrupt unwanted pregnancies. We denounce and reject the violence against women, who are victims of racial and class discrimination and suffer from extreme poverty, who are subjected to coercion, sterilisation abuse, experimental drugs, and lack of proper medical care and information about health risks and alternatives.

We pledge to expose and oppose any coercive population control programmes supported or conducted by governments, funding agencies, multilateral institutions, corporations and NGOs, and to hold them accountable.

We demand women-centred, women-managed and women-controlled comprehensive reproductive health care, including pre- and post-natal care, safe and legal voluntary contraceptives and abortion facilities, sex education and information for girls and boys, and programmes that also educate men on male methods of contraception and their parental responsibilities.

We demand child care facilities, parental leave and care for the elderly and disabled, as family support services.

We demand that scientific experimentation related to reproduction, particularly in the fields of genetic engineering and contraception, be transparent as well as accountable to women's concerns and ethical criteria rooted in the defence of the human species and human rights.
We demand that governments honour international law and commitments on reproductive rights, and fulfil their responsibilities in implementing the Nairobi Forward Looking Strategies, the report of the 1984 Conference on Population and the UNCED agreements. We also demand the urgent and full ratification and implementation of the United Nations Convention on the Elimination of All Forms of Discrimination Against Women.

We demand that national and international communities act now to support community-based responses to the AIDS epidemic, and provide more research, services and information to women, men and children about the prevention and treatment of HIV infection, AIDS and other sexually transmitted diseases, respecting the human rights of those affected.

These demands embody our commitments, and we pledge to integrate them into our lives and our organisations' practices and policies. We further pledge to see that these demands are met at all levels, locally, nationally and internationally. And we pledge to work together on this treaty, affirming our solidarity and our cultural diversity.

International Women's Health Coalition (IWHC), a US-based organisation, to serve as the secretariat. Between October 1992 and March 1993, the Declaration was modified and finalised by over 100 women's organisations in 23 countries.

The Declaration asserted that sexual and reproductive health and rights were fundamental to all people. It spelt out a set of operating principles and programme strategies to ensure that these rights can be exercised. It called on national governments and international agencies to reshape their policies to ensure health and rights.

In the first eight months since the initiative was launched, over 2288 individuals and organisations from more than 105 countries signed and endorsed the Women's Declaration — women and men from many walks of life, professions, cultures and sectors, unions and village associations, major family planning agencies, feminist networks, and human rights groups. They were rich and poor, rural and urban.

They differed as to whether population policies should exist, about the safety and appropriateness of particular methods of contraception, or about the best way to deliver sexual and reproductive health services. But they all — at least according to the sponsors — shared the values and agenda set forth in the Women's Declaration.

Women's groups were also active at the national level as preparations continued for the Cairo conference. In Brazil, for example, in an exceptional move, about 80 per cent of the proposals on population and reproductive health issues, tabled by feminists, were incorporated into the government's official report.

Towards the end of 1993, almost 500 women from every corner of the country attended the 'National Encounter on Women and Development — Our Rights at Cairo '94', held in the capital, Brasilia. It was here that the 'Brasilia Charter' emerged — a document defining women's reproductive rights and outlining the population policies which Brazilian women would like their government to present at ICPD.

The Encounter, a joint effort by seven women's NGOs, brought together representatives of over 70 different women's organisations, experts and institutions specialising in development and demographics. Several deputies and senators from various political parties also participated.

The Brazilian women's movement pressed for women's reproductive rights to be recognised. Equally significant, they campaigned for women's access to education, training and jobs, especially in fields where gender discrimination persisted, and in specialised areas.

Jacqueline Pitanguy, one of the organisers of the Encounter, applauded the Charter as the initiator of the historic process to build women's citizenship. She stressed that it had made the voices of Brazil's women more audible. The organising efforts of the last two years would be evident in the language finally adopted in the Plan of Action.

As 1993 came to an end, it was increasingly apparent that a large number of women around the world were determined that Cairo would not be a re-run of Rio. Arguably, as far as population issues were concerned, the women's groups did not "get their act together" early enough to influence significantly the outcome of the Rio text. Neither Agenda 21's tone, nor its content has much in common with the NGO Treaty on population and the environment. However, after Rio, where their success had been at best partial, the women's groups fixed their sights on Cairo.

WEDO AND THE WOMEN'S CAUCUS

By the time detailed negotiations were under way for the Cairo conference, the NGOs, including the women's groups, were far better organized. The Women's Environment and Development Organisation (WEDO) in particular had begun to play a major role in preparation for the UN International Conference on Population and Development in Cairo, 5–13 September, 1994. WEDO's priorities were to ensure that the ICPD process, which would hopefully culminate in the adoption of a new global population/development policy at Cairo, remained open to women's participation, addressed the rights and needs of women, and recognised the central role of women in every issue related to population and development. As WEDO saw it, these objectives could be accomplished by: effective advocacy efforts at UN and regional and national NGO meetings; generating timely flow of information; and continual dialogue among women's caucus participants and between the caucus and the ICPD secretariat. WEDO also encouraged women's active participation in the preparation and writing of the national reports that governments submitted to the ICPD secretariat.

During PrepCom II, held in May 1993, WEDO organised a women's caucus of 132 women, representing 41 countries from every region of the world. Approximately 50 per cent of the caucus consisted of women from 33 developing countries. The caucus was a focal point for women advocates and strategists. Together they ensured that all delegates and the secretariat were fully informed about women's concerns.

Caucus members produced several documents, including a consensus document entitled, "Suggested Revisions to the Conceptual Framework for the Draft Recommendations of the ICPD, Offered by Women's Groups from All Regions". This was presented to delegates and the ICPD Secretariat. As a result of these efforts, the women's caucus had a substantial influence in the formulation of the Annotated Outline of the

139

final document for the Conference, prepared by the ICPD secretariat and presented to the Second Committee of the UN General Assembly on 4 November, 1993.

WEDO sent the Annotated Outline document to all PrepCom II women's caucus participants for their comments. A WEDO Writing Analysis Group then formulated amendments to the document which better reflected the expressed needs and concerns of women. The revisions were presented to government delegates and the secretariat in November 1993. The preliminary Draft Final Document of the Conference, released by the Secretariat in February 1994, incorporated many suggestions of the caucus.

Prior to PrepCom III, WEDO, calling on the women's caucus and other women's networks, coordinated and prepared an extensive critique of the secretariat's Draft Final Document. The critique was made available to all delegates, NGOs and caucus members at PrepCom III, to facilitate discourse and lobbying.

During PrepCom III, the WEDO-organized women's caucus convened daily, bringing together over 300 women and men from 44 countries. Caucus participants organised themselves into five task forces. Based on the "Women's Caucus Compilation of Proposed Revisions" the task forces produced a set of "Priority Amendments" for each chapter. Throughout the PrepCom, the women's caucus task forces promptly recommended amendments to each draft chapter as they emerged from the secretariat. Caucus task forces produced and distributed to delegates as many as four versions in response to each round of the official discussions. These amendments served as invaluable and effective lobbying tools for caucus participants.

There is little doubt that, overall, women's groups played a major role in the April 1994 meeting of the ICPD Preparatory Committee (PrepCom III).

"The people outside these walls would never have a voice at a conference like this if it weren't for women's groups and other NGOs", said New Zealander Brigid Inder of the Pacific Island NGO group.

She explained that this was "not just because of our work at the grassroots level in our communities but also because of the analysis we were able to provide to government delegations".

"Women's groups have been extremely helpful in keeping delegates on the right track", said Dr Nafis Sadik, conference Secretary General. "They've given their suggestions to the working groups and the working groups have used many of the women's suggestions."

Where views appeared most inflexible, women's groups lobbied the hardest, for example, during the debate on the section of the draft document that dealt with safe motherhood. This section stated that mortality resulting from complications of poorly performed abortions accounted for many maternal deaths in countries where abortions were unsafe and illegal.

The women's caucus drafted its version, emphasising that the women's movement had never advocated abortion as a method of family planning. However, it pointed out that safe abortions should be made available to those seeking them.

Reviewing their success

As a result of all these detailed painstaking efforts during the preparatory process, the women's caucus had substantial influence in shaping the language and content of the Draft Final Document of the Conference released by the ICPD Secretariat in May 1994. WEDO reviewed this document and completed an "Impact Analysis" of the women's caucus at PrepCom III on the Draft Final Document. The Impact Analysis was a chapter-by-chapter account of the status of each of the amendments proposed by the women's caucus at PrepCom III. The analysis indicated whether amendments proposed by the women's caucus were incorporated into the Draft Final Document or whether they remained a point of contention — indicated by bracketed text — to be negotiated in Cairo. This Impact Analysis served not only to document the many achievements of the women's caucus, but also to highlight the parts of the women's caucus agenda that required further political support.

In close collaboration with the PrepCom III task force chairs, chapter monitors and major women's health and reproductive rights networks around the world, WEDO compiled a set of "Women's Caucus Recommendations on the Bracketed Text of the Draft Final Document". This was the key document used by women's groups for their advocacy work in Cairo. A writing analysis group worked hard, during the period between PrepCom III and Cairo, to prepare careful amendments with rationales to all bracketed text in the document. These amendments were widely distributed to delegates at the Informal Consultations which were convened in June 1994 at the UN in New York, to discuss issues that were not thoroughly deliberated upon at PrepCom III: Preamble and Principles (Canada) on 13 July; Goals (Indonesia & India) on 14 July; and Financial Resources (Netherlands) on 15 July. The chair of each of the informal sessions (Ruth Archibald, Ambassador Nicolaas Biegman and Ambassador Nugroho Wisnumurti, respectively) reminded delegates that the consultations were meant to stimulate discussion and not act as negotiating sessions; hence they would not have the power to add or delete brackets in the document.

That said, a careful analysis of the amendments proposed by the women's caucus and the text finally adopted by the conference demonstrates the very high success rate that the women's caucus had in ensuring that its preferred language was supported by delegates.

In advancing their cause, the Women's Caucus did not hesitate to fire all available ammunition. They cited Bucharest and Mexico. They cited the Universal Declaration on Human Rights and the International Covenant on Economic, Social and Cultural Rights. They cited Rio (the Earth Summit Declaration) and Vienna (the Vienna Declaration and Programme of Action adopted at the United Nations Human Rights Conference, June 1993). They cited recommendations from the World Health Organisation (WHO), the International Labour Office Organisation (ILO) and the United Nations Educational, Scientific and Cultural Organisation (UNESCO) and many others besides. The caucus researchers were well aware that the force of precedent is a powerful one. Point out to a dissenting delegate that the form of words he or she is objecting to has already been agreed in another context (or better still that his or her own government has specifically agreed the contested words elsewhere) and you are generally home and dry.

The caucus text was an astonishingly professional document. As far as NGO organisation was concerned, Cairo was light years from Bucharest where NGOs still operating under pre-UNCED rules were at best tolerated as unwelcome irritants to the smooth running of the intergovernmental process.

Some delegates in private questioned the constitutional propriety of allowing NGOs quite so much say in the negotiation of texts for whose implementation they would never be held accountable in the way governments could be held accountable. But they tended not to voice these reservations publicly. NGO participation, particularly when the NGOs in question were highly female and highly articulate, was the flavour of the month, the year, the decade ... who knew? Agenda 21 had devoted whole chapters to the participation of major groups and nobody, two years later, was going to stand up and say Rio got it wrong.

So the timing was right, the politics was right — and the basic research was good. What's more the practical organisation was superb.

At the Cairo meeting itself the women's caucus was well organised, as can be seen from the following announcement posted on both material and electronic bulletin boards.

THE NGO FORUM

The women's caucus was not, of course, the only important NGO gathering "inputting" the conference. At Cairo's covered stadium

Women's Caucus in Cairo, 4–13 September, 1994

An orientation session to the Women's Caucus process is scheduled for Sunday, 4 September, 1994 from 2–3 pm in the NGO Forum Room 3. This session will initiate newcomers into the Women's Caucus process, and update old-timers. During the orientation, we plan to form regional groups (Africa, Asia, Caribbean and Pacific, Europe, Latin America, Middle East, North America) in order to:

- Allow for greater interaction between experienced Women's Caucus members and newcomers;
- Nominate three Women's Caucus chairs from each of the five regions for the six daily Caucus meetings: Arab Region, Africa, Asia & Pacific, Europe & North America, Latin America & Caribbean;
- Nominate two Women's Caucus Lobby Coordinators within each region and two government voting blocs that are not regionally defined: G-77, CANZ;
- Nominate three Chapter Monitors per chapter in the ICPD Draft Document to monitor floor discussions and offer feedback to the lobby coordinators;
- Call for volunteers for a Women's Caucus post-Cairo Task Force to collect ideas out of the rich array of NGO Forum panels and workshops in preparation for the last session of the Women's Caucus at ICPD. (see below)

After meeting in regional groups, we hope to reconvene as a full Women's Caucus to announce the respective regional decisions and gear up for our first Women's Caucus meeting on Monday, 5 September at 10 am.

The Women's Caucus will convene daily from 9–10 am in the NGO Forum Room 3. The strength and momentum of the Caucus depends on your active participation. We have a heavy agenda and collectively we can build support to remove the brackets on language which supports women's perspectives on population and development, as well as continue our struggle for sexual and reproductive rights and health which is at the core of our agenda. One of the main purposes of the daily Caucus will be to brief people on the government process. Many NGOs will focus on activities in the NGO Forum to network, strategise and build an agenda for the future, while a smaller number of accredited NGOs will have access to the governmental negotiations in the conference centre. Our strategy, therefore, is to divide work and maximise power for our common advocacy work. Our sisters who are on government delegations will, no doubt, be key allies in carrying the Women's Caucus concerns on to the floor.

complex, adjacent to the convention centre where ICPD was under way, some 4000 representatives of over 1500 non-governmental organisations from 133 countries exchanged experiences and opinions on a wide range of conference-related topics. The NGO Forum '94, held from 4–12 September, offered a lively, diverse programme, with more than 90 sessions each day. Every morning started with meetings of five caucuses. In addition to the Youth, Environment and Women's caucuses which had met during the third session of the ICPD Preparatory Committee in April, there were a religious caucus made up of mainstream religious groups and a pro-life caucus.

Nevertheless, the women's caucus was the largest, with some 400–500 participants daily. Many women's caucus members were actively involved in lobbying activities at ICPD, and each morning, after an overview was given of the negotiations in the conference's Main Committee, the lobbying priorities for the day were discussed.

On Saturday, 10 September, ICPD Secretary General Dr Nafis Sadik visited the women's caucus to show her appreciation of their work. The crowd gave her a tumultuous welcome, with five standing ovations, sustained applause, foot-stamping and whistling. Many women were very moved by Dr Sadik's spontaneous visit; some said it was the high point of their days in Cairo.

The other caucuses were smaller, ranging from 15 participants in the pro-life caucus to 200–300 in the environment caucus. Most caucuses issued a final declaration or statement, often emphasising the post-Cairo process.

Throughout each day in the complex's various meeting rooms and auditoriums, there were dozens of panel discussions and presentations organised by different NGOs from around the world. These centred on several main themes: empowerment of women, reproductive health, human rights, religion, environment and development.

In the sessions on religion, population and development, many participants reported that for the first time they were able to exchange frank views on population and reproductive health issues both within their denominations and across religious lines. This unprecedented, spontaneous ecumenical assembly was driven in part by what organisers described as the need to put forth mainstream religious views in the face of religious extremism. Some participants voiced frustration over negative media coverage focusing on religious groups whose views were not representative of the majority of parishioners/adherents in their countries.

Interviews with Forum participants revealed a widespread enthusiasm about being able to talk frankly about issues that have not been addressed as openly at past meetings. Many women expressed a great sense of relief and freedom to be able to share their anger and frustration over such problems as unsafe abortion, teenage pregnancy, sex-selection abortion, female infanticide, discrimination against girls, child marriage and prostitution, medical malpractice by reproductive health providers, coercive family planning programmes, female genital mutilation, rape, incest and other violence against women.

Some participants contended, however, that ICPD should have given more emphasis to broader development issues, including poverty alleviation, international economic justice and the impact of structural adjustment programmes. A number of Southern groups decried what they said was a lack of attention to environmental issues, particularly wasteful over-consumption and environmental pollution in the wealthy countries of the North.

Most appeared to appreciate the civility which tended to characterise the Forum's exchanges (notwithstanding some well-publicised clashes between those with opposing views). Despite major differences in the viewpoints of participating groups, their interactions were generally respectful. For example, the display booths of the pro-choice Marie Stopes International and the International Right to Life organisation were adjacent. This contrast attracted the media's attention, and the staff of the two organisations were shown on camera shaking hands.

Forum participants generally seemed pleased with the level of NGO participation in the process leading up to Cairo and during the conference itself. Most seemed satisfied with the services provided in the NGO Forum site and impressed by the organisation of the event and the extensive programme offered. Most of the schedule of events was available before the Forum started. At the same time, organisers from the NGO Planning Committee for the ICPD responded efficiently to a flood of requests for new sessions.

Another positive experience for many was the hospitality of the Egyptian volunteers working in the Forum, and the humane feeling created by the Forum's variety of booths, restaurants and souvenir shops. While many participants were initially worried about their safety in Cairo, most came away impressed with the safety measures taken by the Egyptians.

Much of the talk during the last days of the Forum was about what to do after Cairo — how to ensure implementation of the Programme of Action and how to monitor government actions. In this regard, the women's caucus issued a post-Cairo action agenda. There was also considerable discussion of how to ensure that agreements reached in Cairo on important health and gender equity issues would be carried forward to the Fourth World Conference on Women in Beijing in 1995.

THE DELEGATES' RESPONSE TO THE EMPOWERMENT OF WOMEN THEME

We have already looked at the speeches made on the opening day, particularly those of Gro Harlem Brundtland and Benazir Bhutto, which struck a resounding note in favour of female empowerment. These keynote speeches set the tone for much of the plenary debate. Clearly there were differences of approach between North and South, East and West. Many countries in the so-called WEOG (Western Europe and Other Group) addressed the subject of female empowerment as though it was already axiomatic, part of accepted wisdom.

Johanna Dohnal, for example, Austria's Federal Minister for Women's Affairs, stated most eloquently:

> "The empowerment of women is the key to population and development issues. Empowerment of women means the establishment of equal opportunities between the genders from birth onwards. It means extending choices: choices about if and when to get married; choices about education and development opportunities; choices about their own lives.
>
> "Equality and empowerment of women means more than just the right to birth control. It means power-sharing, it means better access to political leadership, it means economic self-reliance of women. Women want redistribution in all aspects of life. Women want to decide on their future by themslves."

The Swedish government saw the empowerment of women as one of the most important policies on the agenda of this conference. Inger Davidson, Minister of Public Administration and Youth, said:

> "The empowerment of women must however be championed in its own right, not just as a means in a population policy. The competence and potential of both women and men must be recognised in all fields of society. Education for women is just one of many important policies emanating from such a view. Others are the woman's economic independence, her right to land, her right to credit and her sexual and reproductive rights on her own terms. In this context, the right of individuals and couples to make informed choices about the number and spacing of their children constitutes a cornerstone."

The Swedish representative went on to say, possibly more controversially for some of her audience:

> "The empowerment of women will however not come about without corresponding changes in male behaviour and attitudes; men must be prepared to abstain from some of their power in order for power to be truly shared. Men also have to take their part in the work with home and children."

Manfred Kanther, the German Minister of the Interior, speaking on behalf of the European Union, said:

> "Priority should be given to improving primary health care and education with particular emphasis on the health of women and education of women and youth as well as to the reduction of maternal and infant mortality. The promotion of gender equity and the empowerment of women in improving their status in society are priorities."

Several speakers from developing countries recognised that there was still some way to go before "female empowerment", as defined in the Cairo draft programme, became a reality. A particularly thoughtful speech was made by Shri B Shankaranand, India's Minister of Heath and Family Welfare:

> "Gender equality in terms of equal status, and political social and economic right, is a Fundamental Right guaranteed by the Indian Constitution. Various laws have been enacted to provide protection to women against social discrimination and exploitation. To ensure the Constitutional and legal safe-guard provided to women, a National Commission for women has been set up.
>
> "Despite the tremendous progress made in improving the status of women, socio-cultural traditions continue to assign a subordinate role for women. We firmly believe that empowerment of women in terms of literacy, employment and access to quality health and family welfare services will lead not only to greater equality but to faster economic growth as well."

Indonesia took a similar line. Haryono Suyono, State Minister for Population and Chairman of the National Family Planning Coordinating Board said:

> "My delegation is of the firm belief that the empowerment of women should be done through wider provision and access to educational opportunities, skill training and employment opportunities. In this respect, since 1993 the Indonesian Government has increased compulsory education from 6 to 9 years, and this is applied to all Indonesians, regardless of race, sex, religion and ethnic origin. This policy in itself is providing the basic means for empowerment in the sense of empowering women and men to enable them to live and work together in facing the challenges and opportunities based on equality, sharing and caring for each other's dignity and welfare. In addition, special and innovative activities are implemented to keep young girls in school and to motivate them to pursue higher educational attainment as well as expertise and careers in science and technology for development. This is further reinforced by the efforts to create non-discriminatory employment opportunities and treatment which

eventually will result in a more gender-sensitive and responsive employment system."

Among African delegations, Abe Williams, Minister of Welfare and Population Development in South Africa, a country now beginning to play a new role on the world stage, stressed the importance of the "empowerment of women" theme.

"The important linkages of gender equity and the empowerment of women with population and development have been consistently highlighted in the preparatory process for this conference. The importance of this is fully accepted by the government of South Africa.

"The new constitution of South Africa introduces protection for the fundamental rights of all South Africans. The Bill of Rights has specific relevance to the situation of women, as it fully entrenches gender equality, which has great significance for gender equity and the empowerment of women. This new legal position of women is an essential basis for redressing the situation of women in a practical way.

"The government of national unity is giving further impetus to the development of women and elevating their role within the development process and the economy, improving the access of women to education, jobs, land, housing and health services as well as economic empowerment. These will have important spin-offs for individual decision-making power of women, including control over fertility, morbidity, mortality and migration."

Ethiopia was hardly less explicit. Tamirat Layne, Prime Minister, said:

"The adoption of a women's policy occupies a prominent place among these measures. Without the empowerment of women, no population policy can be expected to produce significant results. The promotion of women's rights and the creation of the necessary legal and institutional framework to translate this into reality has now placed the gender issue in its proper perspective."

The Latin American delegations tended to eschew the phrase "empowerment of women" and tended to stress the importance of the family rather than that of women. Nevertheless some delegates from Latin American countries were recognisably talking the language of empowerment. Minister Leonor Franco, for example, the leader of the Brazilian delegation, said:

"Little can be achieved in the population field without improving the status of women. It is our task to improve women's access to education and to the labour market, on the same terms that apply to men. In addition, it is essential to eliminate the barriers limiting women's participation in the political, cultural and economic realms, so that women can realise their full potential, pursue their aspirations, and guarantee their rights. These rights include reproductive rights, which we consider to be fundamental human rights that should not be subject to governmental restrictions."

An intriguing analysis came from Mercedes Pulido, Venezuela's Minister for the Family:

"The occidental civilization has also engendered a binary system of meanings which confront the mind against the body, the reason against the feelings, human beings against nature, male against females, individual against society. So, those that have the privileged properties (mind, reason, human being, male, individual) have, indiscriminately, the right of dominating those that posses the inferior properties (body, feelings, nature, female, society) in an attempt that threatens to destroy the life in our planet. If we keep this outline of consumption and production and this distorted relationship between male and female; if we keep the scheme of exploitation; we will finish transforming the earth in a monumental and useless factory that will increase poverty, migrations and uncertainty."

While these and other speeches were being made in the plenary, the Main Committee considered Chapter IV on Gender Equality, Equity and the Empowerment of Women as it had emerged from the last Preparatory Committee. The chapter contained three sections: empowerment and the status of women; the girl child; and male responsibilities and participation.

With so much of the text already agreed at previous meetings, the Main Committee's consideration of Chapter 4 was relatively painless. The *Earth Negotiations Bulletin* (vol 6, no 39) summarised the debate succinctly:

"Egypt, supported by Jordan, Tunisia and others wanted to amend paragraph 4.17 (value of the girl child) because the word "equitable" in the English text was different in the Arabic translation and Egypt also sought to delete "inheritance rights". The EU agreed to delete the brackets in paragraph 4.18, which states the goal of universal primary education by 2015.

"Egypt and Iran proposed changes to unbracketed text. Egypt wanted to drop "in particular by providing alternatives to early marriage" in paragraph 4.21 (marriage) and the words "alternatives to early marriage, such as" were later dropped. Iran wanted to delete the words "forced prostitution" in paragraph 4.9 (elimination of exploitation) and it was replaced by "exploitation through prostitution". During the discussion, the chair pointed out that unbracketed text could not be reopened and that the English version of the text would be the basis on which translation problems would be worked on. Several countries, including Zimbabwe and the British Virgin Islands supported the Chair's clarification. Algeria and Iran said that at some point it would be a choice whether to save the conference or to save the rules of procedure."

Because the text of Chapter IV as adopted is one of the most significant achievements of the ICPD, it is printed in full in Appendix C.

Summarising the conference's debate on the theme, the *Earth Negotiations Bulletin* reported (vol 6, no 39, p 10 of 14 September 1995):

"EMPOWERMENT OF WOMEN: Many delegates and NGO represent-atives have commented that the language in the Programme of Action on the empowerment of women goes much further than the text prepared for the Beijing Women's Conference. The objectives in the Programme of Action include: to achieve equality and equity based on a harmonious partnership between men and women and enable women to realise their full potential; to ensure the enhancement of women's contributions to sustainable development through their full involvement in policy- and decision-making; and to ensure that all women are provided with the education necessary for them to meet their basic human needs and to exercise their human rights. All countries are urged to ensure the widest and earliest possible access by girls and women in fulfilling the goal of universal primary education before the year 2015. Encouraging the full participation of the girl child and speaking out against patterns of gender discrim-ination is also highlighted. This language finally meets the demands of those who have long argued that any sound population policy has to be implemented through those who are in a position to make a difference — women. ICPD Secretary General Nafis Sadik highlighted that all delegates who took the floor during the general debate endorsed this position, proving that this is no longer a point defended by a minority. Although some countries argued that the language on equal inheritance rights between men and women goes against Islamic Law, none the less, the progress made towards empowerment of women is considered remarkable."

In her final speech to the ICPD, Dr Sadik commented:

"Energetic and committed implementation of the Programme of Action over the next 20 years will bring women at last into the mainstream of development; it will protect their health, promote their education, and encourage and reward their economic contribution; will ensure that every pregnancy is intended, and every child is a wanted child; will protect women from the results of unsafe abortion; will protect the health of adolescents, and encourage responsible behaviour; will combat HIV/AIDS; will promote education for all and close the gender gap in education; will protect and promote the integrity of the family.

Not everyone, of course, was as happy as the conference's Secretary General with the outcome of the ICPD as far as the empowerment of women was concerned. Vandana Shiva, for example, a well-known Indian feminist and ecologist, launched a blistering attack on the supposedly narrow focus of some of the women's groups active in Cairo.

"When 'Choice' is used as a justification for population control, it is an example of Orwellian doublespeak. Thus at Cairo, women's multiple rights as full human beings in society were reduced to 'reproductive rights' alone. The Western women's movement contributed to this biological reductionism in Cairo by failing to focus on women's productive roles and by focusing exclusively on their reproductive roles, by failing to draw attention to denial of women's economic rights through structural adjustment and the General Agreement on Tariffs and Trade (GATT), and allowing 'unmet needs' to be redefined as needs for contraceptives alone, and not needs for food, water and livelihoods."[4]

There was some force in Vandana Shiva's argument that "women's rights" should not be narrowly equated with reproductive rights but an objective reading of the text of Chapter 4 as adopted in Cairo hardly sustained that interpretation. On the contrary, as the UN system moved on to look beyond Cairo towards the Beijing Women's Summit in August 1995 (with several old battlefields being revisited in the process) the ICPD's chapter on Gender Equality, Equity and Empowerment of Women began to seem remarkably forward-looking and comprehensive.

Chapter 8
Adolescence

The debate over abortion was the most publicly visible controversy to mark the ICPD. As we have seen, in the end various forms of words were agreed, at least for the purpose of the Consensus, even though several delegations including the Holy See registered their reservations.

At the end of the day the Vatican's Islamic allies were, arguably, less bothered by what the conference had to say about abortion, than by the way it discussed marriage and the family and the possibilities for individuals outside the context of marriage, including — for example — adolescents to have access to contraceptive information and supplies.

Dr Halfdan Mahler, IPPF's Secretary General, in his speech to the plenary repeated the point he had already made to PrepCom 3, namely that globally there were some 500 million adolescents aged 15 to 19 and that their numbers would keep mounting for a very long time.

> "A tragic expression of the failure to support young people in realising their sexuality with care and responsibility is the high incidence of pregnancies, sexually transmitted diseases and abortions among teenagers world-wide."

Some delegations clearly shared Dr Mahler's assessment of the situation.

As on the abortion issue and the need for the empowerment of women, Gro Harlem Brundtland in her speech to the plenary on the opening day had been firm and forthright in insisting that the conference should focus on youth.

> "Reproductive health services not only deal with problems that have been neglected, they also cater to clients who have previously been

overlooked. Young people and single persons have received too little help, and continue to do so, as family planning clinics seldom meet their needs. Fear of promoting promiscuity is often said to be the reason for restricting family planning services to married couples. But we know that lack of education and services does not deter adolescents and unmarried persons from sexual activity. On the contrary, there is increasing evidence from many countries, including my own, that sex education promotes responsible sexual behaviour, and even abstinence. Lack of reproductive health services makes sexual activity more risky for both sexes, but particularly for women. As young people stand at the threshold of adulthood, their emerging sexuality is too often met with suspicion or plainly ignored. At this vulnerable time in life adolescents need both guidance and independence, they need education as well as opportunity to explore life for themselves. This requires tact and a delicately balanced approach from the parents and from society. It is my sincere hope that the ICPD will contribute to increased understanding and greater commitment to the reproductive health needs of young people, including the provision of confidential health services to them."

As usual, Brundtland had been supported by her Scandinavian colleagues.

Helle Degn, Denmark's Minister for Development Cooperation, for example, said:

"It is against this background that I encourage all of us to rid ourselves of the constraints of the traditional concept of family planning and turn towards the concept of sexual and reproductive health and rights.

"This concept, which we have consistently advocated throughout the preparatory process, deals with population issues within a broader perspective. It addresses questions that are often neglected in more traditional family planning and mother and child health care programmes: persistently high maternal mortality. The continued spread of sexually transmitted diseases, including HIV/AIDS. The sexual and reproductive health problems of adolescents. Let me add that we all know that many young girls die as a result of early pregnancy and unsafe abortion. It is tragic that this can be seen as one of the results of the silence that often prevails on teenage sexuality."

Elizabeth Rehn of Finland had been even more explicit in insisting that:

"Every person — regardless of age or marital status — should have access to information and quality services regarding sexual and reproductive health and rights."

Inger Davidson for Sweden said:

"Adolescents and youth are a key group for the concerns we are gathered here to discuss. They and their children are the agents of change and development. Not least important is the fact that attitudes affecting gender equity are developed during these formative years. The incidence of unsafe abortions, of sexually transmitted diseases including AIDS/HIV makes it even more imperative than ever that young people in society, both boys and girls, receive adequate and confidential guidance — not least through school — with regard to their sexuality, and that they have access to contraceptives."

The Scandinavian countries had a good deal of support in the developing world.

India's Minister of Health and Family Welfare, Shri B Shankaranand, said:

"A special adolescent girl programme has been launched through the ICDS system for reaching out to school drop-out adolescent girls in the age group 11–18 years."

For South Africa, Abe Williams, Minister of Welfare and Population Development, said:

"There will be a programme to improve access to quality antenatal services, delivery services and postnatal services for all women. Special services aimed at adolescents, in particular education campaigns to combat adolescent parenthood, sexually transmitted diseases and substance abuse among the youth, are to be developed. The need to re-orient reproductive health services to include education, counselling and confidentiality and to promote people's right to privacy and dignity is being given special emphasis."

Brazil's Leonor Franco said:

"As regards education of adults or adolescents about reproduction, we hold that governments are obliged to provide means for individuals to make their own decisions freely.

"Adolescents are of special concern to the Brazilian government, since female morbidity and death rates associated with pregnancy and child birth are especially high in this age category. Traditions and prejudices keep adolescents from acquiring the necessary information about the consequences of their sexuality. We believe, therefore, that adolescents deserve preferential treatment in regard to education about reproduction and family planning. The effects of teenage pregnancy and motherhood are harmful for the lives of a great many adolescents. It is necessary to protect them better."

Some of the NGOs went much further than the government delegations, particularly the European NGOs who issued a collective statement:

"European NGOs also want to draw urgent attention to adolescents' reproductive and sexual health. As early as possible young women and men should receive information and education on reproductive and sexual health. Young women should gain skills in order to recognise and prevent sexual abuse and unsafe sex, especially to prevent STDs (sexually transmitted diseases), including HIV/AIDS, and to protect themselves against rape, incest and genital mutilations."

For some other delegations this hard-hitting, almost deliberately provocative language, went too far. The Holy See's point of view was that:

"The task of rearing children belongs in the first place to parents, not to the state. The Holy See hopes that texts clearly endorse the rights, responsibilities of parents in this area, will draw attention to the negative aspects of premature sexual activity for young people and will endeavour to foster mature behaviour on the part of adolescents."

Like the Holy See, the Islamic countries were concerned with the question of permissiveness and the adoption of inappropriate lifestyles and the threat to the family and family values that these represented.

Malaysia agreed that adolescent health was an area requiring due attention as that country now faced the problems of unwanted pregnancies, unsafe abortion, STD and HIV/AIDS. Immediate steps should be taken to strengthen provision of knowledge and education, guidance and counselling services, improve parenting and family life education and skills and instill responsible behaviour among youth and adolescents. However, the Malaysian delegate went on to add:

"In designing programmes and strategies for youth and adolescent sexuality and reproductive health, due caution must be taken so as not to give the connotation of sexual permissiveness and unhealthy sexual and reproductive practices and lifestyles, the undesirable effects of which are evident.

"We also feel that it is time now that we go back to basics of family, family life and values and to strengthen the family institution, particularly as we will encounter even greater challenges within the next century. We believe that the concept of the traditional family must not be lost as there is a need to protect rights and to exercise responsibility of spouses and family members in view of the diversity of families existing today. We support the need for family sensitive policies and the elimination of practices which endanger the health and well-being of women, children and families, such as child marriages, genital mutilation, child prostitution and abuse among the many other forms of domestic and family violence."

Like Malaysia, Indonesia stressed the importance of the family. Dr Haryono Suyono, Indonesia's State Minister for Population and Chairman of the National Family Planning Coordinating Board stressed:

"Indonesia adheres to the belief that the family is the basic unit of society and ought to be continuously strengthened. It is encouraging to note that these issues have been given particular attention in the Draft Programme of Action. The draft does promote the idea of strengthening the family and encourages all governments to formulate policies which are sensitive to the needs of the family and its impact. In this regard, Indonesia has been promoting and implementing family centered development programmes during the last four years. By doing so, we hope that the family will be able to perform its main functions as well as preserve the basic fabric of the society.

"In accordance with the socio-cultural traditions and national laws of our country, we only recognise families which are legally and/or religiously formed between men and women. Under this concept, the family consists of husband and wife or husband and wife and their children or widows with their children and or widowers and their children. We note, however, that other countries recognise other forms of family realising fully that there is no international model of family which is suitable and acceptable to every country."

Dr Haryono went on to say that the right of couples and individuals to decide on the number and spacing of their children clearly had to be seen within the social, cultural and family context.

"Allow me now to address the closely related subjects of sexual and reproductive health, sexual and reproductive rights as well as family planning. I simply wish to caution that we consider these subjects with great sensitivity, understanding and empathy. I believe our approach should be in accordance with each country's own culture, tradition and religion taking into account the level of its development without ignoring their individual and community rights as well as their responsibilities. Underlying the debate on these issues is the basic right of all couples and individuals to decide freely and responsibly the number and spacing of their children and to have the necessary information and means to do so. This is fundamental, and it is upon such a premise that various related notions contained in the Programme of Action should take into account the religion, culture, norms and values, cultures and stages of development of each country. Needless to say that the involvement of the family, particularly the parent, is of critical importance in the provision of such services which should take into account such questions as: who are the clients, what kinds of services are appropriate for certain types of client, in what ways certain services would be best delivered, which channels are effective and when and where certain services should be delivered. Furthermore, it is also our conviction that decisions concerning sexual and reproductive matters are family decisions and therefore are not solely the exclusive rights of an individual. Instead, the exercise of these rights should, to a certain degree, be carried out in consultation with other relevant family members."

The statement by the Head of the Iranian delegation, Mohammad Ali Tashkiri, also stressed the family context but provided an interesting nuance as he referred to young people "at the age of marriage" rather than insisting that only young married people should have access to family planning advice and services:

> "The sexual and reproductive health education for young people, either married or at the age of marriage, can play a significant role in the promotion of health for all, better motherhood and family planning, as well as in reduction of sexually transmitted diseases, morbidity and mortality. Based on this understanding, the Islamic Republic of Iran supports the idea of sexual health education. But the content and beneficiaries of these programmes should be chosen very carefully. One should not overlook the dangerous implications of sexual education for those who are not at the age of marriage."

Mr Tashkiri went on to add:

> "We believe that extending these educations to children and teenagers will lead to many unbearable social problems, which should be avoided."

In keeping with the cooperative tone Iran was adopting at the Cairo conference, Tashkiri refrained from any talk of the "Great Satan" or other finger-pointing admonition. Others were not so circumspect. Pat Buchanan, for example, a celebrated right-wing columnist widely syndicated in the United States, commented just before the ICPD opened:

> "Well, Bill Clinton had better consider the consequences of what his crowd is up to in Cairo. Notes Reuters, Islamic groups 'have worked themselves into a frenzy over the conference, warning that a draft version of its final declaration violates Islamic morals and encourages promiscuity and homosexuality.' Look for big trouble in Cairo in September. After all, we asked for it. There, America's moral authority is being put behind abortion on demand, sterilisation, homosexuality. While this may be a bold agenda at Washington dinner parties, to traditional societies in Latin America, Africa and the Islamic world, it is the essence of decadent, godless Western materialism. The new face Clinton's America is presenting the world is causing millions who once looked to us with affection and admiration to recoil in contempt and disgust. No, friends, it is not the American right that is 'isolating' America."[1]

The devil, of course, was in the detail. Apart from the abortion issue discussed in the previous chapter, what precisely was the objectionable hackle-raising language in the ICPD draft?

LOOKING CLOSER AT THE DRAFT

The crucial language was contained in a special section of Chapter VII dealing with adolescents, bracketed text indicating areas of disagreement.

"7.39 The [reproductive health] needs of adolescents as a group have been largely ignored to date by existing [reproductive health] services. The response of societies to the [reproductive health] needs of adolescents should be based on information that helps them attain a level of maturity required to make responsible decisions. In particular, information and services should be made available to adolescents that can help them understand their sexuality and protect them from unwanted pregnancies, sexually transmitted diseases and subsequent risk of infertility. This should be combined with the education of young men to respect women's self-determination and to share responsibility with women in matters of sexuality and reproduction. This effort is uniquely important for the health of young women and their children, for women's self-determination and, in many countries, for efforts to slow the momentum of population growth. Motherhood at a very young age entails a risk of maternal death much greater than average, and the children of young mothers have higher levels of morbidity and mortality. Early child-bearing continues to be an impediment to improvements in the educational, economic and social status of women in all parts of the world. Overall for young women, early marriage and early motherhood can severely curtail educational and employment opportunities and are likely to have a long-term, adverse impact on their and their children's quality of life.

"7.40 Poor educational and economic opportunities and sexual exploitation are important factors in the high levels of adolescent child-bearing. In both developed and developing countries, adolescents faced with few apparent life choices have little incentive to avoiding pregnancy and child-bearing.

"7.41 In many societies, adolescents face pressures to engage in sexual activity. Young women, particularly low-income adolescents, are especially vulnerable. Sexually active adolescents of both sexes are increasingly at high risk of contracting and transmitting sexually transmitted diseases, including HIV/AIDS, and they are typically poorly informed about how to protect themselves. Programmes for adolescents have shown to be most effective when they secure the full involvement of adolescents in identifying their [reproductive and sexual health] needs and in designing programmes that respond to those needs.

"7.42 The objectives are:

(a) To address adolescent [sexual and reproductive health] issues, including unwanted pregnancy, [unsafe abortion], sexually transmitted diseases and HIV/AIDS, through the promotion of responsible and healthy reproductive and sexual behaviour, including voluntary abstinence, and the provision of appropriate services and counselling specifically suitable for that age group;
(b) To substantially reduce all adolescent pregnancies.

"[7.43   Countries should remove legal, regulatory and social barriers to sexual and reproductive health information and care for adolescents and must ensure that the programmes and attitudes of health care providers do not restrict the access of adolescents to the services and information they need. In doing so, services for adolescents must safeguard their rights to privacy, confidentiality, informed consent and respect.]

"7.44   Countries, with the support of the international community, should protect and promote the rights of adolescents to [sexual and reproductive health] education, information and care and greatly reduce the number of adolescent pregnancies."

With the agreement elsewhere on the definitions of reproductive health and unsafe abortion, paragraphs 7.39 to 7.42 of the ICPD survived intact in the final version, the only change being the removal of brackets. However, paragraph 7.43 suffered a substantial rewrite as a result of the Cairo debate with the role of parents given a substantial upgrade and a potentially fatal "appropriate" being inserted before the word "services". Quite how the responsibility of parents could be combined with the need to respect an adolescent's confidences was not made clear in the final text which read as follows:

"7.45 (ex-7.43)   Recognising the rights, duties and responsibilities of parents and other persons legally responsible for adolescents to provide, in a manner consistent with the evolving capacities of the adolescent, appropriate direction and guidance in sexual and reproductive matters, countries must ensure that the programmes and attitudes of health care providers do not restrict the access of adolescents to appropriate services and the information they need, including on sexually transmitted diseases and sexual abuse. In doing so, and in order to, inter alia, address sexual abuse, these services must safeguard the rights of adolescents to privacy, confidentiality, respect and informed consent, respecting cultural values and religious beliefs. In this context, countries should, where appropriate, remove legal, regulatory and social barriers to reproductive health information and care for adolescents."

The final text of 7.46 (ex-7.44) read as follows:

"7.46   Countries, with the support of the international community, should protect and promote the rights of adolescents to reproductive

159

health education, information and care and greatly reduce the number of adolescent pregnancies."

Though the reference to sexual health is retained elsewhere in the section on adolescents, it is dropped here — a significant watering-down of the draft language.

The other main controversy in the debate on adolescents was in a sense an old chestnut and related to the use and meaning of the word "individuals" in the context of sexual and reproductive health.

In the draft programme paragraph 7.4 read as follows:

"7.4 All countries should strive to make accessible through the primary health care system, [reproductive health] to all individuals [of all ages] as soon as possible [and no later than the year 2015]."

This paragraph contained one of the key goals at least as far as the conference organisers were concerned. Agreeing on the provision of universal access to reproductive health care had been set out as one of the fundamental objectives of the conference by Secretary General Nafis Sadik in her speech to the second meeting of the Preparatory Committee held in May 1993. However, when the paragraph came before the Main Committee, the Holy See, supported by a number of delegates, suggested an amendment replacing "of all ages" with "age-appropriate" before reproductive health. This was agreed (as paragraph 7.6).

Para 7.45 in the draft contained the passage:

"Sexually active adolescents will require special family planning information, counselling and services, including contraceptive services, and those who become pregnant will require special support from their families and community during pregnancy and early child care. Adolescents must be fully involved in the planning, implementation and evaluation of such information and services with proper regard for parental guidance and responsibilities."

The *Earth Negotiations Bulletin* summarised the debate on the above paragraphs in the following terms:

"The issue of adolescent sexuality led to considerable debate within the working group. Though the phrase "including contraceptive services" was not bracketed it was deleted from the final version of the sentence on sexually active adolescents. Whereas the old paragraph ensured that sexual and reproductive health information and care would be available to adolescents, while safeguarding their right to privacy, the new paragraph has an emphasis on the rights, duties and responsibilities of parents. The paragraph also states '... these services must safeguard the rights of adolescents to privacy, confidentiality, respect and informed consent, respecting cultural values and religious beliefs'.[2]

A third area where the draft proved contentious was the use of the phrase "couples and individuals" or "individuals and couples". Though as noted [see page 123], delegations had somewhat grudgingly agreed to leave these words unbracketed where they occurred elsewhere in the text (for example in draft paragraphs 7.12 and 7.14), a bracketed reference to individuals and couples still remained in paragraph 7.2.

"The cornerstone of [sexual and reproductive health] rests on the recognition of the basic right of all couples and individuals to decide freely and responsibly the number, spacing and timing of their children and to have the information and means to do so, [and the right to the enjoyment of the highest attainable standard of sexual and reproductive health]. It also includes respect for [security of the person and] physical integrity of the human body as expressed in human rights documents, [*and the right of couples and individuals to make decisions concerning reproduction free of discrimination, coercion and violence*]. In the exercise of this right, couples and individuals should take into account the needs of their living and future children and their responsibilities towards the community." (author's emphasis)

In discussion in Committee, the brackets around the words "couples and individuals" were removed. Jordan and Syria expressed, however, concern about the use of the term "individuals" in paragraph 7.2.

Other Islamic countries expressed similar concerns when the ICPD programme as a whole was adopted on the final morning of the conference. The representative of Afghanistan stated the following:

"The delegation of Afghanistan wishes to express its reservation about the word "individual" in Chapter VII and also about those parts that are not in conformity with Islamic Sharia."

The representative of Brunei Darussalam stated the following:

"According to our interpretation, one aspect of reproductive rights and reproductive health, referring specifically to paragraphs 7.3 and 7.47 and subparagraph 13.14 (c) of the Programme of Action, contradicts Islamic law and our national legislation, ethical values and cultural background. My country wishes to place on record its reservation on those paragraphs."

The representative of Jordan stated the following:

"The delegation of Jordan, in its deliberations and discussions with all delegations and in a very serious and responsible manner, always wanted to join the consensus on the Programme of Action. While deeply appreciating the great efforts deployed by the Main Committee and the working groups, which have worked for long hours with the aim of achieving consensus on the language, and in full respect of the values of all countries, the delegation of Jordan has reached some compromises regarding the language on all issues.

"We fully believe that the international community respects our national legislation, our religious beliefs and the sovereign right of each country to apply population policies in accordance with its legislation. The delegation of Jordan understands that the final document, particularly chapters IV, V, VI and VII, will be applied within the framework of Islamic Sharia and our ethical values, as well as the laws that shape our behaviour. We will deal with the paragraphs of this document accordingly. Therefore, we interpret the word "individuals" to mean couples, a married couple. I hope that you will put these comments on record."

The representative of Kuwait stated the following:

"The delegation of Kuwait would like to express its support for the Programme of Action, including all its positive points for the benefit of humankind. At the same time, we would like to put on record that our commitment to any objectives on population policies is subject to their not being in contradiction with Islamic Sharia or with the customs and traditions of Kuwaiti society and the Constitution of the State."

The representative of the Libyan Arab Jamahiriya stated the following:

"The delegation of the Libyan Arab Jamahiriya wishes to express a reservation on all terms in the document that are in contravention of Islamic Sharia, such as we see in paragraph 4.17 and in Chapter II of the document, in relation to inheritance and extramarital sexual activities, and the references to sexual behaviour, as in paragraph 8.31.

"I wish to express a reservation, despite the discussion that took place in the Main Committee regarding the basic rights of couples and individuals. We express a reservation regarding the word "individuals"."

The representative of Egypt submitted the following written statement:

"We wish to point out that the delegation of Egypt was among those delegations that registered numerous comments on the contents of the Programme of Action with regard to the phrase 'couples and individuals'.

"While recognising that this expression was adopted by consensus at the two previous population conferences of 1974 and 1984, our delegation called for the deletion of the word 'individuals' since it has always been our understanding that all the questions dealt with by the Programme of Action in this regard relate to harmonious relations between couples united by the bond of marriage in the context of the concept of the family as the primary cell of society."

The representative of the Islamic Republic of Iran submitted the following written statement:

> "There are some expressions that could be interpreted as applying to sexual relations outside the framework of marriage, and this is totally unacceptable. The use of the expression 'individuals and couples' and the contents of principle 8 demonstrate this point. We have reservations regarding all such references in the document.
>
> "We believe that sexual education for adolescents can only be productive if the material is appropriate and if such education is provided by the parents and aimed at preventing moral deviation and physiological diseases."

The Islamic nations clearly felt extremely strongly on this point, even more strongly, perhaps, than they felt on the issue of abortion. In contrast, the Catholic countries had obviously learned to live with the expression "couples and individuals" in the two decades since the phrase was adopted at the World Population Conference in Bucharest in August 1974 and seemed reluctant to make a *casus belli* of it now.

Of the Catholic nations only tiny El Salvador made an explicit reservation on the need for contraceptive education, information and services being available to individuals outside the context of marriage:

> "The delegation of El Salvador endorses the reservations expressed by other nations with regard to the term 'individuals' as we objected to that term in the Main Committee. It is not in conformity with our legislation and therefore could give rise to misunderstanding. We therefore express our reservation with respect to the term 'individuals'."

The representative of El Salvador later corrected his statement as follows:

> "In referring to the family in its various forms, under no circumstances can we change the origin and foundation of the family, which is the union between man and woman from which derive children."

Apart from El Salvador, no Catholic country explicitly reserved its position on the use of the word "individuals" in the context of the provision of contraceptive education, information and services. The Holy See, however, took care to restate its own position:

> "With reference to the term 'couples and individuals', the Holy See reserves its position with the understanding that this term is to mean married couples and the individual man and woman who constitute the couple. The document, especially in its use of this term, remains marked by an individualistic understanding of sexuality which does not give due attention to the mutual love and decision-making that characterises the conjugal relationship."

Reviewing the final statements made by delegations on the question of adolescent sex, we must conclude that genuine consensus on this issue in the conventional sense of the word could scarcely be said to exist. Only semantic hair-splitting permitted agreement and the statements made for the record indicated clearly that this was where the same set of words could be made to have very different meanings with, in turn, drastically different implications for social policy. Fred Sai, Chairman of the Main Committee, attempted to reassure delegates that they were not being forced to agree to anything which they fundamentally objected to because, after all, everything in the whole programme was governed by the famous "chapeau" on national sovereignty at the beginning of Chapter II. But the wily men and women on the delegations, in spite of Sai's authoritative charm, were not so easily foxed.

Bearing in mind the statements made for the record on the final day, the section of the programme as adopted which deals with the needs of adolescents was less radical than people like Dr Halfdan Mahler might have hoped. As Sweden pointed out in the closing plenary, it would have been useful to have focused more on adolescents since there would be over one billion of them in the near future.

Chapter 9

International Migration

Apart from the questions of abortion, the hotly disputed definition of reproductive health and the rights of adolescents to family planning information and services, the issue of international migration generated much interest and not a little controversy. In March 1994, the UN had estimated that there were more than 125 million people living outside their country of birth or citizenship and that half of them were from developing nations. UN Secretary General Boutros Boutros-Ghali said that growing economic interdependence among countries encouraged and was, in turn, encouraged by international migration. "International migration is a rational response of individuals to the real or perceived economic, social and political differences between countries."

The UN Secretary General's report was presented to the final meeting of the ICPD Preparatory Committee which took place in New York in April 1994. It heralded the beginning of a controversy which, if less heated than that which took place over abortion, nevertheless involved some powerful skirmishes and strong language on all sides.

On April 28, 1994, for example, at the end of the Preparatory Committee meeting, a non-governmental organisation representing migrant workers blasted the UN for its cavalier attitude towards the sufferings of expatriates.

Charito Basa of the Rome-based Women's Council — an advocacy group for Filipino migrant workers — said the UN talked a lot but did little or nothing to help the world's migrant workers.

"Our women are being sexually exploited and our families torn apart", she told IPS. "But the United Nations is refusing to recognise even the

165

right to family reunification by migrant workers. With the signing of the new General Agreement on Tariffs and Trade, goods can move freely across borders, but Third World migrants cannot.[1]

Basa said she was very disappointed by a draft action plan which had emerged from the New York meeting to be transmitted to the Cairo meeting September 5–13. "The plight of the migrant workers has no place in the ICPD Programme of Action", she said.

Basa vowed to take her fight all the way to the Egyptian capital come September. Basa, who was from the Philippines, said there were more than 3.5 million Filipino migrant workers in some 120 countries worldwide. In Europe, the Philippines had one of the biggest contingents of migrant workers, after Turkey. In Italy there were about 160,000 Filipino workers, the second largest migrant group, of which 70 per cent were women. Basa said the international community — including "host" countries that employed migrants and "sending" countries where workers originated — were both silent about the plight of these workers.

She singled out India, Bangladesh, Sri Lanka and Thailand — all countries depending heavily on migrant workers' earnings — accusing them of not taking an active role in the ongoing debate on international migration. The phobia of overpopulation had not only distracted policymakers from the actual causes of migration, but had also further victimised the victims. She referred to the overriding social costs of international migration that were breaking up families in Third World nations. Migrant women, long separated from their loved ones at home, were more vulnerable and were being sexually exploited in the countries where they were employed as domestics. In Italy, she said, cases of unwanted pregnancies had become a major concern among Filipino expatriates. In the patriarchal culture of Philippine society, single mothers and women having children out of wedlock were discriminated against.

"And so, thousands of Filipinas have resorted to abortion because of these and other circumstances", Basa said. And to make matters worse, she said, it is the general practice among Italian employers to sack pregnant domestic workers. She said the rich countries were practising double standards on the movement of the world's citizens: between those who were welcome and could afford to move freely and those who were shunned or exploited for their labour.

She also said that employers made a sharp distinction between documented workers and undocumented workers. The undocumented workers got the worst of it, she said, because they had no legal status in the country in which they lived. But still they were exploited to the maximum — long hours, less pay, no vacation and no social security. The draft Cairo Programme of Action, which devoted one chapter to international migration, said that it was the right of every nation state to decide who could enter and stay in its territory and under what conditions.

"Such right, however, should be exercised taking care to avoid racist or xenophobic actions and policies", Basa punchily added.

CHAPTER X OF THE DRAFT

As far as the question of international migration was concerned, the ICPD draft as it came to Cairo was inevitably couched in language far less colourful than that used by Charito Basa.

Chapter X of the draft programme, on international migration, proposed measures aimed at addressing the root causes of migration, especially those relating to poverty. The objective was to encourage more cooperation and dialogue between countries of origin and countries of destination in order to increase the likelihood that migration would have positive consequences for the development of both sending and receiving countries; and to facilitate the reintegration process of returning migrants. Regarding documented migrants, among the actions proposed were that governments of receiving countries must recognise the right to family reunification — a sentence still in brackets — giving priority to programmes and strategies that combatted religious intolerance, racism, ethnocentrism, xenophobia and gender discrimination, and that generated the necessary public sensitivity in that regard.

Governments of both receiving countries and countries of origin, the chapter went on, should adopt effective sanctions against those who organised undocumented migration, exploited undocumented migrants or engaged in their trafficking, especially those who engaged in any form of international traffic in women, youth and children. Proposals for action concerning refugees, asylum-seekers and displaced persons included a call to governments to address the root causes of those movements by taking appropriate measures, particularly with respect to conflict resolution; the promotion of peace and reconciliation; respect for human rights, including those of persons belonging to minorities; respect for independence, territorial integrity and sovereignty of states.

The first paragraph in which bracketed text appeared was paragraph 10.12 which read as follows:

> "10.12 In order to promote the integration of documented migrants having the right to long-term residence, governments of receiving countries are urged to consider giving them civil and political rights and responsibilities, as appropriate, and facilitating their naturalisa-

tion. Special efforts should be made to enhance the integration of the children of long-term migrants by providing them with educational and training opportunities equal to those of nationals, allowing them to exercise an economic activity, and facilitating the naturalisation of those who have been raised in the receiving country. Governments of receiving countries must ensure the protection of migrants and their families, [and recognise the right to family reunification], giving priority to programmes and strategies that combat religious intolerance, racism, ethnocentrism, xenophobia, and gender discrimination and which generate the necessary public sensitivity in that regard."

Bracketed text also appeared in 10.13:

"10.13 Governments of countries of destination should respect the basic human rights of documented migrants as those governments assert their right to regulate access to their territory and adopt policies that respond to and shape immigration flows. With regard to the admission of migrants, governments should avoid discriminating on the basis of race, religion, sex, [age] and disability, while taking into account health and other considerations relevant under national immigration regulations. Governments are urged to promote, through family reunion, the normalisation of the family life of legal migrants who have the right to long-term residence."

In the plenary debate, a number of speakers addressed the problem of international migration directly.

Europe

In Europe the situation was particularly delicate. Individual member states within the European Union (EU) had already implemented policies to limit immigration, with Germany changing its constitution the previous year in an effort to stem the tide.

The EU had thus decided to limit immigration at the same time as its own population was declining. In countries such as Italy, Greece and Spain, women were having fewer children, while overall in the EU, the population was ageing inexorably.

This trend was putting pressure on the social security system in member states, but so far there had been no firm consensus on how to deal with this problem. The one point of agreement was that increased immigration was definitely not the solution.

Manfred Kanther, the German Minister of the Interior speaking on behalf of the European Union, said:

"International migration is clearly an important issue and we welcome the fact that agreement has already largely been reached on Chapter 10 of the document which addresses the sensitive subject in an appropriate manner. A number of countries including EU countries are particularly affected by the consequences of migration."

The sending countries

The sensitivities were not all on the side of the receiving countries. On Thursday 8 September a new controversy was reported to have erupted at the International Conference on Population and Development (ICPD) over the rights of migrants and expatriate workers. Nicolaas Biegman, Vice Chairman of the Main Committee, said at a press conference that Turkey was in the "forefront" of the controversy on whether migrants had the "right" to bring their families to host countries. Biegman, who was responding to a question by a Turkish reporter, declined to specify other countries involved or give further details. But he said he believed recipient countries would find it "very difficult" to accept the amendments demanded by the donors in connection with Chapter X on "International Migration" in the ICPD's draft Programme of Action.

There were indications that the dispute involved not only the Western industrialised countries but the oil-producing Arab countries of the Gulf, which hosted millions of expatriate workers mostly from Asia. The chief of the Philippines delegation had stressed the issue in his speech before the conference on Tuesday, 6 September. He specifically urged the Gulf countries to respect the rights of workers on their territories "not only for the sake of Filipinos but for that of millions of others" employed in the region. Suriname's Minister for Internal Affairs, S Sabiran, took up the issue from a different angle in a speech he delivered on the Thursday. He called for "concerted national, regional and international measures" to address what he described as unprecedented waves of migration aggravating the "brain drain" in the developing countries and North-South disparities.

Ukraine

Ukraine worried that it was losing too many workers to Western Europe.

> "The emigrational potential is fluctuating now within 2–6 per cent of the country's population. According to existing estimates, 120 thousand of Ukrainian citizens were working last year in the European countries. External migration is growing and causes negative social and economic consequences in our country and concern in the countries of entry. In these conditions the problem of regulation of international migration becomes more and more pressing. In particular, it concerns labour migration, the problem which may be solved on

the basis of intergovernmental agreements providing for the restriction of the number of emigrants and the legal protection of the labour migrants' rights."

Tunisia

Tunisia was also concerned to address the root causes of emigration, as well as the conditions under which workers, once they had migrated, were forced to live.

"In some countries, population is dwindling which further affects international migration. Control of such migration will only be possible when internal economic and social conditions in each country reach acceptable levels. The measures proposed in the draft programme of action are insufficient to deal with the problem of migration. Tunisia calls for an international conference to deal with the particular problem of international migration. Greater attention should also be given to the status of migrant communities working abroad."

Korea

"Despite global efforts to resolve population issues, we can see that the problems still exist and are becoming more complex. The growing synergy between population, environment and development, the rapid increase in international migration, and the spread of AIDS have added greater complexity to the population issues, which more than ever require the concerted response of the international community. Thus, greater efforts will be required in the future and into the next century to ensure that what we have gained is not lost and what has yet to be done is achieved successfully by working together in the spirit of true international cooperation."

Malaysia

"The emergence of a borderless world and ensuing present and future problems such as international migration and modern technology and communication will also pose challenges in many facets of population and development."

European NGOs

Not for the first time, the most radical statement was made by a group of European NGOs. For them, the cause of international migration were economic and political circumstances. The inequitable distribution of resources and poverty, and the current economic crisis in the South and

East Europe induced many migration flows. The political causes were war, systematic human rights violations, persecution for political opinions, religious beliefs or ethnic origin and the absence of democratic systems of government. In addition, there were people who migrated as a result of natural disasters and a serious degradation of their environment, caused by desertification, pollution, toxic substances or radioactivity from nuclear testing.

"Women are especially vulnerable victims of the political and economic causes of migration and the abuses of immigrant rights. Abuse of immigrant women's rights may be seen in practices such as trafficking of women as sex workers or mail order brides. The domestic services sector is a growing area of employment of non-white and migrant women where established labour practices are frequently ignored. In the current migration process, women are often at a disadvantage. Though generally, immigration regulations themselves respect individual rights, in practice women face more difficulties in obtaining independent refugee status. Women-specific forms of oppression, such as rape, mutilation or gender based laws are not currently recognised as justification for political asylum.

"As European NGOs, we are concerned about the strict migration controls which promote 'illegal' migration. It seems that cheap 'Third World' and Eastern European labour is still imported when needed. Reduced status and illegality lead to exploitation at work, ie low status jobs with little protection. Such workers are very vulnerable and easily exploited.

"As European NGOs, we need to be especially aware of the specific issues in Europe and of the double standards of our governments in matters of population. Although Europe is amongst the world's most densely populated regions, with an increasing demand for housing, recreations space, roads and parking places due to individualistic lifestyles and ever-growing mobility, there is no explicit population policy. Carrying capacity in terms of population in Europe is seen as a complex relationship between technology, politics and economics, and not simply as a question of numbers. The fact none the less remains that European consumption and consumption patterns contribute to the global population and environmental problem. The European NGOs urge the European Union to take its responsibility in these discussions."

FAMILY UNIFICATION

Earth Negotiations Bulletin reported as follows on the question of the "right to family unification":

"The 'right to family reunification' in paragraph 10.12 proved to be one of the more difficult issues to solve at the conference. Many developing countries wanted to delete the brackets and recognise this right. Canada, Australia, Switzerland and the US commented that their commitment to the objective of family reunification is clear, but their governments retain the ability to define family and limit the number of family members. These countries also thought that family reunification was sufficiently covered in paragraph 10.13. Other countries were concerned since the right to family reunification is not a universally recognised human right, and this Programme of Action should not establish any new rights.

"When it appeared as though the Main Committee was unable to make headway on this issue, a working group, chaired by Soliman Awaad (Egypt), was established. The group met over the course of three days before a compromise emerged. When the new text, which did not refer to the right of family reunification, was announced on Saturday, 10 September, over 35 delegates expressed their regrets, frustration, sadness, difficulties and even reservations including: the Dominican Republic, Zambia, Mali, Benin, Zimbabwe, The Gambia, Cuba, Senegal, Tunisia, Algeria, China, Cameroon, Swaziland, Ecuador, Nicaragua, Guatemala, Mexico, Mauritania, Honduras, Libya, Liberia, Chile, the Philippines, Bangladesh, Bolivia, Uganda, Malawi, Botswana, Peru, El Salvador, Paraguay, the Holy See, Suriname, the Congo, Chad and Haiti. Canada said that for the first time countries have agreed to implement, in practice, family reunification in their national legislation, and this is progress. The chair said that it was sad that the world's divisions are stronger when it comes to migration and related matters. Several delegates asked that the draft be rejected, since it was not fully endorsed. Zimbabwe said that a compromise could be based on reference to Article 10.1 of the Convention on the Rights of the Child. The Chair postponed the chapter's adoption."[2]

The working group reconvened and announced a new compromise on Monday afternoon: "Consistent with Article 10 of the Convention on the Rights of the Child and all other relevant universally recognised human rights instruments, all governments, particularly those of receiving countries, must recognise the vital importance of family reunification and promote its integration into their national legislation in order to ensure the protection of the unity of the families of documented migrants." Egypt added that there was strong support in the working group for a global conference on international migration and development and that the report of the conference should note this support.

As adopted, the final text of paragraph 10.12 read as follows:

"10.12 In order to promote the integration of documented migrants having the right to long-term residence, governments of receiving countries are urged to consider giving them civil and political rights and responsibilities, as appropriate, and facilitating their naturalisation. Special efforts should be made to enhance the integration of the children of long-term migrants by providing them with educational and training opportunities equal to those of nationals, allowing them to exercise an economic activity, and facilitating the naturalisation of those who have been raised in the receiving country. Consistent with article 10 of the Convention on the Rights of the Child and all other relevant universally recognised human rights instruments, all governments, particularly those of receiving countries, must recognise the vital importance of family reunification and promote its integration into their national legislation in order to ensure the protection of the unity of the families of documented migrants. Governments of receiving countries must ensure the protection of migrants and their families, giving priority to programmes and strategies that combat religious intolerance, racism, ethnocentrism, xenophobia and gender discrimination and that generate the necessary public sensitivity in that regard."

In paragraph 10.13 (rights of documented migrants), the word "age" was bracketed. The ENB reported:

"At PrepCom III, the Philippines had asked for this word, since migration patterns are often discriminatory based on age, and Australia had insisted on the brackets. The Philippines suggested deleting 'age' and adding a new phrase at the end of the sentence: 'including the special needs of children and the elderly'. This formulation was approved."

The final text for paragraph 10.13 therefore read as follows:

"10.13   Governments of countries of destination should respect the basic human rights of documented migrants as those governments assert their right to regulate access to their territory and adopt policies that respond to and shape immigration flows. With regard to the admission of migrants, governments should avoid discriminating on the basis of race, religion, sex and disability, while taking into account health and other considerations relevant under national immigration regulations, particularly considering the special needs of the elderly and children. Governments are urged to promote, through family reunion, the normalisation of the family life of legal migrants who have the right to long-term residence."

The Philippines received partial satisfaction with the amendment to paragraph 10.13 as agreed. When the programme as a whole, however, came to be adopted by the plenary on the morning of Tuesday 13 September, 1995, the representative of the Philippines stated the following:

"The Philippine delegation would like to put on record our regret that in paragraph 10.12 of the Programme of Action the originally proposed wording, recognising "the right to family reunification" was

173

toned down to just recognising "the vital importance of family reunification". In the spirit of compromise, we agreed to the revised wording based on the argument forwarded by other delegations that there have been no previous international conventions or declarations proclaiming such a right, and that this is not the appropriate conference to establish this right. For this and other worthy reasons, we wish to reiterate the recommendation made in the Main Committee, supported by many delegations and received positively by the chairman, that an international conference on migration be convened in the near future. We trust that this recommendation will be part of the record of this conference and will be formally referred to the Economic and Social Council and the General Assembly for proper consideration."

In the event, when in November 1994 the Second Committee of the General Assembly considered the report of the ICPD, no decision was taken to hold a world conference on international migration as one of the follow-up actions, the UN Secretary General being merely invited to study the objectives and modalities of such an event and to report to ECOSOC at its substantive session in 1995.[2]

We should not conclude from this that the General Assembly regarded the issue of international migration as being unimportant. On the contrary, the movement of workers across national frontiers, their conditions of life and work, including the right of their families to join them was without question going to be one of the key economic, social and political questions of the age. If the GA failed to follow-up on the ICPD with a decision to call a conference on international migration as some delegations in Cairo wished, the reason was almost certainly not disinterest but a certain "conference fatigue".

By the end of 1994 the cycle of mega-conferences held under UN auspices still had some way to run. The Social Summit to be held in Copenhagen in March 1995 loomed on the immediate horizon; the Beijing Women's Conference was scheduled for August 1995 and Habitat II for June 1976 in Istanbul. An international migration conference was certainly a worthy cause. But it would have to take its turn in the queue.

Chapter 10
Population Stabilisation

One of the paradoxes of the Cairo population conference, at least as far as the man on the Cairo omnibus was concerned, was how little of it seemed to be about population. There was a great deal of talk and some highly emotional exchanges about abortion, about reproductive rights, about the empowerment of women, about immigration and so on, but very few people were talking about the "population explosion" and the need for "population control" in the good old-fashioned sense. Suddenly it had become unfashionable, even unacceptable and politically incorrect, to talk about demographic targets if those targets were then expressed in crude statistics involving family planning "acceptors", couples sterilised, millions or even billions of condoms distributed and so forth.

Worst of all, it seemed, was the approach which somehow assumed that women and women's bodies were merely the instruments through which these over-arching (most often male-determined) demographic goals were to be achieved. Everyone, of course, was against coercion. But even if overt coercion was not involved, there were subtle as well as crude forms of pressure involved in organised family-planning programmes and these pressures most often stemmed from the macro-approach which concentrated on the overall population-resources equation rather than the (new and now fashionable) micro-approach which looked at the health and well-being of individual women, individual families.

There was, of course, a convenient way of squaring the circle, of achieving a neat synthesis. You didn't, as it were, have to throw away the baby with the bathwater. If as part of the overall package involving health (particularly infant and child mortality reduction), education (particularly for girls) and female empowerment more generally, you significantly expanded access to family planning, you would — hopefully — not only be contributing to overall sustainable development (newly empowered women being the key to this); you would also be contributing to continuing important falls in fertility and possibly even population stabilisation.

BEYOND JUST NUMBERS

The phrase which was on everyone's lips at Cairo was "beyond the numbers". The new emphasis was on the "holistic approach" that would take in poverty, women's status and the structure of society as well as fertility *per se*. The argument went that the reason for the emphasis on these new programmes (health, education, women and so on) was that they were good things in and of themselves, not merely as a means to an end. In fact there were large numbers of people present in Cairo, particularly among the women non-governmental contingent, who didn't want to hear about the population problem at all in the sense that Bucharest and Mexico and a hundred other gatherings had addressed that issue

It is quite intriguing to trace the way in which demographic as opposed to welfare objectives were demoted during the Cairo process. As we have noted in an earlier chapter, Nafis Sadik in her speech to the second meeting of the Preparatory Committee on 14 May 1993 "urged the conference to set the goal of attaining the low variant population projection of 7.2 billion for the year 2015". In practice, as we have seen, the draft programme circulated in January 1994 before the third meeting of the Preparatory Committee was somewhat less explicit than Dr Sadik had been. Rather than propose the goal of attaining the UN's low population projection by the year 2015, it spoke of "achieving stabilisation of the world population as soon as possible", of achieving and maintaining "a harmonious balance between population, resources, food supplies, the environment and development". The January 1994 draft did, however, suggest that if the measures proposed in the programme were taken, the result would be levels of population growth "close to the United Nations low variant".

This somewhat indirect and obscure language was maintained in the final draft as it emerged from the third meeting of the PrepCom in April 1994. In other words, the official document that went to Cairo contained no clear proposal that the world as a whole should be aiming at the low projection and the early stabilisation of population (followed by actual reduction in total world population size) that this implied.

Moreover, whereas the January 1994 draft still set out the objective of achieving the stabilisation of world population (paragraph 6.3, see page 52), the corresponding text in the draft programme as it emerged from the final PrepCom was altogether more waffly, speaking not of the objective to stabilise world population but to "facilitate the demographic transition".

The full text of paragraph 6.3 in the May 1994 draft read as follows:

> "Recognising that the ultimate goal is the improvement of the quality of life of present and future generations, the objective is to facilitate the demographic transition as soon as possible in countries where there is an imbalance between demographic rates and social, economic and environmental goals, while fully respecting human rights. This process will contribute to the stabilisation of the world population, and, together with changes in unsustainable patterns of production and consumption, to sustainable development and economic growth."

At the individual country level

So much for the global level. As far as individual countries were concerned and national population targets, the language was again a disappointment. As long ago as 1974, the World Population Conference in Bucharest had invited countries "which consider their birth rates detrimental to their national purposes ... to consider setting quantitative goals and implementing policies that may lead to the attainment of such goals by 1985" (World Population Plan of Action, Paragraph 37). In Mexico City, ten years later, this clear call had been watered down with countries "which consider their population growth rates hinder the attainment of national goals" being "invited to consider pursuing relevant socio-economic policies, within the framework of socio-economic development" (Recommendation 13).

The January 1994 draft still retained some pertinent language. Paragraph 6.4 stated:

> "Countries should give greater recognition to the importance of population trends for development and should take the proven steps needed to accelerate their demographic transition from high to low levels of fertility and mortality."

However, the language which emerged from the last PrepCom, was much vaguer, stating merely:

177

"Countries should give greater attention to the importance of population trends for development. Countries that have not completed their demographic transition should take effective steps in this regard within the context of their social and economic development and with full respect of human rights."

SUPPORT FOR THE GOAL OF POPULATION STABILISATION

What happened at Cairo itself to the idea of global or national demographic targets? Was there ever a chance that those who believed in clear statements about global and national population goals would make their voices heard against, or in addition to, those who were arguing with increasing clamour and confidence that the means (health, education, female empowerment and so on) were in and of themselves ends and not merely the means to an end (viz global or national population targets)?

Ironically, if we review carefully the speeches made in plenary there was far more support for the traditional view of the population problem than one might have supposed from reading the literature and listening to the speeches in the NGO Forum. The term "population explosion" may not have featured much but there were still a surprising number of speakers ready to admit that, yes, rapid population growth was still a problem and that steps had to be taken to curb that growth — whether at the global or national level.

Nick Bolkus, Australia's Minister for Immigration and Ethnic Affairs, put it most succinctly:

"All of us, both developed and developing nations, come here with a common goal — to work together, and independently, to stabilise population growth."

US Vice-President Al Gore said the same thing in a more long-winded way. He had no doubt that rapid population growth was a major problem and that world population stabilisation was a major objective.

"We would not be here today if we were not convinced that the rapid and unsustainable growth of human population was an issue of the utmost urgency . . .

". . . We have reached a new stage of human history — a stage defined not just by the meteoric growth in human numbers but also by the unprecedented Faustian powers of the new technologies we have acquired during these same 50 years — technologies which not only bring us new benefits but also magnify the consequences of age-old behaviours to extremes that all too often exceed the wisdom we bring to our decisions to use them ...

"The world has also learned from developing countries that the wrong kind of rapid economic development — the kind that is inequitable and destructive of traditional culture, the environment and human dignity — can lead to the disorientation of society and a lessened ability to solve all problems — including population. But here, at Cairo, there is a new and very widely shared consensus that no single one of these solutions is likely to be sufficient by itself to produce the pattern of change we are seeking. However, we also now agree that all of them together, when simultaneously present for a sufficient length of time, will reliably bring about a systemic change to low birth and death rates and a stabilised population. In this new consensus, equitable and sustainable development and population stabilisation go together. The education and empowerment of women, high levels of literacy, the availability of contraception and quality health care: these factors are all crucial."

As they had in previous world population conferences, the European nations took a similar line. Some, like Austria, stressed the importance of linking population curbs in the developing world with self-restraint in the rich industrial world and changes in lifestyle to reduce pollution and overconsumption.

Maria Rauch-Kallat, Austria's Federal Minister for Environment, Youth and Family Affairs, said:

"Mr President, as Minister not only in charge of youth and family affairs but also of the environment, I consider it a duty to say a word about the threats of unchecked population growth for the global environment. Although it is impossible to calculate the potential carrying capacity of the earth for human activity, we would be well advised not to test the limits of environmental endurance. In the developed countries of the north the environment is under tremendous stress due to prevailing patterns of production and consumption. Urgent solutions are called for. The change of lifestyles in the industrialised countries is of paramount importance but it is not a subject matter for this conference.

"The environmental degradation due to poverty and rapid population growth in developing countries may be of comparatively lesser proportion at this stage. But in a number of countries the alarm bells are already ringing. Complacency is out of place. The interlinkages between environment and a sustainable resource base to provide for the needs of the living and of future generations are well known. They should motivate governments to adopt measures as rapidly as possible."

Ruth Dreifuss, Head of the Swiss delegation, said:

"The Swiss authorities are convinced that the twin objectives of respect for individual freedom and demographic stabilisation are perfectly compatible."

Elizabeta Rehn of Finland said:

"Policies and actions that we will agree on should result in stabilising population growth to levels that could be maintained in economic, social and environmental terms. They must be based on the full realisation of human rights and fundamental freedoms for all individuals."

Gro Harlem Brundtland, Prime Minister of Norway, in her opening address said:

"Population growth is one of the most serious obstacles to world prosperity and sustainable development. We may soon be facing new famine, mass migration, destabilisation and even armed struggle as peoples compete for ever more scarce land and water resources.

"In the more developed countries the fortunate children of new generations may delay their confrontation with the imminent environmental crisis, but today's new-borns will be facing the ultimate collapse of vital resources bases. In order to achieve a sustainable balance between the number of people and the amount of natural resources that can be consumed, both the peoples of the industrialised countries and the rich in the South have a special obligation to reduce their ecological impact."

Speaking for the 12 nations of the EU as a whole, Manfred Kanther, Germany's Minister of the Interior, said:

"It will be the task of this conference to find ways how a balance between the population growth and development can be brought about, how the disparities between demographic developments as the result of decisions of individuals, on the one hand, and social, economic and ecological objectives, on the other, can be removed. Such a balance can only be established when population policies are an integral part of sustainable development strategies."

Japan's Minister for Foreign Affairs, Yohei Kono, said:

"We should try to maintain the sustainable balance with respect to population growth, natural environment and consumption-production activities. Both developing and developed countries have their own responsibility. Developing countries should reduce the population growth rate, while developed countries should change the production and consumption patterns and develop and diffuse environmentally sound technology such as low-pollution automobiles and renewable energies like solar power."

180

THE ASIAN NATIONS

The emphasis on world population stabilisation and on national strategies to curb population growth was by no means confined to the nations of the industrial world. Historically, the nations of Asia had long taken the lead in urging the issue of rapid population growth should be addressed at global and national level. In November 1993, in the run-up to the Cairo conference, they had signed the Denpasar Declaration calling for rapid progress towards population stabilisation. Now, in Cairo, several of them repeated the call.

Dr Haryono of Indonesia said:

> "President Soeharto has written to the Leaders of the Non-Aligned countries inviting them to sign the Statement on Population Stabilisation. To date, there are 69 Heads of Government representing 3.4 billion people who support the goal of national and international population stabilisation in order to have a sustainable development which gives primacy to human dignity and welfare and addresses human beings in their entirety. The issue of sustainable human development was thus put at the centre of the global agenda."

Peng Peiyun, Minister of China's State Family Planning Commission, said:

> "The stabilisation of the world population and the achievement of sustained development depend not only on the endeavours of governments of nations but also on further strengthening and promotion of international cooperation...
>
> "Tangible progress has been made at global level in reducing the crude birth rate, crude death rate, especially infant mortality rate, and in increasing the average life expectancy at birth. Education level, especially women's education status, in all countries has been upgraded. More people have had accesses to reproductive health and family planning information and services. However, it must be noted, that the world is still faced with severe challenges in the area of population and development. The world still sees a net increase of 90 million people each year, the number of poverty people is still in the increase, the environmental pollution caused by irrational modes of consumption and excessive depletion of natural resources is still increasing. Faced with these challenges we must take actions to reduce the speed of population growth, eliminate poverty and protect ecology and environment in order to achieve sustained development. We must take our due responsibilities in ensuring a beautiful and happy life for all our people and our future generations. This is a sacred mission that history has endowed with us, and is also a common goal that brings us together today."

Shri B Shankaranand of India said:

181

"Poverty as the biggest challenge remains the central issue in developing countries as over 90 per cent of the current growth in population is taking place in the developing countries. High rates of population growth, poverty and under development are all inter-linked. Therefore it is all the more necessary to break the nexus between high fertility poverty, ill health and illiteracy in the context of population stabilisation and sustainable development ... .

"No amount of economic development would suffice to meet the challenges of ever-increasing growth of population unless we succeed in quickly arresting the same. The rate at which our large population is growing eats away almost all the fruits of our developmental efforts. In order to bring about a meaningful and sustained improvement in the quality of life of our people, it is necessary to put an immediate brake on the population growth and break the nexus between overpopulation and poverty."

Pakistan, India's next-door neighbour, took a similar line. In her opening address to the conference, Benazir Bhutto had, with almost her first remarks, addressed the issue:

"The problem of population stabilisation faced by us today cannot be divorced from our yesterdays. Ironically enough, population has risen fastest in areas which were weakened most by the unfortunate experience of colonial domination.

"The Third World communities have scarce resources spread thinly over a vast stretch of pressing human needs. We are unable to tackle questions of population growth on a scale commensurate with the demographic challenge.

"Since demographic pressures, together with migration from disadvantaged areas to affluent states, are urgent problems, trans-cending national frontiers, it is imperative that in the field of population control, global strategies and national plans work in unison.

"Perhaps that is a dream. But we all have a right to dream."

She returned to the theme in the course of her speech, saying: "Our document should seek to promote the objective of planned parenthood, of population control." And she concluded on the same note: "Given that background, I hope that the delegates participating in this conference will act in wisdom, and with vision to promote population stabilisation."

Bangladesh's Minister of Health and Family Welfare, Chowdury Kamal Ibne Yusuf, said:

"Honorable Chairperson, Bangladesh is the ninth most populous country in the world. The population of around 112 million people lives in an area of 144,000 sq km, making Bangladesh the most densely populated country in the world, excepting some island states.

"The population of Bangladesh will increase to around 144 million by the year 2000, and is expected to stabilise at around 240 to 250 million by the year 2025 to 2030. There are serious consequences of this rapid population growth. The land-man ratio continues to decline considerably. The per-capita income remains low. The levels of savings and investment are highly inadequate. There is considerable unemployment and underemployment. There is widespread malnutrition."

For Papua New Guinea, Mr Utula Samana, the country's permanent representative to the United Nations said:

"In March 1991, my government approved an integrated National Population Policy for progress and development. The key objective of the policy is to reduce population growth and to maintain it at a level which is sustainable in terms of the nation's resources and economic development."

For Samoa, Sala Vaimili II, Western Samoa's Minister of Health, said:

"Our coming together in Cairo at such a critical moment reflects the global concern that rapid population growth is straining available resources and leading inextricably to unsustainable development. The growth rate is such that even as I speak, thousands of newborn are brought into a world already beset with problems of hunger, basic sanitation, health services and illiteracy. Population estimates are so startling indeed that on a single day, over 200,000 new human beings enter the world, quite easily exceeding Samoa's population of 163,000. Therefore, the confident expectation of my delegation is that at the end of this conference, the world community would need to agree on an outcome of strategies that will bring about significant impacts on population and development for the next 20 years."

For Fiji, Ratu Jo Nacola, Minister for Regional Development and Multi-Ethnic Affairs, said: "Our current strategy calls for maintaining a population growth rate below 2 per cent per year."

Thailand's Minister for Public Health, Dr Arthit Ourairat, said:

"Our recognition of the importance of population to national development preceded the holding of the World Population Conference at Bucharest. The first statement of the Thai Government's population policy was made in March 1970. It stated clearly that family planning would be the main strategy to reduce the rapid population growth rate. Subsequently, the Ministry of Public Health was given the responsibility for establishing the National Family Planning programme, which has made possible a decline in the population growth rate from around 3 per cent per annum in 1970 to 1.3 per cent in 1994."

For the Republic of Korea, Sang-Mok Suk, Minister of Health and Social Affairs, said:

> "The population policy in the Republic of Korea evolved primarily in response to the high population growth rate in the early 1960s. At that time, the Korean government was strongly aware that, without a suitable population control policy, it could not achieve economic development quickly."

THE AFRICAN STATES

The keynote speech given on the opening day by Prince Mbilini, Prime Minister of Swaziland, was of enormous importance in indicating that, unlike on previous occasions when the Africa-is-full-of-wide-open-spaces mentality tended to prevail, African countries collectively were ready to admit to, and seriously address, problems of rapid population growth.

Prince Mbilini told delegates:

> "The African continent faces extremely serious problems of development. It is our sincere belief that population growth plays a critical role in the continued underdevelopment of our continent. We, therefore, cannot be indifferent when these issues are being discussed. Africa has the highest population and fertility growth rates, the highest levels of poverty, the highest levels of infant and maternal mortality, and this is further complicated by the highest level of HIV/AIDS infections.
>
> "A large number of African countries are currently undergoing the painful exercise of structural adjustment with a view to correcting economic imbalances which have crept up over the years. The rapidly expanding populations of our continent, Swaziland included, are not facilitating this process; instead, they complicate it further. This is especially felt by the vulnerable groups, such as women and children. The effects of population growth rates on land and environmental degradation, national and household food insecurity and the inability of our national budgets to meet immediate social needs, such as the provision of education and health facilities, are very familiar to us. It is for this reason that we strongly suggest that by addressing population issues the prospects for sustained economic growth and development will be enhanced."

For South Africa, Abe Williams said:

> "President Mandela has requested me to convey his greetings to you and to express his sincere regret that he is not able to be present at this important event. He has indicated his strong commitment to the work of this conference by signing the statement on population

stabilisation of the Global Committee of Parliamentarians on Population and Development."

Ethiopia's Prime Minister, Tamirat Layne, said:

> "The problem of rapid population growth has assumed critical proportions in the least developed countries like Ethiopia where, in the face of continuing technological backwardness it has been and continues to be difficult to meet basic human needs."

Delegates from Latin America, at least in their formal speeches to the plenary, were on the whole less concerned with the demographic aspects of population policy, concentrating instead on the social and health aspects. Some, like Dr Mercedes Pulido, Venezuela's Minister for Social Development, still spoke of empty hinterlands waiting to be filled and quoted approvingly Pope Paul VI's famous dictum:

> "In Venezuela, almost the half of our territory is practically uninhabited and there are, however, those who think and say before our demographic growth that the remedy is to limit the population instead of assuming the task of putting the world to the service of the human beings; there are those who, as the Pope Paul the VI has said, want to remedy the scarcity of the bread in the table, not putting more bread, but searching for fewer people to eat."

The Caribbean delegates, like most other representatives of island states, tended to take a different view. Antigua's delegate, Lionel Hurst, said:

> "The beauty of the Caribbean is also legendary. Hundreds of millions have visited us — most from the industrial countries — to marvel at our tropical rainforests, swim on our breathtakingly beautiful white sand beaches, snorkel at our tropical off-shore reefs, and to seek relaxation from a harried life in their developed countries. The creator's planet is meant to be appreciated, and nowhere so like our Caribbean islands. But death results when the carrying capacity of our planet is exceeded; irreversible damage results when the carrying capacity of islands is exceeded by too large a human population. Small Caribbean island states have solved their over-population problem by emigration. But that avenue is now closing, and we must seek to limit population growth while developing."

DRAFTING VS PLENARY SESSIONS

With all these points about the need for global and national population stabilisation being so powerfully made in the plenary, and by leaders of such stature, why was there not a considerable "beefing up" of the Cairo texts to include more explicit global and national demographic objectives? Was there no connection between the proceedings of the plenary and the detailed work of the drafting groups?

There was, admittedly, a working agreement among participants that texts already agreed at the preparatory meetings would not be reopened in Cairo (in other words only bracketed texts would be discussed), but this was not an utterly unbreakable rule. As work proceeded, there were examples of texts devoid of brackets being nevertheless subject to redrafting and of entirely new points being added to a previously discussed draft. Moreover, the preamble itself had not been negotiated by the Preparatory Committee. After an initial round of discussions in the Main Committee, the chair had moved the discussion to the "Friends of the Chair" group which met several times during the week to examine the chapter. It would have been perfectly proper and entirely within the conference's rules of procedure for delegates to insist, in the light of the statements being made in the plenary, on some stronger language about demographic objectives in the preamble.

There were a number of reasons why this did not happen. The first was a purely practical one. At these mega-conferences, what happens in the plenary can often both seem and be divorced from what happens in the drafting committees. Delegates who attend the committees like to believe that this is where the main work of the conference takes place. Heads of state or government may make their speeches and these speeches may achieve a considerable echo in the outside world but they don't usually result in a change to texts under negotiation, whether through the removal of brackets or through the introduction of new material. Most conference organisers and habitues — and certainly the band of professional UN diplomats who had moved en masse from New York to Cairo — would hold up their hands in horror at such a thought. What on earth would happen, they protested, to their carefully crafted compromises if you let the politicians loose? The unwritten rule at all such meetings is that the politicians are only wheeled on when it is too late for them to do much damage.

At Cairo, there was also a substantive reason why population was effectively dropped from the population conference. That substantive reason had to do with the atmosphere of political correctness that was inevitably associated with the massive upgrading of women's issues that had occurred through the Cairo preparatory process and which, if you took account of what was happening at the NGO Forum as well as in the conference centre, continued throughout the conference. As indicated earlier, demographic targets were quite simply not the flavour of the month, year or decade. Female empowerment was. Even if the message from the NGO Forum and the women's caucus was not coming through loud and clear, there were enough "sisters" on the delegations to keep any troublesome delegates in line.

The third reason was of the intellectual nit-picking variety. Whereas Rafael Salas in his speech to the Mexico City Conference in 1984 had courageously proclaimed "our goal is the stabilisation of global population within the shortest period possible before the end of the next century", Nafis Sadik had urged that the conference adopt the goal of attaining the low variant population projection of 7.27 billion for the year 2015, and whereas the final draft before the conference still spoke (as an implied objective) in terms of achieving levels of world population growth "close to the United Nations low variant", paragraph 1.6 as it emerged from the "Friends of the Chair" dropped all reference to the low variant, referring only to levels "below the United Nations medium variant".

The full text of the preamble paragraph 1.6 as adopted read as follows:

> "1.4 During the remaining six years of this critical decade, the world's nations by their actions or inactions will choose from among a range of alternative demographic futures. The low, medium and high variants of the United Nations population projections for the coming 20 years range from a low of 7.1 billion people to the medium variant of 7.5 billion and a high of 7.8 billion. The difference of 720 million people in the short span of 20 years exceeds the current population of the African continent. Further into the future, the projections diverge even more significantly. By the year 2050, the United Nations projections range from 7.9 billion to the medium variant of 9.8 billion and a high of 11.9 billion. Implementation of the goals and objectives contained in the present 20-year Programme of Action, which address many of the fundamental population, health, education and development challenges facing the entire human community, would result in world population growth during this period and beyond at levels below the United Nations medium projection."

Paragraph 1.6 as adopted points out that the difference between the medium and the low variant is 400 million people over the next 20 years and almost two billion people by the year 2050. So this was far more than a drafting change. In so far as there were any global demographic objectives of a quantitative nature, they were to be found in this paragraph. As a result of a totally obscure process closed to any kind of public scrutiny, the objective such as it was had been transformed in a major way. There was all the difference in the world — almost two billion people's worth of difference — between the language contained in the January 1994 draft and repeated in the May 1994 draft and that which the conference finally adopted.

187

The most charitable explanation for the change, which seems to have been introduced on the wing in the "Friends of the Chair" group without any documented proposal or conference paper (certainly none which is traceable today), appears to be a concern among the academics present that, even with implementation of the Cairo programme as envisaged, it might be hard to hit the low target and therefore it was better to err on the side of caution.

This was one moment, of course, where caution was best thrown out of the window. What the Friends of the Chair needed at that moment was delegates who were ready not only to ensure that the reference to the low variant was retained but that all drafting ambiguities were removed in favour of a clear statement in favour of the low population projection target. A clear political statement of that nature could have helped generate the resources necessary to implement the Cairo programme, even to reinforce it, and thus it could have become a sort of self-fulfilling prophecy. If the participants in the friends of the chair group had spared the time to listen to some of the speeches in the plenary described above, they might have agreed to let boldness, rather than caution, be their friend.

If the objective of early population stabilisation at the global level was downgraded at Cairo, what about the national level? In the light of the powerful statements in the plenary about the need to bring down national population growth rates, was there any move to strengthen the language of paragraph 6.4, for example, as described above?

The answer to that is unfortunately no. As adopted by the Cairo conference, the language relating to national population programmes remained woolly and unconvincing. Moreover, paragraph 7.12 as adopted deliberately set out to downgrade national demographic goals in connection with family planning programmes by insisting that:

> "Governmental goals for family planning should be defined in terms of unmet needs for information and services. Demographic goals, while legitimately the subject of government development strategies, should not be imposed on family planning providers in the form of targets or quotas for the recruitment of clients."

In other words, at the national as at the global level, demographic impact in terms of births averted is to be seen as incidental to the main objective.

It remained to be seen to what extent the new paradigm, which effectively dethroned demographic objectives in favour of other social policy goals, would be capable of generating the resources necessary for the attainment of those goals. The importance of the "holistic approach" may now be well understood in UN circles, thanks in part at least to the

"Cairo process". But is it equally recognised in the chancelleries and finance ministries of the nation state?

One may plausibly argue that in demoting population stabilisation to an implicit rather than explicit goal (burying Malthus, as some have put it), the Cairo conference even in terms of its own "holistic" objectives took a step too far. No matter how dramatic and far-reaching the gender revolution may have been (and in some parts of the world, that revolution has certainly been less marked than in others), there are still hard-hearted men in suits out there who need to be convinced that the holistic approach, including as it does major spending on social programmes and social infrastructure, is going to give them real value for money. They do not need to believe, as President Lyndon Johnson reportedly believed, that family planning "gives the biggest bang for a buck". But they will certainly need to be persuaded that they are not pouring resources into a bottomless pit.

One must not, of course, exaggerate the problem. At the time of going to press, it seems clear that – at least as far as the international level is concerned – United Nations leaders have no intention of allowing the UN's specifically demographic objectives (as confirmed by numerous resolutions of the General Assembly and the Economic and Social Council) to be kicked into the long grass. As they see it, the focus of attention may have shifted but essentially the argument is about means, not ends.

Chapter 11

Resources

Chapter 13 of the Draft Programme of Action submitted to the Cairo Conference, on national policies and plans of action, called on countries to formulate and implement human resource development programmes in a manner that explicitly addressed the needs of population and development strategies, policies, plans and programmes. The chapter called for special consideration to be given to the basic education, training and employment of women at all levels, especially at decision-making and managerial levels, and to the incorporation of user and gender perspectives throughout the training programmes.

The proposals concerning resource mobilisation and allocation were heavily bracketed in regard to the estimates of funds needed as well as the methodology used to arrive at the funding levels required to meet the needs of developing countries and of countries with economies in transition in the period 2000–2015 in the following areas: family planning services; reproductive health services; prevention of sexually transmitted diseases, including HIV/AIDS; and population data collection, analysis and dissemination, policy formulation and research. The implementation of programmes in those four areas would cost, according to the draft programme, $17 billion in 2000, $18.5 billion in 2005, $20.5 billion in 2010 and $21.7 billion in 2015.

The chapter stated that domestic resource mobilisation was one of the highest priority areas for focused attention to ensure the timely action to meet the objectives of the conference's Programme of Action. It added that as countries were undergoing painful structural adjustments and experiencing recessionary trends in their economies, their domestic resource mobilisation efforts to implement the Programme of Action would need to be complemented by a significantly greater provision of financial and technical resources by the international community.

Chapter XIV dealt with international cooperation. Among recommendations relating to the aim of increasing the commitment to financial assistance in the population field, a bracketed provision called for avoiding possible reductions in other development areas. The estimates of financial resource needs from donors were also bracketed, as follows: $5.7 billion in 2000; $6.1 billion in 2005; $6.8 billion in 2010; and $7.2 billion in 2015. Also in brackets, donor countries and recipient governments were invited to devote at least 20 per cent of official development assistance (ODA) funds to the social sectors. This was colloquially referred to as the 20/20 proposal. Language on resource flows for population activities in countries with economies in transition, in other words the countries of Central and Eastern Europe, was also not agreed upon. The draft provision that countries in transition should receive temporary assistance in the light of the difficult problems they faced was hotly disputed by developing countries who, understandably, feared that new calls on scarce international resources would result in a smaller share of the cake for them. Also in brackets was a call for innovative financing, including new ways of generating funding resources, such as debt relief, including debt forgiveness in exchange for government investment in population and development programmes.

Addressing the responsibilities of partners in development, the draft stated that numerous experiences of cooperation among developing countries had dispelled the stereotyped view of donors being exclusively developed countries. Difficulties in the process of international cooperation included increasing pressure to decide among a multitude of competing development priorities, as well as a lack of adequate financial resources and effective coordination mechanisms. Among the actions called for were the transfer of technology to developing countries, including countries with economies in transition. The international community should promote a supportive economic environment by adopting favourable macroeconomic policies for promoting sustained economic growth and development.

The key paragraphs in the draft relating to the overall costs of the Cairo programme were 13.15 and 13.16:

> "13.15 It has been estimated that in the developing countries and countries with economies in transition, the implementation of programmes in the area of [reproductive health, including those related to family planning], maternal health and the prevention of

sexually transmitted diseases, as well as other basic actions for collecting and analysing population data, will cost: [$17.0 billion in 2000, $18.5 billion in 2005, $20.5 billion in 2010 and $21.7 billion in 2015]. Of this, approximately 65 per cent is for the delivery system. Programme costs in the closely related components which should be integrated into basic national programmes for population and reproductive health are estimated as follows:

(a) The family planning component is estimated to cost: [$10.2 billion in 2000, $11.5 billion in 2005, $12.6 billion in 2010 and $13.8 billion in 2015]. This estimate is based on census and survey data which help to project the number of couples and individuals who are likely to be using family planning information and services. Projections of future costs allow for improvements in quality of care. While improved quality of care will increase costs per user to some degree, these increases are likely to be offset by declining costs per user as both prevalence and programme efficiency increase.

(b) The [reproductive health] component [(not including the delivery-system costs, which are summarised under the [family planning] component)] is estimated to [add/cost:] [$5.0 billion in 2000, $5.4 billion in 2005, $5.7 billion in 2010 and $6.1 billion in 2015]. The estimate for reproductive health is a global total, based on experience with maternal health programmes in countries at different levels of development, selectively including other reproductive health services. The full maternal and child health impact of these interventions will depend on the provision of tertiary and emergency care, the costs of which should be met by overall health sector budgets.

(c) The sexually transmitted disease/HIV/AIDS prevention programme is estimated by the WHO Global Programme on AIDS to cost: $1.3 billion in 2000, $1.4 billion in 2005 and approximately $1.5 billion in 2010 and $1.5 billion in 2015.

(d) The basic research, data and population and development policy analysis programme is estimated to cost: [$500 million in 2000, $200 million in 2005, $700 million in 2010 and $300 million in 2015].

"13.16   It is tentatively estimated that up to two thirds of the costs will continue to be met by the countries themselves [and up to one third from external sources]. However, the least developed countries and other low-income developing countries will require a greater share of external resources on a concessional and grant basis. Thus, there will be considerable variation in needs for external resources for population programmes, between and within regions.

The estimated global requirements for international assistance were outlined in Chapter XIV, paragraph 14.11.

"14.11   The international community should strive for the fulfilment of the agreed target of 0.7 per cent of GNP for overall ODA and endeavour to increase the share of funding for population and development programmes commensurate with the scope and scale of activities required to achieve the objectives and goals of the present Programme of Action. A crucially urgent challenge to the international donor community is therefore the translation of their commitment to the objectives and quantitative goals of the present Programme of Action into commensurate financial contributions to population programmes in developing countries and countries with economies in transition. Given the magnitude of the financial resource needs for national population and development programmes [as identified in Chapter XIII], and assuming that recipient countries will be able to generate sufficient increases in domestically generated resources, the need for complementary resource flows from donor countries would be (in 1993 US dollars): [\$5.7 billion in 2000; \$6.1 billion in 2005; \$6.8 billion in 2010; and \$7.2 billion in 2015.] [Donor agencies and the recipient governments concerned are further invited to devote at least 20 per cent of ODA funds to the social sectors, including the requirements mentioned above, along with a similar level of domestic expenditure.]"

Paragraphs 14.14 and 14.15 of the draft contained bracketed references to countries with economies in transition. As noted above, this was a contentious issue and it had been contentious for some time. A row had already broken out in the April 1994 meeting of the Preparatory Committee, colourfully summarised in Thalif Deen's 22 April report to the InterPress Service (IPS).

"The world's 130 developing nations and the 50 newly independent countries of Eastern Europe and the former Soviet Union are engaged in a bruising political battle over a shrinking pie: international development assistance.

"The Russians, taking the lead on behalf of the ex-Soviets, are demanding that the 50 "economies in transition" be given the same status as the world's developing nations.

"But the Group of 77, which represents the 130, says the newly independent countries are not as poverty stricken as they claim to be and don't deserve equal treatment in international development assistance.

" 'They are trying to piggyback on us', a G-77 spokesman told IPS today, 'But we have made it clear that we will treat their pleas only on a case-by-case basis.'

" 'If they think they are part of the developing world, they should join the Group of 77. But on the contrary some of them are trying to join the rich man's club, the European Union. They can't have it both ways', he said."

Thalif Deen pointed out that the average per capita incomes of most developing nations ranged from \$400 to \$600 per year while Eastern

European countries such as Poland ($1800), Romania ($1340), Czech Republic ($2500) and Hungary ($2700) had four digit incomes.

At the Cairo conference itself, discussion as to how the countries of Central and Eastern Europe should be treated continued to spark heated debate. Finally, delegates agreed to: include a reference to this group of countries in 14.13 (the need for donor coordination); delete the reference in 14.14 (allocation of external financial resources); and remove the brackets from 14.15, which was amended to read: "Countries with economies in transition should receive temporary assistance for population and development activities .... "

On balance it was a victory for the G-77 group of countries. The spat over the "economies in transition" was symptomatic of a wider concern, namely whether adequate resources, national and international, would be available for the implementation of the Cairo programme.

At Cairo, there were two key questions to be answered. First, were the estimates in the draft programme accurate? Second, what proportion of the Cairo programme would be financed by the developing countries themselves and how much would be financed by the international community, or donor nations?

On the first point, the accuracy of the estimates, the *Earth Negotiations Bulletin reported:*

> "As at PrepCom III, delegates questioned and challenged the secretariat on the methodology used to derive the cost figures in paragraph 13.15, which deals with estimates and allocation of programme costs for four major components of basic reproductive health services: family planning, basic reproductive health services, sexually transmitted disease/HIV/AIDS prevention, and basic research, data and population and development policy analysis. After a lengthy debate in the Main Committee, interested delegates met and worked out a compromise. The chapeau now includes the following: 'These are estimates prepared by experts, based on experience to date of the four components referred to above. These estimates should be reviewed and updated on the basis of the comprehensive approach reflected in paragraph 13.14 of this Programme of Action, particularly with respect to the costs of implementing reproductive health service delivery.' "[1]

A more fundamental point was whether the estimates, limited as they were to the four major components of reproductive health services in fact covered the whole thrust of the Cairo programme. Critics focused in particular on the fact that the estimates failed to include resources for the education of girls, a key element in the programme.

According to Lewis T Preston, the President of the World Bank who addressed the plenary on 6 September:

"Raising girls' primary school enrolment rates to equal boys' would cost just under $1 billion (annually) — or only 2 per cent of annual education spending by the developing world."

And the women's groups, in particular, argued that other costs — involved in empowering women and improving their opportunities — had not been factored in to the totals "approved" by the conference.

As to the question of how the financial burden was to be split between rich and poor countries, delegates agreed finally on the phrase in paragraph 13.16 "and in the order of one-third from external sources", the subtle change being the replacement of "up to" by the words "in the order of". In practice it was recognised that there were some areas, including possibly the whole of sub-Saharan Africa, where finding one-third of the cost of the Cairo programme would be difficult if not impossible and where increased international funding would be required.

Draft paragraph 13.23 (like paragraph 14.11 cited above) contained a reference to the 20/20 proposal.

"13.23 Governments, non-governmental organisations, the private sector and local communities, assisted upon request by the international community, should strive to mobilise the resources to meet reinforcing social development goals, and in particular to satisfy the commitments governments have undertaken previously with regard to Education for All (the Jomtien Declaration), the multisectoral goals of the World Summit for Children, Agenda 21 and other relevant international agreements, and to further mobilise the resources to meet the goals in this Programme of Action. In this regard, governments are urged to devote [at least 20 per cent] [an increased proportion] of public sector expenditures to the social sectors, as well as [20 per cent] [an increased proportion] of official development assistance, stressing, in particular, poverty eradication within the context of sustainable development."

James Grant, Executive Director of UNICEF, speaking in Cairo on 5 September at the beginning of the conference, had claimed that most of the socio-economic ills in Third World countries could be resolved by restructuring North-South budgets in favour of increased spending on basic human services. He expected that the Cairo programme of action would be a landmark document underlining the fact that progress in stabilising global population could be achieved only if countries followed a holistic approach towards human development. "And 20/20 would be the means for funding this holistic strategy", he said.

Grant said that basic social services which warranted increased spending included health and nutrition, reproductive health and population, education, and water supply and sanitation. At a time of scarce resources, he said 20/20 was a means of ensuring that basic social services were provided to all those in need — particularly women and children.

Grant said the great majority of countries at the UN "have either supported the 20/20 concept or made it clear it was worthy of serious consideration".

A coalition of more than 100 North-South non-governmental organisations supported UNICEF's point of view. Indeed, they went further, urging that 50 per cent of resources — not 20 per cent — should be devoted to poverty alleviation and human development.

Another co-sponsor of the 20/20 proposal was the United Nations Development Programme. UNDP Administrator James Gustave Speth said the 20/20 proposal was one of the answers — or perhaps the only answer — to declining development aid and shrinking financial resources world-wide.

Speth said developing nations devoted only 13 per cent annually (about $57 billion) for human priority concerns. The proposed hike to 20 per cent would result in $88 billion being made available for human development. Donor nations now devoted only 7.0 per cent of aid budgets annually for human priority concerns. The proposed increase to 20 per cent would push total spending to about $12 billion.

Speth said the increase would generate about $30 to $40 billion of additional investments in critical human development areas. "This is not new money. This is more efficient spending of existing funds", Speth said.

One practical example of what Speth meant was provided by Bradman Weerakoon of Sri Lanka in his speech to the conference. A former Secretary General of the International Planned Parenthood Federation and now Presidential Adviser on International Affairs, Weerakoon said:

> "As a result of enlightened social and economic policies, Sri Lanka has reached the final stage of its demographic transition. The annual rate of population growth has come down to 1.2 per cent; the total fertility rate is 2.2, and the life expectancy for women is almost 75 years. In spite of a modest per capita income of around $550, Sri Lanka has achieved such progress through the people's participation in decision-making and a receptive political leadership and the resulting allocation of resources to human development. Education and health receive heavy investment. Literacy rates for men and women have reached around 90 per cent. Health investment has achieved an infant mortality rate of 19.4 per 1000 live births and a maternal mortality rate of 40 per 100,000 — one of the lowest in the region. Effective family-planning services have contributed to contraceptive use by 66 per cent of married women in the reproductive age group."

In spite of the stature and clout of its supporters, the 20/20 initiative received a cautious welcome from the developing countries. The 130-member Group of 77 — the Third World caucus at the United Nations — announced that "for such an expenditure (20/20) to be sustained over a period of time, it is essential for the economy to grow and generate the necessary surplus".

Without rejecting the concept outright, the G-77 was firmly of the view that each country had the sovereign right "to evaluate and decide for itself the appropriate incremental levels of expenditure in this (social) sector".

The donor nations were similarly cautious. ENB summarised the debate which took place in the Main Committee in its usual pithy manner.

> "In paragraph 13.23, Senegal, supported by Zimbabwe, Mali and others, proposed an amendment where governments would devote at least 20 per cent of public sector expenditures to the social sectors, and 20 per cent of official development assistance, stressing poverty eradication. Algeria noted that the G-77 did not have a position on this concept — known as the 20/20 Initiative — pending the outcome of discussions at the forthcoming World Summit for Social Development. Sweden highlighted its commitment to social development assistance, but pointed out that adoption of the 20/20 Initiative would require increased understanding. Germany, on behalf of the EU, supported by Japan and others, preferred to use the phrase "an increased proportion" rather than endorsing the 20/20 Initiative. Delegates finally reached a compromise, which was part of a package deal with paragraph 14.11: "In this regard, governments are urged to devote an increased proportion of public sector expenditures to the social sectors, as well as an increased proportion of official development assistance.""

The final text of paragraph 13.23 as adopted read as follows:

> "13.23 Governments, non-governmental organisations, the private sector and local communities, assisted upon request by the international community, should strive to mobilise the resources needed to reinforce social development goals, and in particular to satisfy the commitments Governments have undertaken previously with regard to Education for All (the Jomtien Declaration), the multisectoral goals of the World Summit for Children, Agenda 21 and other relevant international agreements, and to further mobilise the resources needed to meet the goals in the present Programme of Action. In this regard, governments are urged to devote an increased proportion of public-sector expenditures to the social sectors, as well as an increased proportion of official development assistance, stressing, in particular, poverty eradication within the context of sustainable development."

And in 14.11 the bracketed reference to the 20/20 initiative was replaced with the following (painfully) agreed text:

> "The international community takes note of the initiative to mobilise resources to give all people access to basic social services, known as the 20/20 Initiative, which will be studied further within the World Summit for Social Development."

This last amendment was of course a classic example of the "quick side-step and kick for touch" technique perfected by able Western diplomats when confronted with unpalatable demands. In Copenhagen in March 1995, at the Social Summit, a new furore broke out over the 20/20 initiative but, predictably, clear commitments were once again shelved in favour of "compromise language".

DIFFERING PRIORITIES

Leaving aside the 20/20 initiative which admittedly had wide implications for both donor and recipient nations, it is obvious that the financial texts agreed at Cairo were less than watertight. They did not lay down clear binding obligations on nations to put up the whole of the amounts required to implement the Cairo programme.

It was clear that for some countries domestic resources rather than external aid would continue to cover by far the largest proportion of population spending, far greater than the two-thirds figure envisaged as a rough guide in the Cairo programme. An inspiring speech made by Peng Peiyun, Head of the Chinese Delegation, State Councillor and Minister of the State Family Planning Commission of China, made it clear that China's family planning programme would continue to be allocated resources on a priority basis.

> "While concentrating on developing the national economy, the Chinese Government has set family planning and environment protection as two fundamental national policies and has incorporated them into the overall national planning for economic and social development. In implementing population and family planning programs, the Chinese Government has been adhering to the principal of combining government guidance and voluntariness of the people."

Whether the Chinese interpretation of "voluntariness" was precisely the same as that of other delegations was a moot point. In Cairo, there were no direct frontal attacks on China's family planning policies as there had been in Mexico City a decade earlier. On the contrary, there was a general sense that China was the most important player in the population game and that much of the progress over the last three decades, at least as far as the global figures were concerned, was closely correlated with developments in China since China, with 1185 million people at the end of 1993, still accounted for such a large proportion of the world's population.

China spent about 1.1 billion dollars annually, or about one dollar per head, on its family planning programmes. But most of the resources came from the national budget, with only about 15 million dollars in the form of international assistance. Assistance from outside had come primarily from the UN Population Fund (UNFPA), the International Planned Parenthood Federation, the World Health Organisation, the Japan Organisation for International Cooperation in Family Planning, the Rockefeller Foundation, and the Ford Foundation.

Other developing countries besides China — Korea, India, Indonesia, Sri Lanka, Thailand, for example — stressed the high priority that their own domestic budgets accorded to population and family planning programmes. Some recognised that the ability to fund population programmes itself depended on the successful management of the economy. A few made the connection between democratic processes with an emphasis on individual rights, including the empowerment of women, and a nation's economic vitality.

Realistically, though, for many developing countries — especially those of sub-Saharan African — the question of whether external resources would be available was a dominant consideration. External resources might make the difference between a successful programme and no programme at all.

"We simply lack the resources to solve our own problems", Prince Mbilini, Prime Minister of the southern African nation of Swaziland, told the conference on the opening day.

The Economic Commission for Africa and the Organisation of African Unity stated that if any programmes were to work on their continent, it would be necessary for the industrialised world to cover at least half the costs.

Seen in this perspective, the commitment of donors to supporting the Cairo programme was essential. Indeed, without such commitment, the Cairo programme, as Nafis Sadik so cogently put it, could indeed amount to little more than a "paper promise".

The Cairo conference itself was not designed to be the occasion for firm bankable pledges to be made about future spending. It was not a "pledging conference" in the sense that term was used by UN organisations such as UNDP anxious to tap the generosity of donors in an organised recordable fashion. There were none the less some encouraging signs that real external resources would be forthcoming in support of the Cairo programme.

Japan's Minister for Foreign Affairs, Yohei Kono, in his speech to the plenary on 6 September announced that Japan would contribute $US 3 billion over the seven years 1994 to 2000 and he referred at the same time to a US commitment, already discussed with Japan, to provide $US 9 billion during this period.

The United States, the biggest donor to population programmes, clarified that it would devote $595 million in the fiscal year 1995 to such programmes (double the 1992 amount), a figure that was to increase substantially toward 2000. Roughly half of US aid for population programmes was spent in government-to-government aid programmes. About $60 million was earmarked for the purchase of American contraceptives for use in the programmes. Some $50 million was channelled through the United Nations Fund for Population Activities. And the rest was used to support projects run by private organisations.

The World Bank announced that it was currently spending $200 million a year on family planning and reproductive health services and that it planned to increase the amount by 50 per cent over the next three years and spend more on population assistance.

Germany announced that it would spend $2 billion over the next seven years. And the United Kingdom announced that it would spend more than £100 million over the next two years, an increase of 60 per cent.

All this was a good start. It remained to be seen whether over the coming months, the pledges would be made good with hard cash and whether other pledges and contributions would be made to bring up the total of external funding to the levels envisaged.

Not all external funding, actual or pledged, would be on a North-South basis. Paragraphs 14.10 and 14.16 as proposed and adopted called for increased financial assistance to direct South-South cooperation. There were already some practical examples of this. In his speech to the conference, Indonesia's ebullient Minister of Population, Haryono Suyono, noted his country's success in reducing fertility, and said it was already engaged in cooperating on population with other developing countries. As current chair of the Non-Aligned Movement, Indonesia had initiated a unique South-South initiative called "Partners in Population and Development". Under the programme, it was inviting some 2000 persons from 75 countries to examine the country's population experience.

"We emphasise the importance of sharing and not preaching to others on how to get things done. We share both our strengths and weaknesses", Haryono said.

Sri Lanka, too, offered to share its running of effective population programmes with other developing countries. However, given the pressures experienced by most of the developing nations, it seemed unlikely — at least in the short term — that South-South cooperation could replace North-South cooperation to any major extent.

Chapter 12
Closing Session – Looking Ahead

On Tuesday, 13 September, the plenary adopted the report of the conference's Credentials Committee and authorised the Rapporteur General of the conference, Peeter Olesk, Minister for Culture and Education of Estonia, to complete the Report of the Conference and submit it to the UN General Assembly.

The plenary then considered the report of the Main Committee, consisting of the Programme of Action (documents A/CONF.171/L.3 and Adds. 1 to 17). The process involved formal adoption of each chapter. Chapters I, III, VI, and IX through XVI were adopted without reservations. One or more countries voiced reservations on some parts of the other five chapters. Some of those reservations, for examples those relating to Chapters VII and VIII, have been mentioned in previous chapters.

For the waiting world, of course, the key question was whether there would be negative votes when the moment came to adopt the resolution approving the programme as a whole. At the fourteenth plenary meeting, on 13 September, Algeria, on behalf of the G-77 group of developing countries and China, introduced document A/CONF.171/L.5 calling for adoption of the Programme of Action and recommending that the General Assembly endorse the programme and consider the synthesis of national reports on population and development prepared by the conference secretariat.

Before the adoption of the draft resolution, statements were made by the representatives of Argentina, the Dominican Republic, the United Arab Emirates, the Holy See, Nicaragua, Belize, Honduras, Malaysia, El Salvador, Guatemala, Chile, Venezuela, Costa Rica, Paraguay, Pakistan,

Tuvalu, the Libyan Arab Jamahiriya, Guinea, Turkey, Brunei Darussalam, Zambia, Côte d'Ivoire and Cameroon.

The official record of the conference records oral statements and reservations on parts of the Programme of Action from Afghanistan, Brunei Darussalam, El Salvador, Honduras, Jordan, Kuwait, Libya, Nicaragua, Paraguay, the Philippines, Syria, United Arab Emirates, and Yemen. Written reservations on parts of the programme were submitted by Argentina, Djibouti, the Dominican Republic, Ecuador, Guatemala, the Holy See, Malta and Peru.

Notwithstanding the length of the above list, the significant fact was that no voices were raised against the programme as a whole. The fact that the Holy See, rather than disassociating itself from the whole of the programme, limited its reservations merely to parts of the programme was regarded as a considerable triumph. To many it seemed that the Vatican's guns, which had thundered so loudly in August, had by mid-September been reduced to a stutter. Indeed, the text of the Holy See's written statement as submitted seemed curiously emollient, given all that had gone before.

The representative of the Holy See stated:

"As you well know, the Holy See could not find its way to join the consensus of the conferences of Bucharest and Mexico City, because of some fundamental reservations. Yet, now in Cairo for the first time, development has been linked to population as a major issue of reflection. The current Programme of Action, however, opens out some new paths concerning the future of population policy. The document is notable for its affirmations against all forms of coercion in population policies. Clearly elaborated principles, based on the most important documents of the international community, clarify and enlighten the later chapters. The document recognises the protection and support required by the basic unit of society, the family founded on marriage. Women's advancement and the improvement of women's status, through education and better health care services, are stressed. Migration, the all too often forgotten sector of population policy has been examined. The conference has given clear indications of the concern that exists in the entire international community about threats to women's health. There is an appeal to greater respect for religious and cultural beliefs of persons and communities."

After the good news, came the bad news.

"But there are other aspects of the final document which the Holy See cannot support. Together with so many people around the world, the Holy See affirms that human life begins at the moment of conception. That life must be defended and protected. The Holy See can therefore never condone abortion or policies which favour abortion. The final document, as opposed to the earlier documents of the Bucharest and Mexico City conferences, recognises abortion as a dimension of population policy and, indeed of primary health care, even though it does stress that abortion should not be promoted as means of family planning and urges nations to find alternatives to abortion. The preamble implies that the document does not contain the affirmation of a new internationally recognised right to abortion."

The Holy See indicated that while it was able to join the consensus in respect of Chapters II, III, IV, V, IX and X, it would not join in the consensus on Chapters VII, VIII and XII to XVI.

On Chapters VII and VIII, which had been the subject of so much heated debate, the Holy See said:

"Since the approval of Chapters VII and VIII in the Committee of the Whole, it has been possible to evaluate the significance of these chapters within the entire document, and also within health care policy in general. The intense negotiations of these days have resulted in the presentation of a text which all recognise as improved, but about which the Holy See still has grave concerns. At the moment of their adoption by consensus by the Main Committee, my delegation already noted its concerns about the question of abortion. The chapters also contain references which could be seen as accepting extramarital sexual activity, especially among adolescents. They would seem to assert that abortion services belong within primary health care as a method of choice.

"Despite the many positive aspects of Chapters VII and VIII, the text that has been presented to us has many broader implications, which has led the Holy See to decide not to join the consensus on these chapters. This does not exclude the fact that the Holy See supports a concept of reproductive health as a holistic concept for the promotion of the health of men and women and will continue to work, along with others, towards the evolution of a more precise definition of this and other terms.

"The intention therefore of my delegation is to associate itself with this consensus in a partial manner compatible with its own position, without hindering the consensus among other nations, but also without prejudicing its own position with regard to some sections.

"Nothing that the Holy See has done in this consensus process should be understood or interpreted as an endorsement of concepts it cannot support for moral reasons. Especially, nothing is to be understood to imply that the Holy See endorses abortion or has in any way changed its moral position concerning abortion or on contraceptives or sterilisation or on the use of condoms in HIV/AIDS prevention programmes."

When all the statements and reservations had been made, the Programme of Action was adopted by acclamation, as delegates applauded. Several more countries then made closing statements.

Next, the conference formally thanked the government and people of Egypt for their hospitality. In turn, Amr Moussa, Minister of Foreign Affairs of Egypt, congratulated delegates on their agreement.

In her concluding statement, Nafis Sadik praised participants for overcoming their differences to produce a "historic" Programme of Action which "places women and men, and their families, at the top of the international development agenda". She added, "Without resources, however, the Programme of Action will remain a paper promise".

"Compared with any earlier document on population and development", she stated, "this programme is detailed in its analysis, specific in its objectives, precise in its recommendations and transparent in its methodology. In our field it represents a quantum leap to a higher state of energy. Thanks to the media, it has already drawn the interest of people world-wide."

Because she summarised with commendable clarity, the events of the previous ten days, we include here some substantial excerpts from Dr Nafis Sadik's speech:

"This has been an outstandingly successful conference. President Mubarak told us that it should be a bridge between North and South, East and West; and you have made it so. It was attended by 183 countries and addressed by 249 speakers. Altogether, 10,757 people took part ..."

"The Secretary General of the United Nations said you should seek consensus in a spirit of rigor, tolerance and conscience. That describes very well the process of the last ten days ..."

"You have crafted a Programme of Action for the next 20 years that starts from the reality of the world we live in, and shows us the path to a better reality ..."

"This Programme of Action has the potential to change the world."

"Nothing in the Programme of Action limits the freedom of nations to act individually within the bounds of their laws and cultures ..."

"You have demonstrated once more the value of the United Nations process of consensus-building .... In the end, this apparently divisive process, this activity of chopping up sentences and stitching them together again, draws us closer together. Our chopping and stitching has produced a coat of many colours; but it is a garment that will fit us all ..."

"The Programme of Action you are about to adopt puts people first. Energetic and committed implementation of the Programme of Action over the next 20 years: will bring women at last into the mainstream of development; it will protect their health, promote their education, and encourage and reward their economic contribution; will ensure that every pregnancy is intended, and every child is a wanted child; will protect women from the results of unsafe abortion; will protect the health of adolescents, and encourage responsible behaviour; will combat HIV/AIDS; will promote education for all and close the gender gap in education; will protect and promote the integrity of the family ...

"You have spent a long time discussing how the Programme of Action should deal with abortion. I think your conclusion is highly satisfactory. It fulfils the original intention of concentrating on unsafe abortion as a serious and preventable health problem. Abortion is not a means of family planning. There will be fewer abortions in future, because there will be less need for abortion ..."

"You have recognised that poverty is the most formidable enemy of choice .... Without resources however, the Programme of Action will remain a paper promise. We need a commitment from all countries, industrialised countries as well as developing countries, that they will take their full responsibility in this regard ..."

"It is important to remember that the Programme of Action does not stand on its own ..."

"Excellencies, honourable delegates, practical implementation now depends on you ... . You should not be modest about your achievements. Compared with any earlier document on population and development, this Programme of Action is detailed in its analysis; specific in its objectives; precise in its recommendations and transparent in its methodology. In our field it represents a quantum leap to a higher state of energy ... . The Programme of Action deserves your highest commitment and your full-hearted support. You have produced a document you can be proud of. I wish you the greatest success in its implementation."

Delegates gave her a standing ovation when she finished.

Dr Mahran, Egypt's Minister for Population, closed the conference with a statement hailing the conference for the "cooperative spirit" which made it possible to reach agreement "while respecting the diversity of viewpoints".

An article in *Earth Times*, a newspaper which had been produced for delegates and others throughout the conference, summed things up on the last day. The article, by Vir Singh, was entitled: "What really happened at Cairo?"

"When Maher Mahran banged down his gavel Tuesday at the Cairo International Conference Centre, he ended not only the 1994

205

International Conference on Population and Development but also more than three years of rigorous and often disputatious preparations.

"So what did Cairo achieve? To assess the conference, one must first look at the various Preparatory Committee meetings, where participants addressed a variety of issues. The range of the agenda — spanning nutrition, child survival, women's health, gender inequalities, environmental sustainability and much more — indicates the complexity of the links between population and development. More than that, it suggests that examining this relationship means adopting a special solution-oriented perspective on almost all of the world's problems.

"It is hardly surprising, then, that ambassadors of almost every cause flocked to Cairo to offer or impose their perspectives. Barring abortion, the long, drawn-out redrafting of the document was a product mainly of concerns over interpretation and clarification.

"Many delegates said the document already was a success, noting that during the PrepComs, participants had agreed on a large part of it. One NGO delegate noted 'major' changes in the document by PrepCom III, held last March, mostly due to NGO lobbying. Many countries invited NGO members to join their official delegations. Others chose not to involve their NGOs, many of whom then took their grievances to the world press. Time and again, delegates and UN officials praised NGOs for highlighting population and development in the context of women's needs and women's rights, although the document does not mention 'rights'. NGOs, aware of their growing strength, are already planning for next year's World Summit for Social Development in Copenhagen and the Global Conference on Women in Beijing.

"The main theme of the Cairo document — the empowerment of women — calls for profound changes in many societies. Many talked of boycotting Cairo. Some did. But in the end, more than 180 countries attended. Even Iran, which still has strong reservations over the implicit acceptance of sex before marriage, decided to attend, to join other objectors in 'blocking the weak parts of the document'. It could have joined the boycott by some other Islamic states, but chose instead to address the issues at an international forum.

"The abortion controversy may have dominated media coverage, but most delegates worked hard to highlight implementation issues, especially funding. Donor commitments became a major theme, prompting questions at almost every press conference. Delegates were asked: why will things be different this time? By endorsing the Cairo document, donors have publicly stated their commitment; the goal is to increase annual population spending to $17 billion by the end of the century, or three times the current expenditure. In the future, NGOs and other governments can use the document to pressure them to come up with the money. Conversely, developing countries also must implement the programme or risk criticism for reneging on their pledge.

"Money aside, 'one of the greatest gains from the Cairo process may be the whole new orientation of population aid', a NGO delegate said. NGOs, especially women's groups, emphasised funding not just for family planning; meaning sterilisation, contraception and other measures aimed at demographic targets — but also at narrowing the gender gap in nutrition and education, child survival programmes and providing health care to women beyond their reproductive years. Major donors constantly stressed the equal importance of these programmes.

"Doubtless, they will take this strong message home. But some African delegates complained that the conference did not sufficiently address development. Why, they asked, will donors come up with money if they don't fully understand the problems? Referring to those who had not yet embraced sexual health and reproductive rights, a delegate told reporters that 'the train had already left the station'."

THE 49TH GENERAL ASSEMBLY

The Cairo conference had its origin, as we have seen, in a resolution of the General Assembly. It is fitting to end this account of the conference by summarising the debate which took place in the General Assembly in October, 1994, a few weeks after the end of the conference. The item relating to the conference was considered during the recent general debate at the start of the Assembly's forty-ninth session. Many countries referred to the objectives and outcome of ICPD. Some examples follow:

Norway said ICPD "will be looked upon as a turning point in the history of population policy as it relates to social development and women's rights. The conclusion will have wide-ranging impact on democracy-building, educational policies, health-care programmes and the status of women."

Mozambique called ICPD a landmark event in the effort to address population in the context of sustainable development and said that its Programme of Action responds to the challenges ahead.

The Netherlands termed ICPD a "success . . . built on a formula which essentially amounted to common decency; to face the population problem not through coercion and discrimination, but by giving people the means to follow the path of their own choice, freely and responsibly."

A number of statements praised ICPD's emphasis on empowering women. Barbados said ICPD "spoke volumes about the changing nature of international dialogue, and the changing role of women". The Commonwealth of Dominica stressed the ICPD consensus that "sustainable development cannot be realised without the full engagement and complete empowerment of women".

Nepal expressed satisfaction with ICPD's "focus given to the empowerment of women in decision-making, especially in planning the size of a family"; but it also voiced concern about increased costs of population activities at a time when developing countries face "severe resource constraints".

Canada emphasised the urgent need to cope effectively with population and development problems, "giving full recognition to the essential role of women. Our ability to translate into reality the concept of sustainable development will have a direct impact on the daily lives of our fellow citizens". Spain stated that the ICPD Programme of Action "paves the way for a new demographic policy and places women at the heart of every population policy".

The Solomon Islands called education "a priority sector", key to effective management of natural resources as well as "a means of advancing women to take their rightful place in society. There is a direct link between the education of women and population".

Several speakers including Cyprus praised the ICPD Programme of Action's integrated approach to population, environmental protection and economic growth. Hungary said ICPD had raised awareness of sustainable development issues "at a time when contrasts between requirements of human development and limited resources become more and more evident".

The Federated States of Micronesia said the international community "faces a massive sense of urgency and obligation to radically reform and redirect its role and resources to address population growth and sustainable resource use". Jamaica called the Programme of Action "a landmark document highlighting the inextricable linkage between population, sustained economic growth and sustainable development".

Saint Kitts and Nevis said that while it supported the need to address population issues, "a concerted attempt to redeploy much of the world's resources, to discover new resources and use them more equitably would better serve the interest of development for all people". Gambia cited the correlation between desertification and rapid population growth and said that ICPD "demonstrated the importance of population policy as an essential ingredient of social and economic development planning".

Sweden said that ICPD and other conferences "contribute to the achievement of human security in a broader sense. The Cairo conference established that questions of population and development must be treated together. The starting point must be the human being and the rights and security of the individual."

Grenada said that after ICPD it was "hopeful that increasingly balanced development will be viewed as the essential basis on which to treat the issue of population".

Many countries noted the continuity among the 1990 World Summit for Children, the 1992 UN Conference on Environment and Development, ICPD, and the World Summit for Social Development in Copenhagen and the Fourth World Conference on Women in Beijing next year. Armenia said they all were "key events for international consensus building".

Suriname said that ICPD, along with the Conference on Women and the Social Summit, "should afford to us all the opportunity to address in an integrated manner the issues of poverty, unemployment and social integration". Namibia spoke of the linkage among the Cairo, Copenhagen and Beijing conferences and the need for "greater and systematic coordination ... to ensure economy and efficiency".

Iceland stated that with the focus of ICPD and the Social Summit on women's issues, "we must once again realise that women share much of the burden in a family and society". Burkina Faso referred to the need for "new and additional resources" to carry out the decisions of ICPD, adding that the Fourth World Conference on Women should "continue the in-depth work initiated in Cairo ... under the theme that the woman is the best link to development".

Germany said ICPD reflected a "growing recognition that we must tackle global problems together". Slovakia said that the fact that ICPD succeeded in reaching agreement and adopted the Programme of Action "is a signal that the international community is aware of its responsibility for global issues of humanity". Kenya said that ICPD "clearly underlines the resolve of the international community to coordinate actions and strategies on social development as envisaged in the UN Charter".

Slovenia observed that ICPD had contributed significantly towards "a global consensus" on fundamental problems, and had "involved a whole new constituency". Cameroon welcomed the Programme of Action's focus on humans in all their diversity — religious, cultural and social.

El Salvador stressed the need for reforms and increased investments in health and education sectors, which would result in lower infant mortality and illiteracy rates. Saint Vincent and the Grenadines said it hoped ICPD would contribute to greater understanding of problems developing countries face and help create a global consensus and mobilise adequate resources to address those problems effectively.

Cuba said the ICPD debate regarding migration showed "the growing concerns of industrialised countries", pointing up the urgent need for action to promote development. The Philippines reiterated the call by many delegations at ICPD for a global conference on international migration and development.

St Lucia described ICPD as "a powerful initiative, however contentious some of the issues may have been". Paraguay pointed out that it had expressed two reservations when the ICPD Programme of Action was adopted.

The Marshall Islands praised ICPD's "expanded international population strategy", but voiced concern "that so much of the costs involved in the implementation of the Plan of Action will be borne by individual countries".

The forty-ninth session of the General Assembly concluded its deliberations on the ICPD by adopting, on 19 December 1995, a comprehensive resolution on the results of the conference. The resolution endorsed Cairo Programme of Action; affirmed that governments should commit themselves at the highest political level to achieving its goals and objectives; stressed the need for resources to be made available, both domestically and externally; renamed the UN's Population Commission — a body which had existed since 1946 — the Population and Development Commission and charged it with reviewing and assessing the implementation of the Cairo programme and reporting to the UN's Economic and Social Council. The full text of the General Assembly's resolution 49/128 is set out in Appendix B.

The terms of the GA resolution inevitably fail to catch the drama and the conflict of the Cairo meeting. UN resolutions are seldom entertaining or easy reading. And it is also true that many conferences which seem to the participants at the time, and even to outside observers, "pathbreaking" or "historic" or whatever, can come to seem but a few short months later fairly run-of-the-mill happenings, soon to be overtaken in the public mind by other more significant or at least more recent events.

Yet the International Conference on Population and Development which took place in Cairo in September 1994 does seem in its way to have been something special. More than 4000 print and electronic media representatives (that is journalists and so on) were accredited and attended the conference. Thousands of stories were filed and screened. More than 4200 individuals representing 1500 non-governmental organisations from 133 countries participated in the NGO forum and took their experiences back home with them at the end of the conference.[1] Though there is probably no sound polling data on the point, the likelihood is that the average man or woman in the street is more than vaguely aware that in Cairo, Egypt, in September 1994, as in Rio de Janeiro, Brazil, in June 1992, something quite significant happened.

Appendix A:

Summary of the Programme of Action of the International Conference on Population and Development

Contents

INTRODUCTION

The International Conference on Population and Development (ICPD) was held in Cairo, Egypt, from 5–13 September 1994. Delegations from 179 States took part in negotiations to finalise a Programme of Action in population and development for the next 20 years.

The 115-page document, adopted by acclamation on 13 September, endorses a new strategy which emphasises the numerous linkages between population and development and focuses on meeting the needs of individual women and men rather than on achieving demographic targets.

Key to this new approach is empowering women and providing them with more choices through expanded access to education and health services and promoting skill development and employment. The programme advocates making family planning universally available by 2015 or sooner as part of a broadened approach to reproductive health and rights, provides estimates of the levels of national resources and international assistance that will be required, and calls on governments to make these resources available.

The Programme of Action includes goals in regard to education, especially for girls, and for the further reduction of infant, child and maternal mortality levels. It also addresses issues relating to population, the environment and consumption patterns; the family; internal and international migration; prevention and control of the HIV/AIDS pandemic; information, education and communication; and technology, research and development.

After a week of intense negotiations, the conference reached general agreement on the Programme of Action. During the two final plenary meetings in which this agreement was reached, 13 countries (Afghanistan, Brunei Darussalam, El Salvador, Honduras, Jordan, Kuwait, Libyan Arab Jamahiriya, Nicaragua, Paraguay, the Philippines, Syrian Arab Republic, United Arab Emirates and Yemen) made statements expressing reservations or comments on specific chapters, paragraphs or phrases in the programme which they requested be recorded in the final report of the conference (A/CONF.171/13). Ten States (Argentina, Djibouti, the Dominican Republic, Ecuador, Egypt, Guatemala, the Holy See, Iran, Malta and Peru) submitted written statements for inclusion in the report.

ICPD was a United Nations conference, organised principally by the United Nations Population Fund (UNFPA) and the Population Division of the UN Department for Economic and Social Information and Policy Analysis.

The UN Economic and Social Council in 1991 explicitly linked population and development when it decided on the name of the ICPD. The same year, as preparations for the 1992 UN Conference on Environment and Development (UNCED) focused attention on how to achieve sustainable development, the first session of the ICPD Preparatory Committee resolved that population, sustained economic growth and sustainable development would be the themes of the Cairo conference.

The ICPD draft Programme of Action builds upon the World Population Plan of Action adopted at the 1974 World Population Conference in Bucharest, and the 88 recommendations for its further implementation approved at the International Conference on Population in Mexico City in 1984.

It also builds on UNCED's outcomes, Agenda 21 and the Rio Declaration, as well as on the agreement reached at the 1990 World Summit for Children and the 1993 World Conference on Human Rights. In turn, ICPD's emphasis on meeting people's needs and empowering women are influencing preparations for the World Summit for Social Development, the Fourth World Conference on Women, and the celebration of the United Nations' fiftieth anniversary, all scheduled to take place in 1995.

Of key importance in helping to shape the Programme of Action were the recommendations made at five regional population conferences (for Asia and the Pacific, Africa, Europe and North America, Latin America and the Caribbean, and the Arab States) in 1992 and 1993, and a number of subregional preparatory meetings; expert group meetings on six issues identified by ECOSOC as requiring the greatest attention; and a series of ad hoc round tables on other important conference themes. Important input also came from the second meeting of the Preparatory Committee, from discussion in the UN General Assembly in 1993, and from national population reports prepared in more than 140 countries.

At its forty-eighth session in 1993, the General Assembly (in resolution 48/186) strongly endorsed ICPD by deciding to make the Preparatory Committee a subsidiary body of the Assembly, giving ICPD a status comparable to that of UNCED. Debate in the General Assembly's Second Committee on a proposed annotated outline of the Programme of Action further guided the secretariat in preparing the draft final document for negotiation at the Preparatory Committee's third session (PrepCom III) in April 1994.

Delegations from 170 States took part in PrepCom III, held at UN headquarters in New York. Negotiation of the draft Programme of Action to be finalised in Cairo was the central activity.

The conference itself had 10,757 registered participants — from governments, intergovernmental organizations, UN programmes and specialised agencies, non-governmental organisations (NGOs) and the news media — and received an unprecedented level of press coverage. Dr Nafis Sadik, Executive Director of UNFPA, was Secretary General of ICPD. Egyptian President Mohamed Hosni Mubarak was President of the conference; Dr Maher Mahran, Minister of Population and Family Welfare of Egypt, was ex officio Vice Chairman. Dr Fred Sai of Ghana was Chairman of the Main Committee, which negotiated the final Programme of Action.

Some 249 speakers addressed the week-long plenary, including: UN Secretary General Boutros-Ghali; Prime Minister Benazir Bhutto of Pakistan; Prime Minister Gro Harlem Brundtland of Norway; Prime Minister Tamirat Layne of Ethiopia; Prime Minister George Cosmas Adyebo of Uganda; Prime Minister Francisque Ravony of Madagascar; Prince Mbilini, the Prime Minister of Swaziland; and Vice President Al Gore of the United States.

In addition, more than 4200 representatives of over 1500 non-governmental organisations from 133 countries attended the NGO Forum '94, an independent gathering held alongside the conference.

Other parallel activities were: the International Youth NGO Consultation on Population and Development, held from 31 August to 4 September and organised by nine youth and youth-related NGOs; the International Conference of Parliamentarians on Population and Development, held 3 and 4 September and organised by five international organisations of parliamentarians; and the 1994 Parliamentarians' Day assembly organised by the Inter-Parliamentary Union.

In addition, the Population Division's Population Information Network provided an electronic communication and reference centre at the conference site. Four independent daily newspapers on ICPD were produced in Cairo for distribution at the Conference. And the UN Department of Public Information and UNFPA co-sponsored a 3–4 September Encounter for Journalists on ICPD issues.

CHAPTER I: PREAMBLE

The Preamble provides an overview of the main issues covered in the ICPD Programme of Action and sets the context for action in the field of population and development. It stresses that the ICPD is not an isolated event and that its Programme of Action builds on the considerable international consensus that had developed since the World Population Conference in Bucharest in 1974 and the International Conference on Population at Mexico City in 1984.

The 1994 conference was explicitly given a broader mandate on development issues than previous population conferences, reflecting the growing awareness that population, poverty, patterns of production and consumption and the environment are so closely interconnected that none of them can be considered in isolation.

The Preamble points out that the ICPD follows and builds on other important recent international activities, and that its recommendations should be supportive of, consistent with and based on agreements reached at a series of earlier conferences. It further notes that the conference outcomes are closely related to and will make significant contributions to other major conferences in 1995 and 1996, such as the World Summit for Social Development, the Fourth World Conference on Women, the Second United Nations Conference on Human Settlements (Habitat II), the elaboration of the Agenda for Development, as well as the fiftieth anniversary of the United Nations.

The Preamble points out that the objectives and actions of the Programme of Action collectively address the critical challenges and interrelationships between population and sustained economic growth in the context of sustainable development. In order to do so, adequate mobilisation of resources at the national level will be required, as well as new and additional resources to the developing countries from all available funding mechanisms, including multilateral, bilateral and private sources. Financial resources are also required to strengthen the capacity of international institutions to implement the Programme of Action.

The Programme of Action recommends to the international community a set of important population and development objectives, including both qualitative and quantitative goals that are mutually supportive and are of critical importance to these objectives. Among these objectives and goals are: sustained economic growth in the context of sustainable development; education, especially for girls; gender equity and equality; infant, child and maternal mortality reduction; and the provision of universal access to reproductive health services, including family planning and sexual health.

The Programme of Action recognises that over the next 20 years governments are not expected to meet the goals and objectives of the ICPD single-handedly. All members of and groups in society have the right, and indeed the responsibility, to play an active part in efforts to reach those goals.

CHAPTER II: PRINCIPLES

The set of fifteen principles contained in this chapter provides a careful balance between the recognition of individual human rights and the right to development of nations. The wording of most principles is directly derived from agreed international language from relevant international declarations, conventions and covenants.

In the chapeau of this chapter, clear recognition is given to the fact that the implementation of the recommendations contained in the Programme of Action is the sovereign right of each country, consistent with its national laws and development priorities, with full respect for the various religious and ethical values and cultural backgrounds of its people, and in conformity with universally recognised international human rights. International cooperation and universal solidarity, guided by the principles of the United Nations Charter, and in a spirit of partnership, are regarded crucial in order to improve the quality of life of all people.

The Principles touch upon the main issues in the field of population and development, such as: gender equality and equity and the empowerment of women; the integration of population into sustainable development policies and programmes; poverty eradication; access to reproductive health care and family planning; the role of the family; the right to education; the situation of children; the rights of migrants and refugees; and the population and development needs of indigenous people.

The principles reaffirm that human beings are at the centre of concerns for sustainable development, since people are the most important and valuable resource of any nation. Consequently, the right to development must be fulfilled so as to equitably meet the population, development and environment needs of present and future generations. In addition, to achieve sustainable development and a higher quality of life for all people, States should reduce and eliminate unsustainable patterns of production and consumption and promote appropriate policies, including population-related policies.

According to the principles, advancing gender equality and equity and the empowerment of women, and the elimination of all kinds of violence against women, and ensuring women's ability to control their own fertility, are cornerstones of population and development-related programmes. In addition, states should take all appropriate measures to ensure, on a basis of equality of men and women, universal access to health-care services, including those related to reproductive health care, which includes family planning and sexual health. The principles reaffirm the basic right of all couples and individuals to decide freely and responsibly the number and spacing of their children and to have the information, education and means to do so.

The chapter emphasises that the family is the basic unit of society and as such should be strengthened. It also acknowledges that there are various forms of the family in different cultural, political and social systems.

CHAPTER III:
INTERRELATIONSHIPS BETWEEN POPULATION, SUSTAINED ECONOMIC GROWTH AND SUSTAINABLE DEVELOPMENT

A Integrating population and development strategies

There is general agreement that persistent widespread poverty as well as serious social and gender inequities have significant influences on, and are in turn influenced by, demographic factors such as population growth, structure and distribution. There is also general agreement that unsustainable consumption and production patterns are contributing to the unsustainable use of natural resources and to environmental degradation. Section A seeks to integrate population concerns fully into development strategies and into all aspects of development planning at all levels. The sustained economic growth that results will help meet the needs and improve the quality of life of present and future generations. It will also promote social justice and help eradicate poverty.

Governments should seek to strengthen political commitment to such integration in three ways: (a) by undertaking public education and information programmes; (b) by increasing resource allocations, in cooperation with NGOs and the private sector; and (c) by improving the knowledge base through research and national and local capacity-building. They should also reduce and eliminate unsustainable patterns of consumption and production and promote appropriate demographic policies.

B Population, sustained economic growth and poverty

Efforts to slow population growth, reduce poverty, achieve economic progress, improve environmental protection, and to reduce unsustainable consumption and production patterns are mutually reinforcing. Sustained economic growth within the context of sustainable development is essential to eradicate poverty. Eradicating poverty will contribute to slowing population growth and to achieving early population stabilisation. Women are generally the poorest of the poor. They are also key actors in the development process. Eliminating all forms of discrimination against women is thus a prerequisite for eradicating poverty, promoting sustained economic growth, ensuring quality family planning and reproductive health services, and achieving balance between population and available resources.

The aim of section B is to raise the quality of life for all people through population and development policies and programmes that seek to eradicate poverty, sustain economic growth in the context of sustainable development, achieve sustainable patterns of consumption and production, develop human resources, and guarantee all human rights, including the right to development.

Governments must give priority to investment in human resource development in their population and development strategies and budgets. Programmes should seek to increase people's access to information, education, skill development, employment opportunities, and high-quality general and reproductive health services, including family planning. Existing inequities and barriers to women's participation in all policy-making and policy implementation should be promoted and strengthened. So should their access to productive resources, their ability to own land, and their right to inherit property.

Governments should invest in, promote, monitor and evaluate the education and skill development of women and girls and the legal and economic rights of women. They should do likewise with all aspects of reproductive health, including family planning. The international community should continue to promote a supportive economic environment, particularly for developing countries and countries with economies in transition in their attempt to eradicate poverty and achieve sustained economic growth within the context of sustainable development.

C Population and environment

Meeting the basic needs of growing populations is dependent on a healthy environment. Such needs must be addressed when developing comprehensive policies for sustainable development. The aim of section C is two-fold: (a) to ensure that population, environmental and poverty-eradication factors are integrated into sustainable development policies, plans and programmes; and

(b) to reduce both unsustainable consumption and production patterns as well as negative impacts of demographic factors. Governments should formulate and implement population policies to support the objectives and actions agreed upon in Agenda 21, in the outcomes of other conferences and in other international environmental agreements.

In specific, Governments should: (a) integrate demographic factors into environment impact assessments and other planning and decision-making processes aimed at achieving sustainable development; (b) take measures aimed at eradicating poverty, giving special attention to income-generation and employment strategies directed at the rural poor and those living within or on the edge of fragile ecosystems; (c) use demographic data to promote sustainable resource management, especially of ecologically fragile systems; (d) modify unsustainable consumption and production patterns through economic, legislative and administrative measures aimed at fostering sustainable resource use and preventing environmental degradation; and (e) implement policies to address the ecological implications of inevitable future increases in population numbers and changes in population concentration and distribution, particularly in ecologically vulnerable areas and urban agglomerations.

CHAPTER IV:
GENDER EQUALITY, EQUITY AND EMPOWERMENT OF WOMEN

A Empowerment and status of women

The empowerment of women and improvement of their status is an important end in itself and is essential for the achievement of sustainable development. The objectives are: to achieve equality and equity between men and women and enable women to realise their full potential; to involve women fully in policy and decision-making processes and in all aspects of economic, political and cultural life as active decision-makers, participants and beneficiaries; and to ensure that all women, as well as men, receive the education required to meet their basic human needs and to exercise their human rights. Recommended actions include, among others, establishing mechanisms for women's equal participation and equitable representation at all levels of the political process and public life; promoting women's education, skill development and employment; and eliminating all practices that discriminate against women, including those in the workplace and those affecting access to credit, control over property and social security. Countries should take full measures to eliminate all forms of exploitation, abuse, harassment and violence against women, adolescents and girls. In addition, development interventions should take better account of the multiple demands on women's time, with greater investments made in measures to lessen the burden of domestic responsibilities, and with attention to laws, programmes and policies which will enable employees of both sexes to harmonise their family and work responsibilities.

B The girl child

The objectives are to eliminate all forms of discrimination against the girl child, to eliminate the root causes of son preference, to increase public awareness of the value of the girl child and to strengthen her self-esteem. To these ends, leaders at all levels of society should speak out and act forcefully against gender discrimination within the family, based on preference for sons. There should be special education and public information efforts to promote equal treatment of girls and boys with respect to nutrition, health care, education, and social, economic and political activity, as well as equitable inheritance. Governments should develop an integrated approach to the special health, education and social needs of girls and young women, and should strictly enforce laws to ensure that marriage is entered into only with the free and full consent of the intending spouses. Governments are urged to prohibit female genital mutilation and to prevent infanticide, prenatal sex selection, trafficking of girl children and use of girls in prostitution and pornography.

C Male responsibilities and participation

Men play a key role in bringing about gender equality since, in most societies, they exercise preponderant power in nearly every sphere of life. The objective is to promote gender equality and to encourage and enable men to take responsibility for their sexual and reproductive behaviour and their social and family roles. Governments should promote equal participation of women and men in all areas of family and household responsibilities including, among others, responsible parenthood, sexual and reproductive behaviour, prevention of sexually transmitted diseases, and shared control and contribution to family income and children's welfare. Governments should take steps to ensure that children receive appropriate financial support from their parents and should consider changes in law and policy to ensure men's support for their children and families. Parents and schools should ensure that attitudes that are respectful of women and girls as equals are instilled in boys from the earliest possible age.

CHAPTER V: THE FAMILY, ITS ROLES, RIGHTS, COMPOSITION AND STRUCTURE

The family is the basic unit of society. The process of rapid demographic and socio-economic change has influenced patterns of family formation and family life and has generated considerable change in the composition and structure of families. Traditional notions of parental and domestic functions do not reflect current realities and aspirations, as more and more women in all parts of the world take up paid employment outside the home. At the same time, various causes of displacement have placed greater strain on the family, as have social and economic changes.

The objectives are, inter alia: (a) to develop policies and laws that better support the family, contribute to its stability and take into account its plurality of forms, particularly the growing number of single-parent families; (b) to promote equality of opportunity for family members, especially the rights of women and children in the family; and (c) to ensure that all social and development policies provide support and protection for families and are fully responsive to the diverse and changing needs of families.

A   Diversity of family structure and composition

Governments are called upon to cooperate with employers to provide and promote means to make participation in the labour force more compatible with parental responsibilities, especially for single-parent households with young children. Governments should take effective action to eliminate all forms of coercion and discrimination in policies and practices.

B   Socio-economic support to the family

It is recommended that governments should formulate policies that are sensitive and supportive of the family and to develop, along with NGOs and concerned community organisations, innovative ways to provide more effective assistance to families and individuals within them who may be affected by such problems as extreme poverty, chronic unemployment, and domestic and sexual violence, among others.

CHAPTER VI: POPULATION GROWTH AND STRUCTURE

A   Fertility, mortality and population growth rates

The objective is to facilitate the demographic transition as soon as possible in countries where there is an imbalance between demographic rates and social, economic and environmental goals. This process will contribute to the stabilisation of the world population. Governments are urged to give greater attention to the importance of population trends for development. In attempting to address concerns with population growth, countries should recognize the interrelationships between fertility and mortality levels and aim to reduce high levels of infant, child and maternal mortality.

B   Children and youth

Attention is drawn to the major challenges created by the very large proportions of children and young people in the populations of a large number of developing countries. The aims are to promote the health, well-being and potential of all children, adolescents and youth; to meet their special needs, including social, family and community support, as well as access to education, employment, health, counselling and high-quality reproductive health services; and to encourage them to continue their education. Countries are urged to give high priority to the protection, survival and development of children and youth, and to make every effort to eliminate the adverse effects of poverty on children and youth. Countries are further called upon to enact and strictly enforce laws against economic exploitation and the physical and mental abuse or neglect of children. Countries are urged to create a socio-economic environment conducive to the elimination of all child marriages and should also discourage early marriage.

C   Elderly people

Governments are called upon to develop social security systems that ensure greater equity and solidarity between and within generations and that provide support to elderly people through encouragement of multigenerational families. Governments should also seek to enhance the self-reliance of elderly people so that they can lead healthy and productive lives and can benefit society by making full use of the skills and abilities they have acquired in their lives. Governments should strengthen formal and informal support systems and safety nets for elderly people and eliminate all forms of violence and discrimination against them.

D Indigenous people

Indigenous people have a distinct and important perspective on population and development relationships, frequently quite different from those of the populations with whom they interrelate within national borders. The specific needs of indigenous people, including primary health care and reproductive health services, should be recognised. In full collaboration with indigenous people, data on their demographic characteristics should be compiled and integrated into the national data-collection system. The cultures of indigenous people need to be respected. Indigenous people should be able to manage their lands and the natural resources and ecosystems upon which they depend should be protected and restored.

E Persons with disabilities

Although awareness has been raised about disability issues, there remains a pressing need for continued action to promote effective measures for prevention and rehabilitation of disabilities. Governments are called upon to develop the infrastructure to address the needs of persons with disabilities, in particular with regard to their education, training, and rehabilitation; to recognise their needs concerning, inter alia, reproductive health, including family planning and HIV/AIDS; and to eliminate specific forms of discrimination that persons with disabilities may face with regard to reproductive rights, household and family formation, and international migration.

CHAPTER VII: REPRODUCTIVE RIGHTS AND REPRODUCTIVE HEALTH

A Reproductive rights and reproductive health

Reproductive health is a state of complete physical, mental and social well-being in all matters relating to the reproductive system and to its functions and processes. It implies that people have the capability to reproduce and the freedom to decide if, when and how often to do so. Implicit in this is the right of men and women to be informed and to have access to safe, effective, affordable and acceptable methods of family planning of their choice, as well as other methods of their choice for regulation of fertility, which are not against the law, and the right of access to health care services that will enable women to go safely through pregnancy and childbirth. Reproductive health care also includes sexual health, the purpose of which is the enhancement of life and personal relations.

Reproductive rights embrace certain human rights that are already recognised in national laws, international human rights documents and other relevant UN consensus documents. These rights rest on the recognition of the basic right of all couples and individuals to decide freely and responsibly the number, spacing and timing of their children and to have the information and means to do so, and the right to attain the highest standard of sexual and reproductive health. It also includes the right of all to make decisions concerning reproduction free of discrimination, coercion and violence. Full attention should be given to promoting mutually respectful and equitable gender relations and particularly to meeting the educational and service needs of adolescents to enable them to deal in a positive and responsible way with their sexuality.

All countries are called upon to strive to make reproductive health accessible through the primary health-care system to all individuals of appropriate age as soon as possible and no later than 2105. Such care should include, inter alia: family planning counselling, information, education, communication and services; education and services for prenatal care, safe delivery and post-natal care, especially breast-feeding, infant and women's health care; prevention and treatment of infertility; abortion as specified in paragraph 8.25; treatment of reproductive tract infections, sexually transmitted diseases (STDs) and other reproductive health conditions; and information, education and counselling on human sexuality, reproductive health and responsible parenthood.

Reproductive health-care programmes should be designed to serve the needs of women, including adolescents, and must involve women in the leadership, planning, decision-making, management, implementation, organisation and evaluation of services. Innovative programmes must be developed to make information, counselling and services for reproductive health accessible to adolescents and adult men. Such programmes must both educate and enable men to share more equally in family planning, domestic and child-rearing responsibilities and to accept major responsibility for the prevention of STDs.

B Family planning

Actions are recommended to help couples and individuals meet their reproductive goals; to prevent unwanted pregnancies and reduce the incidence of high-risk pregnancies and morbidity and mortality; to make quality services affordable, acceptable and accessible to all who need and want them; to improve the quality of advice, information, education, communication, counselling and services; to increase the participation and sharing of responsibility of men in the actual practice of family planning; and to promote breast-feeding to enhance birth spacing. The text emphasises that governments and the international community should use the full means at their disposal to support the principle of voluntary choice in family planning. As part of the effort to meet unmet needs, all countries are asked to identify and remove all major remaining barriers to the use of family planning services. Governments are urged to provide a climate that is favourable to good-quality public and private family planning and reproductive health information and services through all possible channels. The international community is urged to move, on an immediate basis, to establish an efficient coordination system and global, regional and subregional facilities for the procurement of contraceptive and other commodities essential to reproductive health programmes of developing countries and countries with economies in transition.

C   STDs and HIV prevention

Section C recommends actions designed to prevent, reduce the incidence of, and provide treatment for STDs, including HIV/AIDS, and the complications of STDs such as infertility. Such actions include: increasing efforts in reproductive health programmes to prevent, detect and treat STDs and other reproductive tract infections; providing specialised training to all health-care providers in the prevention and detection of, and counselling on, STDs, especially infections in women and youth; making information, counselling for responsible sexual behaviour and effective prevention of STDs and HIV integral components of all reproductive and sexual health services; and promoting and distributing high-quality condoms as integral components of all reproductive health-care services.

D   Human sexuality and gender relations

The objective is two-fold: to promote the adequate development of responsible sexuality that permits relations of equity and mutual respect between the genders; and to ensure that women and men have access to information, education and services needed to achieve good sexual health and exercise their reproductive rights and responsibilities. Recommended actions include giving support to integral sexual education and services for young people, with the support and guidance of their parents and in line with the Convention on the Rights of the Child, that stress male responsibility for their own sexual health and fertility and that help them exercise those responsibilities. Educational efforts should begin within the family unit, but must also reach adults, in particular men, through non-formal education and a variety of community-based activities. Educational programmes should also encourage and support active and open discussion of the need to protect women, youth and children from abuse, including sexual abuse, exploitation, trafficking and violence. Governments and communities are advised to urgently take steps to stop the practice of female genital mutilation and protect women and girls from all similar unnecessary and dangerous practices.

E   Adolescents

Adolescent sexual and reproductive health issues, including unwanted pregnancy, unsafe abortion (as defined by WHO), and STDs and HIV/AIDS, are addressed through the promotion of responsible and healthy reproductive and sexual behaviour, including voluntary abstinence, and the provision of appropriate services and counselling specifically suitable for that age group. It also seeks to substantially reduce all adolescent pregnancies. The text stresses that countries must ensure that programmes and attitudes of health-care providers do not restrict adolescents' access to the services and information they need. These services must safeguard the right of adolescents to privacy, confidentiality, respect and informed consent, while respecting cultural values and religious beliefs as well as the rights, duties and responsibilities of parents. Countries, with the support of the international community, should protect and promote the rights of adolescents to reproductive health education, information and care, and greatly reduce the number of adolescent pregnancies. Governments are urged, in collaboration with NGOs, to establish appropriate mechanisms to respond to the special needs of adolescents.

223

CHAPTER VIII: HEALTH, MORBIDITY AND MORTALITY

A Primary health care and the health care sector

The increases in life expectancy recorded in most regions of the world in the past half century reflect significant gains in public health and in access to primary health care services. Notable achievements include the vaccination of children and widespread use of low-cost treatments such as oral rehydration therapy. Yet these achievements have not been realised in all countries, and preventable or treatable illnesses are still the leading killers of young children. Moreover, large segments of many populations remain at risk of infectious, parasitic, and water-borne diseases. Section A recommends actions to increase the accessibility, availability, acceptability and affordability of health-care services and facilities, and to increase the healthy life-span and improve the quality of life of all people, as well as to reduce the disparities in life expectancy between and within countries.

Section A stresses that all countries should make access to basic health care and health promotion the central strategies for reducing mortality and morbidity. Sufficient resources should be assigned so that primary health services cover the entire population. All countries should reduce mortality and morbidity and seek to make primary health care, including reproductive health care, universally available by the end of the current decade. Countries should aim to achieve by 2005 a life expectancy at birth greater than 70 years and by 2015 a life expectancy at birth greater than 75 years. Countries with the highest levels of mortality should aim to achieve by 2005 a life expectancy at birth greater than 65 years and by 2015 a life expectancy at birth greater than 70 years. Governments should ensure community participation in the planning of health policies, especially with respect to the long-term care of the elderly, those with disabilities and those infected with HIV and other endemic diseases. Access to health-care services for all people and especially for the most underserved and vulnerable groups must be ensured. Governments should seek to make basic health-care services more sustainable financially, while ensuring equitable access.

B Child survival and health

Important progress has been made in reducing infant and child mortality everywhere. However, the mortality of children under age 5 varies significantly between and within countries and regions. Poverty, malnutrition, a decline in breast-feeding, and inadequacy or lack of sanitation and of health facilities are all associated with high infant and child mortality. Child survival is closely linked to the timing, spacing and number of births and to the reproductive health of mothers. Early, late, numerous and closely spaced pregnancies are major contributors to high infant and child mortality and morbidity, especially where health-care facilities are scarce. Section B thus recommends actions to reduce the disparities in mortality rates between and within developed and developing countries, with particular attention to eliminating the pattern of excess and preventable mortality among girl infants and children. Also recommended are actions to improve the health and nutritional status of infants and children and promote breast-feeding as a child survival strategy.

Section B contains the following specific targets: Countries should strive to reduce their infant and under-5 mortality rates by one-third, or to 50 to 70 per

1000 live births, respectively, whichever is less, by the year 2000. By 2005, countries with intermediate levels should aim to achieve an infant mortality rate below 50 deaths per 1000 and an under-5 mortality rate below 60 deaths per 1000 births. By 2015, all countries should aim to achieve an infant mortality rate below 35 per 1000 live births and an under-5 mortality rate below 45 per 1000. Countries with indigenous people should achieve infant and under-5 mortality rates among their indigenous people that are the same as those of the general population.

Section B calls on all governments to assess the underlying causes of high child mortality and to extend, within the framework of primary health care, integrated reproductive health-care and child-health services, including safe motherhood (defined in a footnote), child-survival programmes and family planning services, to all the population and particularly to the most vulnerable and underserved groups. All countries should give high priority to efforts to reduce the major childhood diseases, particularly infectious and parasitic diseases, and to prevent malnutrition among children, especially the girl child.

C Women's health and safe motherhood

Complications related to pregnancy and childbirth are among the leading causes of mortality for women of reproductive age in many parts of the developing world. About half a million women die each year, 99 per cent of them in developing countries. The age at which women begin or stop child-bearing, the interval between each birth, the total number of lifetime pregnancies and the socio-cultural and economic circumstances in which women live all influence maternal morbidity and mortality. Although approximately 90 per cent of the countries of the world have policies that permit abortion under varying legal conditions to save the life of the mother, a significant proportion of the abortions carried out are self-induced or otherwise unsafe, leading to a large fraction of maternal deaths or to permanent injury to the women involved.

The objectives are: to promote women's health and safe motherhood; to achieve a rapid and substantial reduction in maternal morbidity and mortality and to reduce the difference between and within developed and developing countries; and, on the basis of a commitment to women's health and well-being, to reduce greatly the number of deaths and morbidity from unsafe abortion. Actions that improve the health and nutritional status of women, especially of pregnant and nursing women, were also recommended.

The document calls for a reduction in maternal mortality by one half of the 1990 levels by the year 2000 and a further half by 2015. Countries with intermediate levels of mortality should aim to achieve by the year 2005 a maternal mortality rate below 100 per 100,000 live births and by 2015 a rate below 60 per 100,000. Countries with the highest levels of mortality should aim to achieve by 2005 a maternal mortality rate below 125 per 100,000 live births and by 2015 a rate of below 75 per 100,000. All countries should reduce maternal morbidity and mortality to levels where they no longer constitute a public health problem. All countries are called upon, with the support from the international community, to expand the provision of maternal health services in the context of primary health care. All countries should also aim to further reduce maternal mortality through measures to prevent, detect and manage high-risk pregnancies and births, particularly those to adolescents and late-parity women. Programmes and education to engage men's support for maternal health and safe motherhood should be developed; all countries are urged to seek changes in high-risk sexual behaviour and to devise strategies to ensure that men share responsibility for sexual and reproductive health.

The full text of paragraph 8.25, dealing with abortion, reads as follows: "In no case should abortion be promoted as a method of family planning. All governments and relevant intergovernmental and non-governmental organisations are urged to strengthen their commitment to women's health, to deal with the health impact of unsafe abortion (defined in a footnote) as a major public health concern and to reduce the recourse to abortion through expanded and improved family planning services. Prevention of unwanted pregnancies must always be given the highest priority and all attempts should be made to eliminate the need for abortion. Women who have unwanted pregnancies should have ready access to reliable information and compassionate counselling. Any measures or changes related to abortion within the health system can only be determined at the national or local level according to the national legislative process. In circumstances in which abortion is not against the law, such abortion should be safe. In all cases, women should have access to quality services for the management of complications arising from abortion. Post-abortion counselling, education and family planning services should be offered promptly, which will also help to avoid repeat abortions."

D HIV/AIDS

The AIDS pandemic is a major concern in both developed and developing countries. As of mid-1993, about four-fifths of all persons ever infected with HIV lived in developing countries where the infection was being transmitted mainly through heterosexual intercourse and the number of cases was rising most rapidly among women. The main objectives in section D are to prevent, reduce the spread of, and minimise the impact of HIV infection, and to ensure that HIV-infected individuals have adequate medical care and are not discriminated against. A third objective is to intensify research on methods to control the HIV/AIDS pandemic and to find an effective treatment for the disease.

Section D calls on governments to mobilise all segments of society to control the AIDS pandemic and to give high priority to IEC campaigns in programmes to reduce the spread of HIV infection. Sex education and information should be provided to both those infected and those not infected, and especially to adolescents. Responsible sexual behaviour, including voluntary sexual abstinence, should be promoted and included in education and information programmes. Among the aims are to raise awareness and to emphasise behavioural change. The international community is called upon to mobilise the human and financial resources required to reduce the rate of transmission of HIV infection.

CHAPTER IX: POPULATION DISTRIBUTION, URBANISATION AND INTERNAL MIGRATION

A Population distribution and sustainable development

The process of urbanisation is intrinsic to economic and social development and, in consequence, both developed and developing countries are in the process of shifting from predominantly rural to predominantly urban societies.

The objective is to foster a more balanced distribution of population by promoting sustainable development in both major sending and receiving areas. Such development should be ecologically sound and promote economic, social and gender equity. A related aim is to reduce the various factors that push people to migrate. These include, among others, the inequitable allocation of development resources, the use of inappropriate technologies, and the lack of access to available land. Countries should adopt strategies that encourage the growth of small or medium-sized urban centres and seek to develop rural areas. In order to develop rural areas, governments should actively support access to landownership and to water resources, especially for family units and should also make or encourage investments for increased rural productivity.

B Large urban agglomerations

In many countries, a single city dominates the urban system. This poses specific economic, social and environmental challenges. But large urban agglomerations often also represent the most dynamic centres of economic and cultural activity. The objective is to help countries better manage these large urban agglomerations in order to improve the security and quality of life of both the rural and urban poor. The text calls on governments to increase the capacity and competence of city and municipal authorities to manage urban development and to respond to the needs of all citizens. It also urges them to give migrants, especially females, greater access to work, credit, basic education, health services, child care centres and vocational training, among others. In order to finance the needed infrastructure and services in a balanced manner, it is recommended that government agencies, bearing in mind the interests of the poor segments of society, consider introducing equitable cost-recovery schemes and other measures to increase revenues.

C Internally displaced persons

The objective is to offer adequate protection and assistance to persons displaced within their own countries, particularly women, children and the elderly and to find solutions to the root causes of their displacement, with a view to preventing it in future, and to facilitate their return or resettlement. The document further seeks to put an end to all forms of forced migration, including "ethnic cleansing". Countries are called upon to address the causes of internal displacement, including environmental degradation, natural disasters, armed conflict and forced resettlement, and to establish the necessary mechanisms to protect and assist displaced persons. It further calls for measures to ensure that internally displaced persons receive basic education, employment opportunities, vocational training and basic health care services, including reproductive health services and family planning. Measures should also be taken, at the national level with international cooperation, as appropriate, in accordance with the United Nations Charter, to find lasting solutions to questions related to internally displaced persons, including their right to voluntary and safe return to the home of origin.

CHAPTER X: INTERNATIONAL MIGRATION

International economic, political and cultural interrelations play an important role in determining the flow of people between countries. In its diverse types, international migration is linked to such interrelations and both affects and is affected by the development process. Poverty and environmental degradation, combined with the absence of peace and security, and human rights violations are all factors affecting international migration.

A International migration and development

Orderly international migration can have positive effects on both communities of origin and those of destination. Governments are urged to address the root causes of migration, to make remaining in one's country a viable option for all people. Inflows of remittances should be fostered by sound economic policies and adequate banking facilities. Countries of destination should consider the use of temporary migration, while countries of origin should collaborate in promoting voluntary return. The exchange of information on migration policies and the monitoring of stocks and flows of migrants through adequate data gathering should be supported.

B Documented migrants

Governments of receiving countries are urged to consider extending to documented migrants who meet appropriate length-of-stay requirements, and to members of their families, regular treatment equal to that accorded their own nationals with regard to basic human rights. Women and children who migrate as family members should be protected from abuse or denial of their human rights. All governments, particularly those of receiving countries must recognise the vital importance of family reunification and promote its integration into their national legislation in order to protect the unity of the families of documented migrants in a manner consistent with the universally recognised human rights instruments.

C Undocumented migrants

The document recalls the right of every nation state to decide who can enter and stay in its territory and under what conditions, and urges governments to exercise such right taking care to avoid racist or xenophobic actions and policies. Section C recommends actions to reduce the number of undocumented migrants; prevent their exploitation and protect their basic human rights; prevent international trafficking in migrants; and protect them against racism, ethnocentrism; and xenophobia. These actions include identifying the causes of undocumented migration and its economic, social and demographic impact; adopting effective sanctions against those who organise, exploit or traffic in undocumented migration; deterring undocumented migration by making potential migrants aware of the legal conditions for entry, stay and employment in host countries; and trying to find solutions to the problems of undocumented migrants through bilateral or multilateral negotiations on, inter alia, readmission agreements that protect the basic human rights of persons involved in accordance with relevant international instruments.

D Refugees, asylum-seekers and displaced persons

Governments are urged to address the root causes of movements of refugees and displaced persons by taking appropriate measures with respect to the resolution of conflict, the promotion of peace and reconciliation, respect for human rights, and respect for independence, territorial integrity and the sovereignty of States. Governments should also address the factors that contribute to forced displacement and strengthen their support for international activities to protect and assist refugees and displaced persons. Adequate international support should be extended to countries of asylum to meet the basic needs of refugees and to assist in the search for durable solutions. Refugees should be provided with access to adequate accommodation; education; health services, including family planning; and other necessary social services.

CHAPTER XI: POPULATION, DEVELOPMENT AND EDUCATION

A Education, population and sustainable development

Education is a key factor in sustainable development. It is a component of well-being and a means to enable the individual to gain access to knowledge. It also helps reduce fertility, morbidity and mortality rates; empower women; improve the quality of the working population; and promote genuine democracy. The increase in the education of women and girls contributes to women's empowerment, to postponement of marriage, and to reductions in family size. When mothers are better educated, their children's survival rate tends to increase.

Section A has four main objectives, each of which is also a recommended action: (a) to achieve universal access to quality education, in particular to primary and technical education and job training; (b) to combat illiteracy (the eradication of which is one of the prerequisites of human development) and to eliminate gender disparities in educational opportunities and support; (c) to promote non-formal education for young people; and (d) to introduce and improve the content of the curriculum so as to promote greater responsibility towards, and awareness of, the interrelationships between population and sustainable development; health issues, including reproductive health, and gender equity.

Section A stresses that investments in education and job training should be given high priority in development budgets and take into account the range and level of future workforce skill requirements. It also emphasises that education about population issues must begin in primary school and continue through all levels of formal and non-formal education, taking into account the rights and responsibilities of parents and the needs of children and adolescents.

B Population information, education and communication

Greater public knowledge, understanding and commitment at all levels, from the individual to the international, are vital to the achievement of the goals and objectives of the Programme of Action. A primary aim, therefore, is to increase such knowledge, understanding and commitment. Other aims are: (a) to encourage attitudes in favour of responsible behaviour in such areas as the environment, family, sexuality, reproduction, gender, and racial sensitivity; (b) to ensure governments' commitment to promote private- and public-sector participation in the design, implementation and monitoring of population and development policies and programmes; and (c) to enhance the ability of couples

229

and individuals to exercise their basic right to decide freely and responsibly the number and spacing of their children, and to have the information, education and means to do so.

Countries should seek to raise awareness on priority issues through public education campaigns. The media should be a major instrument in such efforts. It is especially important that IEC strategies are linked to, and complement, national population and development policies and strategies, as well as a full range of services in reproductive health, including family planning and sexual health, in order to enhance the use of such services and improve the quality of counselling and care. Governments, NGOs and the private sector should make greater and effective use of the entertainment media, including radio and television, folk theatre and other traditional media.

CHAPTER XII: TECHNOLOGY, RESEARCH AND DEVELOPMENT

This chapter stresses the importance of valid, reliable, timely, culturally relevant and internationally comparable population data for policy and programme development, implementation, monitoring and evaluation. It also emphasises that research, in particular biomedical research, has been instrumental in giving more and more people access to a greater range of safe and effective modern methods for regulation of fertility. The chapter further stresses that social and economic research is also needed to enable programmes to take into account the views of their intended beneficiaries, especially women, adolescents and other less empowered groups.

A Basic data collection, analysis and dissemination

Governments should strengthen their national capacity to carry out sustained and comprehensive programmes to collect, analyse, disseminate and utilise population and development data. Particular attention should be given to the monitoring of population trends and the preparation of demographic projections. Governments should also monitor progress towards the attainment of the goals and objectives set forth in the Programme of Action. The data collected should be disaggregated by gender in order to provide a more accurate picture of women's current and potential contribution to economic development.

B Reproductive health research

Governments, assisted by the international community and others, including NGOs and the private sector, are called upon to increase support for basic and applied biomedical, technological, clinical, ment processes. Women should be involved at all stages in the planning of research on gender issues, and efforts should be made to recruit and train more female researchers.

CHAPTER XIII: NATIONAL ACTION

A National policies and plans of action

Where leadership is strongly committed to economic growth, human resource development, gender equality and equity and meeting the health and in particular the reproductive health needs of the population, countries have been able to mobilise sustained national commitment to make population and development programmes successful. Population and development are intrinsically interrelated and progress in any area can catalyse improvement in others. Recognition is given to the need to involve intended beneficiaries in the design and subsequent implementation of population-related policies, plans, programmes and projects. Non-governmental organisations and the private sector are acknowledged as partners in national policies and programmes. Members of national legislatures can have a major role to play, especially in enacting domestic legislation for implementing the Programme of Action, allocating appropriate financial resources, ensuring accountability of expenditure and raising public awareness of population issues. The main objectives are to foster active involvement of elected representatives of people, particularly parliamentarians and concerned groups and individuals, especially at the grassroots level, and to build up the capacity and self-reliance to undertake concerted national actions.

B Programme management and human resource development

The document encourages governments to increase the skill level and accountability of managers and others involved in the implementation, monitoring and evaluation of national population and development strategies, policies, plans and programmes. The trend to decentralisation of authority in national population and development programmes is appreciated to require new skills, better information and communication systems, and strategies to increase and retain the numbers of trained staff, particularly women. Governments are called upon to give special attention to client-centred management information systems for population and development, particularly for reproductive health programmes, covering both governmental and non-governmental activities and providing updated data on clientele, expenditures, infrastructure, service accessibility and output and quality of services.

C Resource mobilisation and allocation

The document includes estimates of the funding levels required to meet developing countries' needs and the needs of countries with economies in transition in the period 2000–2015 for basic reproductive health services, including family planning; prevention of sexually transmitted diseases, including HIV/AIDS; and population data collection, analysis and dissemination, policy formulation and research. Based on past experience, experts have estimated that the implementation of programmes in these areas will cost $17.0 billion in 2000, $18.5 billion in 2005, $20.5 billion in 2010 and $21.7 billion in 2015. It is tentatively estimated that up to two-thirds of the costs will continue to be met by the countries themselves and in the order of one third from external sources, with considerable variations between and within regions. In order to meet reinforcing social development goals and satisfy previously undertaken intergovernmental commitments, governments are urged to devote an increased proportion of their public sector expenditures to the social sectors, stressing in particular poverty eradication in the context of sustainable development.

CHAPTR XIV: INTERNATIONAL COOPERATION

This chapter recommends actions to clarify the reciprocal responsibilities consistent with national population and development priorities. National capacity building and the transfer of technology and knowhow are held as the core objectives of international cooperation at the programme level.

The international community should strive for the fulfilment of the agreed target 0.7 per cent of GNP for overall official development assistance (ODA) and endeavour to increase the share of funding for population and development programmes commensurate with the scope and scale of activities required to achieve the objectives and goals of the Programme of Action. A crucially urgent challenge to the international donor community is therefore the translation of their commitment to the objectives and quantitative goals of the Programme of Action into commensurate financial contributions to population programmes in developing countries and countries with economies in transition. Given the magnitude of the financial resource needs for national population and development programmes, and assuming that recipient countries will be able to generate sufficient increases in domestically generated resources, the need for complementary resource flows from donor countries would be (in 1993 US dollars): in the order of $5.7 billion in 2000; $6.1 billion in 2005; $6.8 billion in 2010; and $7.2 billion in 2015. These figures include the needs of the countries with economies in transition, which should receive temporary assistance for population and development activities in light of the difficult economic and social problems that they face at present. The international community should urge donor agencies to facilitate and give higher priority to supporting direct South-South collaborative arrangements. Recipient countries should ensure that international assistance for population and development activities is used effectively to meet population and development objectives so as to assist donors to secure commitment to further resources for programmes.

CHAPTER XV:
PARTNERSHIP WITH THE NON-GOVERNMENTAL SECTOR

The primary objective of this chapter is to promote an effective partnership between government, non-governmental organisations, local community groups and the private sector in the discussion and decisions on the design, implementation, coordination, monitoring and evaluation of programmes relating to population, development and environment. Governments and intergovernmental organisations should integrate NGOs and local community groups into their decision-making and facilitate the contribution that NGOs can make towards finding solutions to population and development concerns and, in particular, to ensure the implementation of the Programme of Action.

Governments should ensure the essential roles and participation of women's organisations in the design and implementation of population and development programmes. Involving women at all levels, especially the managerial level, is critical to meeting the objectives and implementing the Programme of Action. Governments and donor countries should ensure that NGOs and their networks are able to maintain their autonomy and strengthen their capacity through regular dialogue and consultations, appropriate training and outreach activities, and thus play a greater role in the partnership.

The private, profit-oriented sector, which is discussed in section B, plays an important role in social and economic development, including production and delivery of reproductive health care services and commodities, including appropriate education and information relevant to population and development programmes. The aim is to strengthen the partnership between governments, international organisations and the private sector in identifying new areas of cooperation and to promote the role of the private sector in service delivery and in the production and distribution of high-quality reproductive health and family-planning commodities and contraceptives. The profit-oriented sector should consider how it might better assist non-profit NGOs in playing a wider role in society by enhancing or creating mechanisms to channel financial and other support to NGOs and their associations.

CHAPTER XVI: FOLLOW-UP TO THE CONFERENCE

A National-level activities

The willingness of Governments, local communities, the non-governmental sector, the international community and others to integrate population concerns into all aspects of economic and social activity will greatly assist in improving the quality of life for all individuals and future generations.

Extensive international, regional, subregional, national and local preparatory processes have strongly contributed to the formulation of the Programme of Action. Considerable institutional development has taken place in many countries in order to steer the national preparatory process; public information and education campaigns have fostered greater awareness of population issues, and comprehensive national reports have been prepared for the conference.

Conference follow-up should include policy guidance, including building political support for population and development; resource mobilisation; coordination and mutual accountability of implementation efforts; problem solving and sharing of experience within and between countries; and monitoring and reporting of progress in implementation.

Implementation of the Programme of Action must be part of an integrated follow-up effort to major international conferences, including ICPD, the World Conference on Health for All, the World Conference on Education for All, the World Summit for Children, the Conference on Least Developed Countries, the United Nations Conference on Environment and Development, the International Conference on Nutrition, the World Conference on Human Rights, the Global Conference on the Sustainable Development of Small Island Developing States, the World Social Summit, the Fourth World Conference on Women, and Habitat II.

Governments, UN system organisations and NGOs are urged to disseminate the Programme of Action widely and seek public support for its goals, objectives and actions. All countries should consider making additional contributions for implementation of the Programme of Action, taking into account the provisions of Chapters XIII and XIV and the economic constraints faced by developing countries.

All countries are urged to establish appropriate national follow-up, accountability and monitoring mechanisms, in partnership with NGOs, organisations, community groups, the media and the academic community, and with the support of parliamentarians. The international community should assist governments in organising national-level follow-up, including capacity-building for project formulation and programme management, and in strengthening coordination and evaluation mechanisms.

Governments are urged to set up or enhance national databases to provide baseline data and information that can be used to measure or assess progress towards the achievement of the goals and objectives of ICPD. All countries are urged to regularly assess and periodically report their progress, outlining successes, problems and obstacles.

B Subregional and regional activities

Implementation must address specific subregional and regional strategies and needs. Regional commissions, UN system organisations at the regional level and other relevant subregional and regional organisations should be active in coordinated implementation. Governments and relevant organisations are urged to reinforce existing follow-up mechanisms. Multidisciplinary expertise should be utilised in implementation and follow-up. Cooperation in capacity-building, the sharing and exchange of information and experiences, knowhow and technical expertise should be strengthened with the assistance of the international community and in partnership with NGOs. Governments are urged to strengthen training and research in population and development issues, and widely disseminate research findings.

C Activities at the international level

While some of the resources required for implementation could come from reordering priorities, developing countries, particularly the least developed, will require new and additional financial resources from the public and private sectors, NGOs and the international community, including on concessional and grant terms, according to sound and equitable indicators, provided through bilateral and multilateral channels and NGOs. There should be a coordinated approach and a clearer division of labour in population-relevant policy and operational aspects of development cooperation, and enhanced coordination and planning in resource mobilisation.

The General Assembly should organise a regular review of implementation of the Programme of Action. ECOSOC should promote an integrated approach and provide system-wide coordination and guidance in monitoring implementation, and should review the UN reporting system.

The Assembly during its forty-ninth session and ECOSOC in 1995 should review the roles, responsibilities, mandates and comparative advantages of intergovernmental bodies and UN system organs addressing population and development, to: ensure effective implementation, monitoring and evaluation of activities based on the Programme of Action; improve the effectiveness of implemention and monitoring activities; and ensure recognition of the interrelationships between policy guidance, research, standard-setting and operations.

ECOSOC should, in the context of Assembly resolution 48/162, consider the respective roles of the UN organs dealing with population and development, including the United Nations Population Fund (UNFPA) and the Population Division. The General Assembly at its forty-ninth session, in accordance with its resolution 48/162, should consider establishing a separate Executive Board of UNFPA, bearing in mind the administrative, budgetary and programme implications.

The UN Secretary General is urged to promote an exchange of information among the various UN bodies, international financial institutions and bilateral aid organisations and agencies, on international assistance required for regularly reviewing countries' population and development needs, including emergency and temporary needs, and maximising the availability and effective utilisation of resources.

UN specialised agencies and related organisations should strengthen and adjust their activities, programmes and medium-term strategies as follow-up to the conference; governing bodies should review their policies, programmes, budgets and activities in this regard.

Appendix B:

United Nations General Assembly Resolution 49/128: Report of the International Conference on Population and Development

Adopted 19 December 1994

The General Assembly,

Recalling its resolutions 47/176 of 22 December 1992 and 48/186 of 21 December 1993 on the International Conference on Population and Development, and 48/162 of 20 December 1993 on the restructuring and revitalisation of the United Nations in the economic, social and related fields,

Recalling also Economic and Social Council resolutions 1989/91 of 26 July 1989, 1991/93 of 26 July 1991, 1992/37 of 30 July 1992, 1993/4 of 12 February 1993, and 1993/76 of 30 July 1993, in which the Council decided on the convening, mandate and preparatory process of the International Conference on Population and Development,

Recalling further Economic and Social Council decision 1994/227 of 14 July 1994, by which the Council approved the provisional agenda and documentation for the twenty-eighth session of the Population Commission, including discussion of the implications of the recommendations of the International Conference on Population and Development,

Recalling further Economic and Social Council resolutions 3 (III) of 3 October 1946, 150 (VII) of 10 August 1948 and 1985/4 of 28 May 1985 on the mandate of the Population Commission, as well as 1763 (LIV) of 18 May 1973 and 1986/7 of 21 May 1986 on the aims and purposes of the United Nations Population Fund,

Having considered the report of the International Conference on Population and Development [1] which took place in Cairo, Egypt, from 5 to 13 September 1994,

Reaffirming the importance of the outcome of the World Population Conference held in Bucharest in 1974 and the International Conference on Population held in Mexico City in 1984 and acknowledging fully the integrated approach taken during the International Conference on Population and Development which recognises the interrelationship among population, sustained economic growth and sustainable development,

Recognising that the implementation of the recommendations contained in the Programme of Action of the International Conference on Population and Development [2] is the sovereign right of each country, consistent with national laws and development priorities, with full respect for the various religious and ethical values and cultural backgrounds of its peoples, and in conformity with universally recognised international human rights,

Expressing its belief in the contribution that the outcome of the International Conference on Population and Development will make to the forthcoming World Summit for Social Development, the Fourth World Conference on Women and the second United Nations Conference on Human Settlements (Habitat II), in particular relating to the call for a greater investment in people and for the empowerment of women to ensure their full participation at all levels in the social, economic and political lives of their communities,

Expressing its satisfaction at the fact that the International Conference on Population and Development and its preparatory process enabled the full and active involvement of States Members of the United Nations and the specialised agencies, and of observers and various intergovernmental organisations as well as representatives of non-governmental organisations, representing all regions of the world.

Expressing its profound gratitude to the government and people of Egypt for the hospitality extended to the participants at the conference and for the facilities, staff and services placed at their disposal,

1 Takes note with satisfaction of the report of the International Conference on Population and Development: [1]
2 Endorses the Programme of Action of the International Conference on Population and Development [2] as adopted on 13 September 1994;
3 Acknowledges the contribution made by the Secretary General of the United Nations and the Secretary General of the Conference to the successful organisation of the conference;
4 Affirms that, in the implementation of the Programme of Action, governments should commit themselves at the highest political level to achieving its goals and objectives, which reflect a new, integrated approach to population and development, and take a lead role in coordinating the implementation, monitoring and evaluation of follow-up actions;
5 Calls upon all governments, organisations of the United Nations system and other major groups concerned with population and development issues, including intergovernmental and non-governmental organisations, parliamentarians and other community leaders, to give the widest possible

dissemination to the Programme of Action and to seek public support for its goals, objectives and actions;

6 Fully acknowledges that the factors of population, health, education, poverty, patterns of production and consumption, empowerment of women, and the environment are closely interconnected and should be considered through an integrated approach and that the follow-up to the conference must reflect this fact;

7 Urges all countries to consider their current spending priorities with a view to making additional contributions for the implementation of the Programme of Action, taking into account the provisions of Chapters XIII and XIV of the Programme of Action, and the economic constraints faced by developing countries, in particular the least developed among them;

8 Acknowledges the importance of the subregional and regional activities undertaken during the preparations for the conference, including the regional strategies, plans and declarations adopted as part of this process, and invites the regional commissions, other regional and subregional organisations and the development banks to examine the results of the conference held at Cairo within their respective mandates, for the follow-up and implementation of the Programme of Action, at the regional level:

9 Emphasises that international cooperation in the field of population and development is essential for the implementation of the recommendations adopted at the conference and, in this context, calls upon the international community to provide, both bilaterally and multilaterally, adequate and substantial international support and assistance for population and development activities including through the United Nations Population Fund and other organs and organisations of the United Nations system and the specialized agencies that will be involved in the implementation, at all levels, of the Programme of Action;

10 Calls upon the organs and organisations of the United Nations system and the specialised agencies to undertake the actions required to give full and effective support to the implementation of the Programme of Action;

11 Emphasizes the need to maintain and enhance effective partnership with non-governmental groups and organisations so as to ensure their continued contributions and cooperation within all aspects of population and development, and urges all countries to establish appropriate national follow-up mechanisms, in partnership with non-governmental organisations, community groups and representatives of the media and the academic community, as well as to seek the support of parliamentarians, so as to ensure the full implementation of the Programme of Action;

12 Recognises the importance of South-South cooperation in the implementation of the Programme of Action;

13 Recognises that the effective implementation of the Programme of Action will require an increased commitment of financial resources, both domestically and externally, and in this context calls upon the developed countries to complement the national financial efforts of developing countries on population and development and intensify their efforts to transfer new and additional resources to the developing countries, in accordance with the relevant provisions of the Programme of Action, in order to ensure that population and development objectives and goals are met;

14 Acknowledges that countries with economies in transition should receive temporary assistance for population and development activities in light of

the difficult economic and social problems faced by these countries at present, and therefore suggests that the specialised agencies and all related organisations of the United Nations system should adjust, on this basis, their programmes and activities in line with the Programme of Action and take appropriate measures to ensure its full and effective implementation;

15 Emphasises the importance of the early identification and allocation of financial resources by all members of the international community, including regional financial institutions, to enable them to fulfil their commitments to the implementation of the Programme of Action;

16 Requests the Secretary General to consult with the various bodies of the United Nations system, as well as with international financial institutions and various bilateral aid organisations and agencies, with a view to promoting an exchange of information among them on the requirements for international assistance, reviewing on a regular basis the specific needs of countries in the field of population and development and maximising the availability of resources and their most effective utilisation;

17 Invites the Secretary General to ensure that adequate resources are provided for the conference follow-up activities of the United Nation Secretariat during 1995;

18 Requests the Secretary General to prepare periodic reports for the substantive sessions of the Economic and Social Council on the flow of financial resources for assisting in the implementation of the Programme of Action and to promote the exchange of information on the requirements for international assistance among the members of the donor community;

19 Urges the international community to promote a supportive international economic environment by adopting favourable macroeconomic policies for promoting sustained economic growth and sustainable development;

20 Stresses the importance of continued and enhanced cooperation and coordination by all relevant organs, organisations and programmes of the United Nations system and the specialised agencies in the implementation of the Proqramme of Action;

21 Emphasises the need for follow-up activities relating to the conference and the Programme of Action so as to utilise, to the fullest extent possible, existing capacity within the United Nations system in the area of population and development, including the Population Commission, the Population Division of the Department for Economic and Social Information and Policy Analysis of the Secretariat and the United Nations Population Fund, and other organisations, programmes and funds of the United Nations and specialised agencies whose support and commitment are required to successfully implement the full range of activities outlined in the Programme of Action;

22 Requests the specialised agencies and all related organisations of the United Nations system to review and where necessary adjust their programmes and activities in line with the Programme of Action and take appropriate measures to ensure its full and effective implementation, taking into account the specific needs of developing countries, and invites them to report to the Economic and Social Council at its substantive session of 1995 for coordination purposes and to the General Assembly at its fiftieth session for policy implications;

23 Decides that the General Assembly through its role in policy formulation and the Economic and Social Council through its role in overall guidance and

coordination, in accordance with Assembly resolution 48/162, and a revitalised Population Commission shall constitute a three-tiered inter-governmental mechanism that will play the primary role in the follow-up of the implementation of the Programme of Action, keeping in mind the need to develop a common framework for a coherent follow-up to United Nations summits and conferences, and to this end:

(a) The General Assembly, being the highest intergovernmental mechanism for the formulation and appraisal of policy on matters relating to the follow-up of the International Conference on Population and Development, will organise a regular review of the implementation of the Programme of Action;

(b) The Economic and Social Council, in assisting the General Assembly, will promote an integrated approach, provide system-wide coordination and guidance in the monitoring of the implementation of the Programme of Action and make recommendations thereon;

(c) The revitalised Population Commission, as a functional commission assisting the Economic and Social Council, will monitor, review and assess the implementation of the Programme of Action at the national, regional and international levels and advise the Council thereon;

24 Also decides that, to emphasise the new and comprehensive approach to population and development embodied in the Programme of Action, the revitalised Population Commission shall be renamed the Commission on Population and Development;

25 Decides that the Commission on Population and Development shall meet on an annual basis, beginning in 1996;

26 Recommends that the Economic and Social Council review, at its substantive session of 1995, the Commission's terms of reference and mandate so as to bring these fully into line with the provisions of operative paragraph 23 (c) above;

27 Also recommends that the Economic and Social Council, pursuant to the decision made on the terms of reference and enhanced mandate of the revitalised Commission, should consider at its substantive session of 1995 the composition of the Commission, in order to ensure that the Commission fully fulfils its functions as provided in operative paragraph 23 above, taking into account the integrated multidisciplinary and comprehensive approach of the Programme of Action as well as the membership of the other functional commissions of the Council;

28 Requests the Economic and Social Council, at its substantive session of 1995, to consider:

(a) The establishment of a separate executive board of the United Nations Population Fund;

(b) Recommendations to the Secretary General concerning secretariat support and coordination arrangements for the United Nations system;

(c) Recommendations to the Secretary General regarding the establishment of an appropriate inter-agency coordination, collaboration and harmonisation mechanism for the implementation of the Programme of Actions;

29 Also requests the Economic and Social Council, at its substantive session of 1995, to review the reporting procedures within the United Nations system regarding population and development issues, including a quinquennial review and appraisal of the progress made in achieving the goals and objectives of the Programme of Action, in order to ensure full support for its

implementation, bearing in mind the reporting procedures for all United Nations conferences in the economic and social field;

30 Requests the Secretary General, in consultation with States, to prepare a report on institutional follow-up issues and reporting procedures in the United Nations system to be submitted to the Economic and Social Council at its substantive session of 1995;

31 Requests the Economic and Social Council:

(a) To discuss the relevant matters concerning the implementation of population and development programmes, as well as matters concerning harmonisation, cooperation and collaboration within the United Nations system regarding the implementation of the Programme of Action;

(b) To discuss the reports submitted by the different bodies and other bodies and organs on various matters related to the Programme of Action:

32 Invites the governing body of the United Nations Population Fund to oversee, on a regular basis, the response of the Fund to the needs of countries regarding activities to strengthen national population and development programmes, including the specific requests from developing countries for assistance in the preparation of national reports, within its area of competence, and to report to the Economic and Social Council on this matter;

33 Calls upon the programmes of the United Nations system and the regional commissions and funds to provide their full and active support to the implementation of the Programme of Action, particularly at the field level, through the United Nations resident coordinator system, and invites the relevant specialised agencies to do the same;

34 Requests the Population Commission, at its twenty-eighth session, to review, within its area of competence, the Programme of Action and its implications and to transmit its views to the Economic and Social Council at its substantive session of 1995;

35 Requests the Secretary General to report, through the Economic and Social Council, to the General Assembly at its fiftieth session on the implementation of the present resolution;

36 Decides to include in the agenda of its forthcoming sessions, within existing clusters, an item entitled "Implementation of the Programme of Action of the International Conference on Population and Development".

Appendix C:

Cairo Programme of Action – Chapter IV, Gender Equality, Equity and Empowerment of Women

A EMPOWERMENT AND STATUS OF WOMEN

Basis for action

4.1   The empowerment and autonomy of women and the improvement of their political, social, economic and health status is a highly important end in itself. In addition, it is essential for the achievement of sustainable development. The full participation and partnership of both women and men is required in productive and reproductive life, including shared responsibilities for the care and nurturing of children and maintenance of the household. In all parts of the world, women are facing threats to their lives, health and well-being as a result of being overburdened with work and of their lack of power and influence. In most regions of the world, women receive less formal education than men, and at the same time, women's own knowledge, abilities and coping mechanisms often go unrecognised. The power relations that impede women's attainment of healthy and fulfilling lives operate at many levels of society, from the most personal to the highly public. Achieving change requires policy and programme actions that will improve women's access to secure livelihoods and economic resources, alleviate their extreme responsibilities with regard to housework, remove legal impediments to their participation in public life, and raise social awareness through effective programmes of education and mass communication. In addition, improving the status of women also enhances their decision-making capacity at all levels in all spheres of life, especially in the area of sexuality and reproduction. This, in turn, is essential for the long-term success of population programmes. Experience shows that population and development programmes are most effective when steps have simultaneously been taken to improve the status of women.

4.2 Education is one of the most important means of empowering women with the knowledge, skills and self-confidence necessary to participate fully in the development process. More than 40 years ago, the Universal Declaration of Human Rights asserted that "everyone has the right to education". In 1990, governments meeting at the World Conference on Education for All in Jomtien, Thailand, committed themselves to the goal of universal access to basic education. But despite notable efforts by countries around the globe that have appreciably expanded access to basic education, there are approximately 960 million illiterate adults in the world, of whom two-thirds are women. More than one-third of the world's adults, most of them women, have no access to printed knowledge, to new skills or to technologies that would improve the quality of their lives and help them shape and adapt to social and economic change. There are 130 million children who are not enrolled in primary school and 70 per cent of them are girls.

Objectives

4.3 The objectives are:
(a) To achieve equality and equity based on harmonious partnership between men and women and enable women to realise their full potential;
(b) To ensure the enhancement of women's contributions to sustainable development through their full involvement in policy- and decision-making processes at all stages and participation in all aspects of production, employment, income-generating activities, education, health, science and technology, sports, culture and population-related activities and other areas, as active decision makers, participants and beneficiaries;
(c) To ensure that all women, as well as men, are provided with the education necessary for them to meet their basic human needs and to exercise their human rights.

Actions

4.4 Countries should act to empower women and should take steps to eliminate inequalities between men and women as soon as possible by:
(a) Establishing mechanisms for women's equal participation and equitable representation at all levels of the political process and public life in each community and society and enabling women to articulate their concerns and needs;
(b) Promoting the fulfilment of women's potential through education, skill development and employment, giving paramount importance to the elimination of poverty, illiteracy and ill health among women;
(c) Eliminating all practices that discriminate against women; assisting women to establish and realise their rights, including those that relate to reproductive and sexual health;
(d) Adopting appropriate measures to improve women's ability to earn income beyond traditional occupations, achieve economic self-reliance, and ensure women's equal access to the labour market and social security systems;
(e) Eliminating violence against women;
(f) Eliminating discriminatory practices by employers against women, such as those based on proof of contraceptive use or pregnancy status;

(g) Making it possible, through laws, regulations and other appropriate measures, for women to combine the roles of child-bearing, breast-feeding and child-rearing with participation in the workforce.

4.5   All countries should make greater efforts to promulgate, implement and enforce national laws and international conventions to which they are party, such as the Convention on the Elimination of All Forms of Discrimination against Women, that protect women from all types of economic discrimination and from sexual harassment, and to implement fully the Declaration on the Elimination of Violence against Women and the Vienna Declaration and Programme of Action adopted at the World Conference on Human Rights in 1993. Countries are urged to sign, ratify and implement all existing agreements that promote women's rights.

4.6   Governments at all levels should ensure that women can buy, hold and sell property and land equally with men, obtain credit and negotiate contracts in their own name and on their own behalf and exercise their legal rights to inheritance.

4.7   Governments and employers are urged to eliminate gender discrimination in hiring, wages, benefits, training and job security with a view to eliminating gender-based disparities in income.

4.8   Governments, international organisations and non-governmental organisations should ensure that their personnel policies and practices comply with the principle of equitable representation of both sexes, especially at the managerial and policy-making levels, in all programmes, including population and development programmes.
   Specific procedures and indicators should be devised for gender-based analysis of development programmes and for assessing the impact of those programmes on women's social, economic and health status and access to resources.

4.9   Countries should take full measures to eliminate all forms of exploitation, abuse, harassment and violence against women, adolescents and children. This implies both preventive actions and rehabilitation of victims. Countries should prohibit degrading practices, such as trafficking in women, adolescents and children and exploitation through prostitution, and pay special attention to protecting the rights and safety of those who suffer from these crimes and those in potentially exploitable situations, such as migrant women, women in domestic service and schoolgirls. In this regard, international safeguards and mechanisms for cooperation should be put in place to ensure that these measures are implemented.

4.10   Countries are urged to identify and condemn the systematic practice of rape and other forms of inhuman and degrading treatment of women as a deliberate instrument of war and ethnic cleansing and take steps to assure that full assistance is provided to the victims of such abuse for their physical and mental rehabilitation.

4.11   The design of family health and other development interventions should take better account of the demands on women's time from the responsibilities of child-rearing, household work and income-generating activities. Male responsibilities should be emphasised with respect to child-rearing and housework. Greater investments should be made in appropriate measures to lessen the daily

244

burden of domestic responsibilities, the greatest share of which falls on women. Greater attention should be paid to the ways in which environmental degradation and changes in land use adversely affect the allocation of women's time. Women's domestic working environments should not adversely affect their health.

4.12 Every effort should be made to encourage the expansion and strengthening of grass-roots, community-based and activist groups for women. Such groups should be the focus of national campaigns to foster women's awareness of the full range of their legal rights, including their rights within the family, and to help women organise to achieve those rights.

4.13 Countries are strongly urged to enact laws and to implement programmes and policies which will enable employees of both sexes to organise their family and work responsibilities through flexible work-hours, parental leave, day-care facilities, maternity leave, policies that enable working mothers to breastfeed their children, health insurance and other such measures. Similar rights should be ensured to those working in the informal sector.

4.14 Programmes to meet the needs of growing numbers of elderly people should fully take into account that women represent the larger proportion of the elderly and that elderly women generally have a lower socio-economic status than elderly men.

B THE GIRL CHILD

Basis for action

4.15 Since in all societies discrimination on the basis of sex often starts at the earliest stages of life, greater equality for the girl child is a necessary first step in ensuring that women realise their full potential and become equal partners in development. In a number of countries, the practice of prenatal sex selection, higher rates of mortality among very young girls, and lower rates of school enrolment for girls as compared with boys, suggest that "son preference" is curtailing the access of girl children to food, education and health care. This is often compounded by the increasing use of technologies to determine foetal sex, resulting in abortion of female foetuses. Investments made in the girl child's health, nutrition and education, from infancy through adolescence, are critical.

Objectives

4.16 The objectives are:
(a) To eliminate all forms of discrimination against the girl child and the root causes of son preference, which results in harmful and unethical practices regarding female infanticide and prenatal sex selection;
(b) To increase public awareness of the value of the girl child, and concurrently, to strengthen the girl child's self-image, self-esteem and status;
(c) To improve the welfare of the girl child, especially in regard to health, nutrition and education.

Actions

4.17 Overall, the value of girl children to both their family and society must be expanded beyond their definition as potential child-bearers and caretakers and reinforced through the adoption and implementation of educational and social policies that encourage their full participation in the development of the societies in which they live. Leaders at all levels of the society must speak out and act forcefully against patterns of gender discrimination within the family, based on preference for sons. One of the aims should be to eliminate excess mortality of girls, wherever such a pattern exists. Special education and public information efforts are needed to promote equal treatment of girls and boys with respect to nutrition, health care, education and social, economic and political activity, as well as equitable inheritance rights.

4.18   Beyond the achievement of the goal of universal primary education in all countries before the year 2015, all countries are urged to ensure the widest and earliest possible access by girls and women to secondary and higher levels of education, as well as to vocational education and technical training, bearing in mind the need to improve the quality and relevance of that education.

4.19   Schools, the media and other social institutions should seek to eliminate stereotypes in all types of communication and educational materials that reinforce existing inequities between males and females and undermine girls' self-esteem. Countries must recognise that, in addition to expanding education for girls, teachers' attitudes and practices, school curricula and facilities must also change to reflect a commitment to eliminate all gender bias, while recognising the specific needs of the girl child.

4.20   Countries should develop an integrated approach to the special nutritional, general and reproductive health, education and social needs of girls and young women, as such additional investments in adolescent girls can often compensate for earlier inadequacies in their nutrition and health care.

4.21   Governments should strictly enforce laws to ensure that marriage is entered into only with the free and full consent of the intending spouses. In addition, governments should strictly enforce laws concerning the minimum legal age of consent and the minimum age at marriage and should raise the minimum age at marriage where necessary. Governments and non-governmental organisations should generate social support for the enforcement of laws on the minimum legal age at marriage, in particular by providing educational and employment opportunities.

4.22   Governments are urged to prohibit female genital mutilation wherever it exists and to give vigorous support to efforts among non-governmental and community organisations and religious institutions to eliminate such practices.

4.23   Governments are urged to take the necessary measures to prevent infanticide, prenatal sex selection, trafficking in girl children and use of girls in prostitution and pornography.

C   MALE RESPONSIBILITIES AND PARTICIPATION

Basis for action

4.24   Changes in both men's and women's knowledge, attitudes and behaviour are necessary conditions for achieving the harmonious partnership of men and women. Men play a key role in bringing about gender equality since, in most societies, men exercise preponderant power in nearly every sphere of life, ranging from personal decisions regarding the size of families to the policy and programme decisions taken at all levels of government. It is essential to improve communication between men and women on issues of sexuality and reproductive health, and the understanding of their joint responsibilities, so that men and women are equal partners in public and private life.

Objective

4.25   The objective is to promote gender equality in all spheres of life, including family and community life, and to encourage and enable men to take responsibility for their sexual and reproductive behaviour and their social and family roles.

Actions

4.26   The equal participation of women and men in all areas of family and household responsibilities, including family planning, child-rearing and house-work, should be promoted and encouraged by governments. This should be pursued by means of information, education, communication, employment legislation and by fostering an economically enabling environment, such as family leave for men and women so that they may have more choice regarding the balance of their domestic and public responsibilities.

4.27   Special efforts should be made to emphasise men's shared responsibility and promote their active involvement in responsible parenthood, sexual and reproductive behaviour, including family planning; prenatal, maternal and child health; prevention of sexually transmitted diseases, including HIV; prevention of unwanted and high-risk pregnancies; shared control and contribution to family income, children's education, health and nutrition; and recognition and promotion of the equal value of children of both sexes. Male responsibilities in family life must be included in the education of children from the earliest ages. Special emphasis should be placed on the prevention of violence against women and children.

4.28   Governments should take steps to ensure that children receive appropriate financial support from their parents by, among other measures, enforcing child-support laws. Governments should consider changes in law and policy to ensure men's responsibility to and financial support for their children and families. Such laws and policies should also encourage maintenance or reconstitution of the family unit. The safety of women in abusive relationships should be protected.

4.29   National and community leaders should promote the full involvement of men in family life and the full integration of women in community life. Parents and schools should ensure that attitudes that are respectful of women and girls as equals are instilled in boys from the earliest possible age, along with an understanding of their shared responsibilities in all aspects of a safe, secure and harmonious family life. Relevant programmes to reach boys before they become sexually active are urgently needed.

Notes

CHAPTER 1:   SETTING THE SCENE

1 United Nations (1971) *A Concise Report on the World Population Situation in 1970*, United Nations, New York, January.
2 Gille, Halvor (Deputy Executive Director, UNFPA) (1979) 'Recent Trends in International Assistance' in Salas, Rafael M *International Population Assistance: the First Decade*, Pergamon Press, Oxford.
3 Speech published in booklet form by the World Bank, Washington DC, May 1969.
4 United Nations (1994) *A Concise Report on the World Population Situation in 1983*, United Nations, New York, April.
5 United Nations (1991) *World Population Prospects 1990*, United Nations, New York (sales no E.91.XIII.4).
6 World Bank (1993) *Effective Family Planning Programmes*, World Bank, Washington DC.
7 The Reproductive Revolution: New Survey Findings. Johns Hopkins University Population Information Program, Baltimore, December 1992.
8 A Survey by Johns Hopkins University for the National Academy of Sciences, Baltimore 1972.

CHAPTER 2:   PREPARING FOR THE ICPD

1 E/CONF.84/PC/14, 29 April 1993.
2 E/CONF.84/PC/13, 27 April 1993.
3 Dakar/Ngor Declaration, para 1.
4 Op cit, para 3b.
5 E/CONF.84/PC.16, para. 19.
6 E/CONF.84/PC/17, 10 May 1993.
7 "Population, Social Equity and Changing Production Patterns", ECLAC and CELADE, Santiago, Chile, 1993.

8 Op cit, para 6.
9 "Experiences in Population in Latin America and the Caribbean: Historical Perspective and Current Challenges", UNFPA, 1993.
10 "Population, Social Equity and Changing Production Patterns", as cited, p 61.
11 See especially Agenda 21, Chapter 4, Changing Production Patterns.
12 According to the United Nations World Population Prospects 1990 even a total fertility rate (TFR) of 2.62 for developing countries as a whole by 2015 is still above the required TFR of 2.19 (for the quinquennium 2010–2015) if the low variant is to be attained.
13 *Earth Negotiations Bulletin*, vol 6, no 11, 2 June 1993.
14 Op cit, p 3.
15 E/CONF.84/PC/L.9 of 20 May 1993.
16 Op cit, para 62.
17 Op cit, para 59.
18 See *International Cooperation in the Field of Population*, by Halvor Gille, former Deputy Executive Director, UNFPA, E/CONF.84.RM.EUR.WP.5, of 15 December 1992.
19 "Global Population Assistance: A Report Card on the Major donors"; Shanti R. Conly, and J. Joseph Speidel, Population Action International, Washington, June 1993.

CHAPTER 3:
THE THIRD MEETING OF ICPD'S PREPARATORY COMMITTEE

1 A/CONF.171/PC/5.
2 E/CONF.60/19. See Chapter 6.
3 E/CONF.76/19. See Chapter 8.
4 See "The Earth Summit: The United Nations Conference on Environment and Development (UNCED)", Stanley P. Johnson, Graham and Trotman/Martinus Nijhoff, 1993, p 126.
5 See, for example, Chapter 8 and Rafael Salas' speech to the International Conference on Population, Mexico City, August 1994.
6 Op cit, para 6.3.
7 Op cit, para 3.21.
8 Op cit, para 3.23.
9 Op cit, para 3.16.
10 Op cit, para 8.5.
11 Op cit, para 1.10.
12 Op cit, para 8.15.
13 Op cit, para 7.10.
14 Op cit, para 7.13.
15 Op cit, para 11.5.
16 Op cit, para 12.10.
17 Op cit, paras 13.14–13.20.
18 *Children by Choice, not Chance*, UK Overseas Development Administration, August 1991.
19 'Op cit,' para 4.4.
20 *Earth Negotiations Bulletin*, vol 6, no 23, 14 April 1994.
21 See *World Population and the United Nations: Challenge and Response*, Stanley P. Johnson, Cambridge University Press, 1987, p 116.

22 E/CONF.60/19, p 7.
23 E/CONF.76/19, p 24.
24 See *Youth at Risk: Meeting the Sexual Health Needs of Adolescents*, Stephanie L. Koontz and Shanti R. Conly, Population Action International, April 1994.

CHAPTER 4: THE GUNS OF AUGUST, 1994

1 Deutsche Press Agentur, Cairo, 12 August, 1994.
2 Deutsche Press Agentur, Cairo, 22 August, 1994.
3 Cited in BBC Summary of World Broadcasts, 6 September 1994.
4 UPI, Dhaka, 28 August, 1994.
5 UPI, 28 August, 1994.
6 Deutsche Press Agentur, Islamabad, 1 September, 1994.
7 London *Financial Times*, 1 September, 1995.
8 *New York Times*, 18 August, 1994.
9 Associated Press, Manila, 9 August, 1994.
10 Reuters, Rome, 26 August, 1994.
11 UPI, Washington, 25 August, 1994.
12 *San Diego Union Tribune*, 6 September, 1994.
13 *San Diego Union Tribune*, 27 August, 1994.
14 BBC Summary of World Broadcasts, 25 August, 1994.
15 Peter Stafford, the *Guardian*, 25 August, 1994.
16 Xinhua News Agency, 25 August, 1995.
17 Deutsche Press Agentur, Cairo, 23 August, 1994.
18 Kyodo News Service, Tokyo, 27 August, 1994.

CHAPTER 5: THE OPENING OF THE CAIRO CONFERENCE

1 UN Secretary General Boutros Ghali's speech, together with the opening statements made by President Mubarak, Gro Harlem Brundtland, Benazir Bhutto, Dr Sadik and Prince Mbilini, Prime Minister of Swaziland, are printed at Annex II to the official Report of the ICPD (A/CONF.171/Add.1).
2 *Los Angeles Times*, Associated Press byline, 4 September 1994.
3 UN Press Release POP/CAI/8, 5 September 1994.

CHAPTER 6: THE CONTROVERSY OVER ABORTION

1 Women's Feature Service, 8 September, 1994.
2 Reuters, Cairo, 7 September, 1994.
3 Reuters, Cairo, 7 September, 1994.
4 *Earth Negotiations Bulletin* vol 6, no 39, 14 September 1994.
5 UPI, Cairo, 6 September, 1994.
6 *Earth Negotiations Bulletin* vol 6, no 39, 14 September 1994.

CHAPTER 7: THE EMPOWERMENT OF WOMEN

1 World Population Plan of Action, paragraph 29 (a). Report of the United Nations World Population Conference, 1974. E/CONF.60/19. United Nations publications sales No. E.75.XIII.3.

2 Article reviewing outcome of UNCED, as far as population questions were concerned, by Dr Nafis Sadik, Executive Director of UNFPA, published in *People and the Planet*, vol 1, no 4, 1992, p 7.
3 "Alternative Treaties: Synergistic Processes for Sustainable Communities and Global Responsibility", International NGO Forum, Rio de Janeiro, June 1–14, 1992. Edited by Robert Pollard, Ruth West and Will Sutherland. Published by Ideas for Tomorrow Today and International Synergy Institute.
4 Vandana Shiva's article entitled "Women's rights reduced to reproduction issues" was published by Third World Network features on 1 September, 1994.

CHAPTER 8:   ADOLESCENCE

1 *Houston Chronicle*, 30 August, 1994.
2 *Earth Negotiations Bulletin* vol 6, no 39, 14 September 1994.

CHAPTER 9:   INTERNATIONAL MIGRATION

1 InterPress Service, 28 April 1994.
2 *Earth Negotiations Bulletin* vol 6, no 39, 14 September 1994.
3 Resolution A/C.2/49/L.74.

CHAPTER 11:   RESOURCES

1 *Earth Negotiations Bulletin* vol 6, no 39, 14 September 1994.

CHAPTER 12:   CLOSING SESSION — LOOKING AHEAD

1 See A/CONF.171/13/Add.1: Report of the ICPD, Annex IV, 18 October 1994.

APPENDIX B

1 A/CONF.171/13 and Add.1.
2 Ibid, Chap I, Resolution 1, annex.

Index

International conferences are indexed by the name of the city involved, e.g. Cairo, Copenhagen. Details of the Programme of Action text etc are to be found in the individual subject entries, e.g. abortion, adolescence.